# HENRY DAVID THOREAU'S

# KALENDAR

# HENRY DAVID THOREAU'S

# KALENDAR

---

*CHARTS and*

*OBSERVATIONS*

*of NATURAL*

*PHENOMENA*

---

## KRISTEN CASE

MILKWEED EDITIONS

Published 2025 by Milkweed Editions
Printed in Canada
Cover design by Mary Austin Speaker
Cover image of chart by Henry David Thoreau
Photographs of Kalendar by The Morgan Library & Museum
25 26 27 28 29   5 4 3 2 1
*First Edition*

Library of Congress Cataloging-in-Publication Data

Names: Case, Kristen, 1976- author.
Title: Henry David Thoreau's Kalendar : charts and observations of natural
    phenomena / Kristen Case.
Description: Minneapolis, Minnesota : Milkweed Editions, [2025] | Includes
    bibliographical references. | Summary: "A gorgeously crafted book
    pairing reproductions of Thoreau's hand-drawn Kalendar with
    transcriptions and essays by Kristen Case"-- Provided by publisher.
Identifiers: LCCN 2025002275 (print) | LCCN 2025002276 (ebook) | ISBN
    9781571311597 (hardcover) | ISBN 9781571317858 (ebook)
Subjects: LCSH: Thoreau, Henry David, 1817-1862--Knowledge and learning. |
    Thoreau, Henry David, 1817-1862--Criticism and interpretation. |
    Thoreau, Henry David, 1817-1862--Diaries. | Natural
    history--Massachusetts--Concord. | Seasons--Massachusetts--Concord. |
    Ecoliterature, American--History and criticism. | Concord
    (Mass.)--Environmental conditions--19th century.
Classification: LCC PS3057.N3 C37 2025  (print) | LCC PS3057.N3  (ebook) | DDC
    818/.309--dc23/eng/20250528
LC record available at https://lccn.loc.gov/2025002275
LC ebook record available at https://lccn.loc.gov/20

Milkweed Editions is committed to ecological stewardship. We strive to align our book production practices with this principle, and to reduce the impact of our operations in the environment. We are a member of the Green Press Initiative, a nonprofit coalition of publishers, manufacturers, and authors working to protect the world's endangered forests and conserve natural resources. *Henry David Thoreau's Kalendar* was printed on acid-free 100% postconsumer-waste paper by Friesens Corporation.

*for AEJ and WCJ, in all seasons*

# Contents

# INTRODUCTION:

# *To Keep Time*

---

This is June–the month of grass & leaves  The deciduous trees are investing the evergreens & revealing how dark they are  Already the aspens are trembling again, and a new summer is offered me– I feel a little fluttered in my thoughts as if I might be too late. Each season is but an infinitesimal point. It no sooner comes than it is gone. It has no duration. It simply gives a tone & hue to my thought. Each annual phenomenon is a reminiscence & prompting  Our thoughts & sentiments answer to the revolutions of the seasons, as 2 cog wheels fit into each other– We are conversant with only one point of contact at a time–from which we receive a prompting & impulse & instantly pass to a new season or point of contact. A year is made up of a certain series & number of sensations & thoughts–which have their language in nature. Now I am ice–now I am sorrel. Each experience reduces itself to a mood of the mind.
– *Journal*, June 6, 1857

IN THE SPRING OF 1860, AT THE HEIGHT OF HIS INTELLECTUAL powers and the peak of his political engagement, Henry David Thoreau created something new. Part blueprint for a grand new work, part scientific chart, part picture of temporal experience, this *something*—which, following a suggestive Journal entry from October 1859 has come to be called his Kalendar—was more a tool than a text. Comprised of six multipage charts of general phenomena, the Kalendar was an instrument for recording and perceiving not just annual, weather-related phenomena themselves, but also the hidden relations between them—between the skies of one June and the skies of past and future Junes—relations we often feel but can't quite *hold*, stuck as we usually are in our own brief moment of linear time.

"Each season," Thoreau observed in his Journal in June of 1857, "is but an infinitesimal point. It no sooner comes than it is gone. It has no duration." In other words, loss is fundamental to our experience of time: every moment we experience is already passing away. However, even as Thoreau acknowledges that "we are conversant with only one point of contact at a time," he also gestures toward another truth about time—that "each annual phenomenon is a reminiscence & prompting," that our experiences of the world are connected, pointing backward toward past experiences and forward toward future ones. This double nature of our experience of time as simultaneously linear and embedded within cycles of related and recurrent experiences is particularly evident in the natural world, where the trembling aspens of June and the frozen lakes of December can be experienced as both fleeting and timeless.

The Thoreau who created the charts of general phenomena was now several years beyond the publication of *Walden* and still further from his two-year experiment in living in the woods. He lived now in his family home on Main Street in Concord and was an active participant in both family and community life—lecturing at the lyceum, speaking at abolitionist events, and working as a surveyor. In the early 1850s, he had committed to a pattern of walking (typically for several hours each day) and writing (usually about the previous day's walk) that he would continue as long as his health allowed, which turned out to be about a decade. His extraordinary Journal is the record of these practices, and the Kalendar is their culminating gesture: the final major endeavor of his life.

## Structure and Sources

The charts of general phenomena derived from Thoreau's long-held sense that "our thoughts & sentiments answer to the revolution of the seasons, as 2 cog wheels fit into each other," and his equally long-standing desire to more fully experience and comprehend the complex network of relations—what we would now call the *ecosystem*—of which he knew himself to be a part. Though Thoreau had for many years been keeping lists and charts of individual observations of the natural world—bird migration times, the flowering and leafing out of trees—the Kalendar was a discovery: a crystallization of his long-developing ideas about time, the natural world, and the nature of perception. If in 1857 Thoreau lamented that "we are conversant with only one point of contact at a time," by 1860 he had begun to imagine ways of multiplying those points of contact and perceiving them simultaneously, within a single frame.

The frame itself was borrowed from naturalists before him: a simple chart derived from two axes, one measuring time, the other indexing seasonal phenomena. In October of 1859 he had written, "For 30 years I have annually observed about this time, or earlier—, the freshly erected winter lodges of the musquash along the river side. . . . This may not be an annual phenomenon to you – It may not be in the Greenwich almanack– or ephemeris–but it has an important place in my Kalendar" (10/16/1859, Journal Transcript 30:57). These allusions—*Greenwich almanack*, *ephemeris*, and *Kalendar*—tell the story of the predecessors of and models for Thoreau's Kalendar. As a classics student at Harvard, Thoreau was no doubt familiar with the ancient Roman ephemera of Ptolemy—charts tracking the movement of astronomical objects over time. He also knew of the modern versions of these charts published by the Royal Greenwich Observatory beginning in the eighteenth century. The conspicuous spelling of Kalendar points to John Evelyn's *Kalendarium Hortense*, a gardener's almanac in the classical tradition of Hesiod's *Works and Days* and Cato's *De Re Rustica*. A more immediate predecessor, the English naturalist Gilbert White's *Natural History of Selborne*—probably the most significant in terms of its influence on Thoreau—contained a naturalist's calendar, with observations about local species and their first appearances in a given season. Each of these models provided Thoreau with tools for thinking about the intersection of place and time, and for understanding the way the particular species of a place actually construct time: dictating the changes in the landscape by which we mark the year.

Another model, not for the Kalendar's formal structure but for the expanded ecological vision it reflects, was Indigenous knowledge. As John Kucich notes, Thoreau was a dedicated student of native cultures but largely relied on ethnographic accounts written from a settler-colonial perspective. However, Thoreau's participation in the savagist ideology of his time exists alongside his real commitment to learning from Indigenous cultures, and in particular from learning new ways of conceiving of the relationship between humans and a more-than-human world. In an 1858 Journal entry, Thoreau writes,

> How much more conversant was the Indian with any wild animal or plant than we are– and in his language is implied all that intimacy as much as ours is expressed in our language– How many words in our language about a moose–or birch bark! & The like. The Indian stood nearer to wild-nature than we. . . . It was a new light when my guide

gave me Indian names for things, for which I had only scientific ones before. In proportion as I understood the language I saw them from a new point of view. (3/5/1858, Journal Transcript 25:107–108)

The passage demonstrates the way Thoreau's knowledge of Indigenous culture informs one of the driving forces of the Kalendar—Thoreau's desire to both achieve and represent a more intimate relationship between human and more-than-human life. I follow Kucich in his contention that the two sides of Thoreau's relationship to Indigenous culture pose a unique problem for Thoreau scholars, and that part of the explanation for this seeming paradox lies in the particular way in which Thoreau sought to make use of Indigenous epistemology in his late natural history projects, including the Kalendar.

## PROCESS AND PURPOSE

Thoreau's ultimate intentions for the Kalendar remain unknown, however, we do have several suggestive pieces of evidence. The April charts, the first that Thoreau created, contain a column on the far left that includes what seem to be average dates for each phenomenon. This column is empty in the May and June charts, filled in in October and November, and almost entirely empty again in December. The column numbers are often written in pencil, suggesting that they were determined and added at a later date. Much here remains unclear. Why did Thoreau skip the ordering step for certain months? What is the meaning of the superscript numbers next to some dates in this column, particularly in 1861? What does seem clear is that the column represents an initial step toward yet another form of organization. But what?

Here we have some clues, most significantly the "Story of March," an extended Journal entry from 1860, just before the creation of the charts, in which Thoreau sets out the general phenomena of March in a narrative sequence (Journal Transcript 31:95–109). During this same period Thoreau created a chart of spring phenomena—February through April, with clearly delineated composite or average dates written along the vertical axis of the chart. Taken together, the average column and the two texts from the spring of 1860 suggest that Thoreau was working out ideas for the presentation of seasonal phenomena in narrative form. It seems likely that the charts were originally pieces of a plan for a larger work, perhaps the "Book of Concord" that Bronson Alcott had commissioned him to create for local schoolchildren.

From the posthumously published late manuscript *Wild Fruits*, we can get a sense of what such a book might have looked like. Organized by date like the almanacs that inspired it, the text likely would have unfolded in the present tense, providing the reader with a real-time narrative tour of Concord through the seasons.

> By the thirteenth of May I notice the green fruit; and perhaps two or three days later, as I am walking perhaps, over the southerly slope of some dry and bare hill, or where there are bare and sheltered spaces between the bushes, it occurs to me that strawberries have possibly set; and looking carefully in the most favorable places, just beneath the top of the hill, I discover the reddening fruit, and at length, on the very driest and sunniest spot or brow, two or three berries which I am forward to call ripe, though generally only their sunny cheek is red.

Unlike the Journal, which documents Thoreau's experience day by day in linear time, *Wild Fruits* consolidates experience into a temporality that is at once precise ("by the thirteenth of May") and general—a habitual present that also encompasses Mays past and future. This is the temporal space of the Kalendar.

In its articulation of an alternative to the forward march of linear time, the Kalendar can be understood as part of Thoreau's critique of the "restless, nervous, bustling, trivial Nineteenth Century" and its organization of human life. Intimately linked to the rise of industrialization and capitalism, "standard time" or "clock time" began in the early modern period to gain ascendancy over the cyclical, seasonal temporal structures that had governed life in the agricultural societies of Europe in the medieval period. Thoreau made the link between the "bustling" speed of life in the second half of the nineteenth century and the rise of industrial capitalism and its ever-increasing regimentation of labor: "Where is this division of labor to end?" he asks in *Walden*, "and what object does it finally serve? No doubt another may also think for me; but it is not therefore desirable that he should do so to the exclusion of my thinking for myself." Here, Thoreau perceives the connection between the division of labor and its alienation from intellectual thought and natural processes that would become increasingly common features of working life in the twentieth and twenty-first centuries. As Jenny Odell details in *Saving Time: Discovering a Life Beyond the Clock*, the rise of the mechanized, assembly-line style workplace popularized by Frederick Winslow Taylor was accompanied by deliberate "de-skilling" of the workforce—the active suppression of the worker's knowledge of the overall process to which they contribute. Anticipating the way that clock time would be harnessed to control human labor and thought, Thoreau sought an alternative to living that is also an alternative to his culture's temporal conventions. At Walden Pond, Thoreau designed a life, an *economy*, outside of the constraints of clock time, a way of being in which "both place and time were changed." Connecting his own daily habits to the rhythms of the natural world, Thoreau had discovered the plasticity of time. Just as the plants and animals that constituted his world at Walden created the seasons with their appearances and disappearances, Thoreau learned that he, too, could *make* time through a different mode of living in and recording it. The Kalendar represents the last and most elaborate of his many experiments in temporal arrangement.

Thoreau's process in creating the charts of general phenomena involved several steps, some of which were adapted from previous chart-making activities. He'd begun tracking leaf fall, first flowering times, bird migration, and other seasonal phenomena in the spring of 1851 (see fig. 1). As Bradley Dean notes,

> that same spring the Smithsonian Institute sent to scientists across the country a circular titled "Registry of Periodical Phenomena," which invited "all persons who may have it in their power, to record their observations [of "periodical phenomena of Animal and Vegetable life"], and to transmit them to the Institution." The circular lists 127 species of plants, using in most cases both common and Latin names, and asks observers to mark opposite each species its date of flowering.

Though we have no evidence that Thoreau answered the Smithsonian's call, we do know that he was aware of it, and it seems likely that the project may have inspired Thoreau's own list- and chart-making practices.

The innovation represented by the charts of *general* phenomena, which Thoreau developed in 1860, had to do with the variety of phenomena observed—and with the inclusion of his own habits of seasonal behavior within their scope. This inclusion marked a significant shift, not only because it provided Thoreau with the synthetic, comprehensive seasonal view that he sought, but also because it reflected his epistemology: the idea that what mattered was not the distantly observed, objective "fact," but the fact *in relation* to other facts—including those pertaining to its human observer. Structurally, the

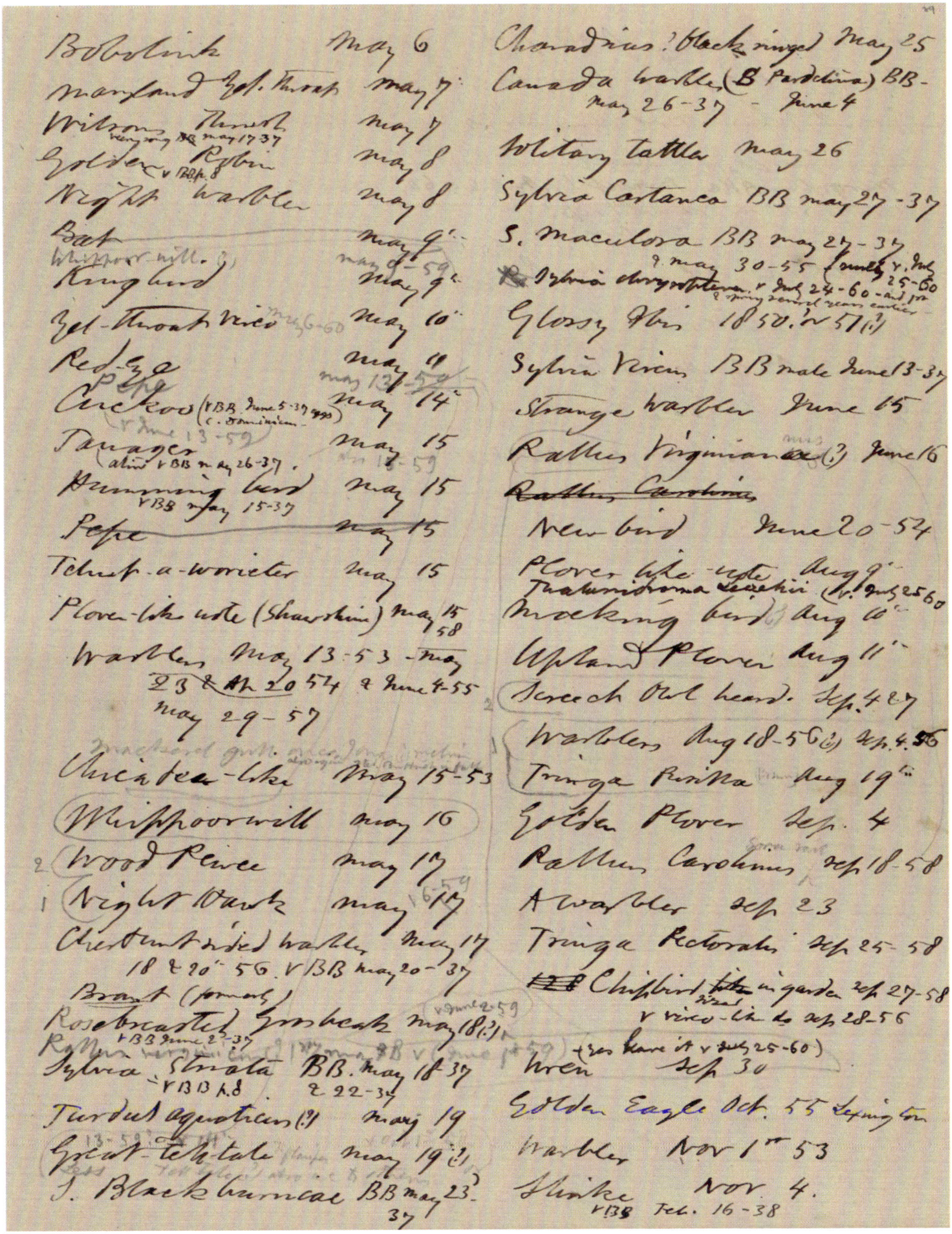

Bobolink  May 6
Maryland Yel. throat  May 7
Wilson's Thrush  May 7
Golden Robin  May 8
Night Warbler  May 8
Bat  May 9
Whippoorwill (?)  May 9-59
Kingbird  May 9
Yel-throat Vireo  May 10
Red-eye  May 11
Cuckoo  May 14
Tanager  May 15
Humming bird  May 15
Pewee  May 15
Tchuck-a-worrier  May 15
Plover-like note (Shawshin)  May 15 '58
Warblers May 13-53 — May 23 & Ap 20 54 & June 4 55  May 29-57
Chickadee-like  May 15-53
Whippoorwill  May 16
Wood Pewee  May 17
Night Hawk  May 17
Chestnut-sided warbler  May 17
Brown (female)
Rosebreasted Grosbeak  May 18
Sylvia Striata BB  May 18 37
Turdus aquaticus (?)  May 19
Great-tell-tale  May 19
S. Blackburniae BB  May 23-37

Charadrius? black ringed  May 25
Canada Warbler (S Pardelina) BB  May 26-37 — June 4
Solitary tattler  May 26
Sylvia Castanea BB  May 27-37
S. maculosa BB  May 27-34
Sylvia chrysoptera
Glossy Ibis  1850 or 57 (?)
Sylvia Virens BB male  June 13-37
Strange warbler  June 15
Rallus Virginianus (?)  June 16
Rallus Carolinus
New bird  June 20-54
Plover like note  Aug 9
Mocking bird  Aug 10
Upland Plover  Aug 11
Screech Owl heard  Sep. 4 & 7
Warblers  Aug 18-56 & Sep 4 56
Tringa Pusilla  Aug 19
Golden Plover  Sep. 4
Rallus Carolinus  Sep 18-58
A warbler  Sep 23
Tringa Pectoralis  Sep 25-58
Chipbird in garden  Sep 27-58  & vireo-like do  Sep 28-56
Wren  Sep 30
Golden Eagle  Oct. 55 Lexington
Warbler  Nov 1 53
Shrike  Nov 4

Figure 1. Birds observed, by date.

charts mimic those he'd been making of discrete seasonal phenomena for some time, but the creative leap that led to the more inclusive Kalendar charts was profound. In 1852, he'd written, "I have a common place book for facts and another for poetry– but I find it difficult always to preserve the vague distinction which I had in my mind–for the most interesting & beautiful facts are so much the more poetry and that is their success." (2/18/1852, *Journal* 4:356). Though Thoreau had long desired and moved toward such a breakdown of the fact/poetry binary, his chart and list making remained largely repositories of facts until 1860. Adapting the objective scientific form of the chart to include subjective experience, he arrived at a technological solution to the divide between "scientific" modes of attention to the natural world and his lived experience of interrelation with it. Seeing the months as the charts of general phenomena presented them allowed Thoreau to envision his world as what Darwin called "a web of complex relations" over time.

To compose his charts—those of individual as well as general phenomena—Thoreau relied on his Journal, a storehouse of observations painstakingly gathered through the 1850s. Thoreau was aided in his backward navigation of the Journal by his habit of indexing his text as he wrote—making notes in the back of his notebooks about the page-locations of descriptions of particular phenomena. Sometime in the early 1850s Thoreau's indexing habit gave way to a more efficient system of hash marks made in the margins of the Journal next to descriptions of phenomena he might wish to record in a given chart (see fig. 2). This system allowed Thoreau to navigate quickly through the Journal in the next stage of the process: the creation of lists of compelling phenomena organized by year and date. These lists, often scrawled on the back of business letters or other ready-to-hand scrap paper, were an intermediate stage between Journal and chart: a first winnowing of the volume of seasonal observations contained in each month of the Journal. (Interestingly, while lists exist for all months except July, August, and September, Thoreau seems to have only drafted *charts* of general phenomena for the months of April, May, June, October, November, and December.) Finally, Thoreau winnowed once again, translating some, but not all, of the list items to his charts of general phenomena, and carefully noting the dates on which each phenomenon occurred in the spaces of the grid. The chain—or more accurately, the network—of textual transmission involved in the production of the charts of general phenomena was complex. Thoreau's habit was to take field notes on small scraps of paper he carried with him when walking. The next day, he would use these notes to reconstruct the day's experiences, indexing

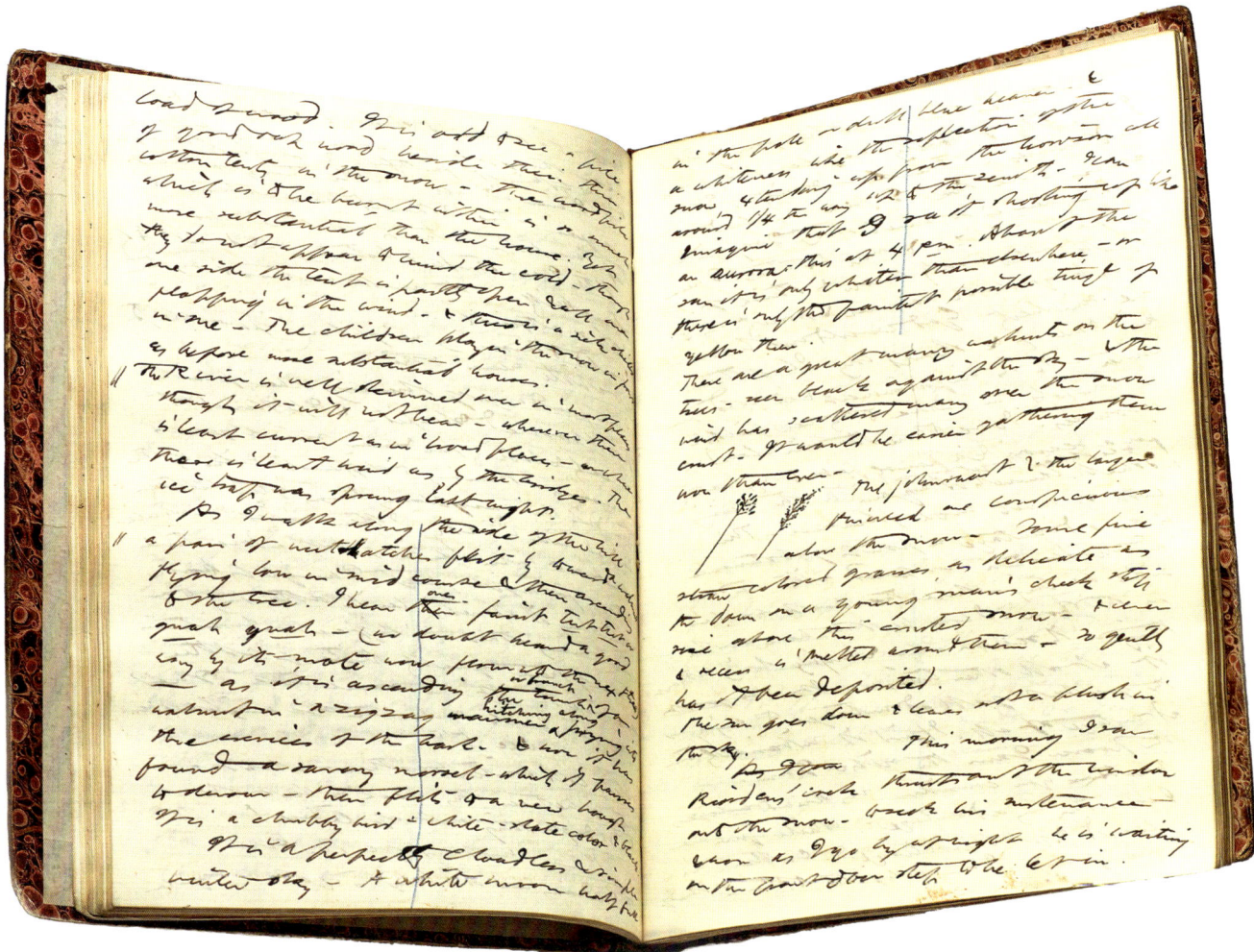

Figure 2. Journal, December 5, 1856, with hash marks indexing
"The river is well skimmed over in most places" and "A pair of nuthatches flit by."

as he went. When, beginning in 1860, he began drawing up the charts, he consulted the indexes of the many volumes of his Journal, then created the yearly lists, then transferred this information to the charts. Field notes, Journal, hash marks, lists, charts—a textual ecosystem. (See fig. 3 for a partial illustration of one such chain.) H. Daniel Peck observes,

> By the fall of 1851 the Journal is already what might be called a material memory, a book deliberately conceived to "keep" time by enlarging the temporal view of reality through the process of cross-reference. Increasingly, this process becomes Thoreau's major strategy for translating facts into truths—the imperative first publicly proclaimed in his early essay "A Natural History of Massachusetts" (1842). Facts would, that is, gain spiritual significance through their gradually revealed placement along the span of time. The disciplined recording of alert observation would provide an invaluable record of facts that, when later remembered (or, reconfigured) in relation to other facts, might reveal the direction and nature of change. When the past was viewed in this way—and *viewing* is indeed the right word—it might become possible to "see" time, and to see it whole, as a full matrix of past, present, and even future.

The charts of general phenomena never became the "Book of Concord." Thoreau charts the spring of that year with enthusiasm, then apparently sets the project aside. In December of 1860, Thoreau contracts a cold, almost certainly exacerbated by underlying tuberculosis, from which he never fully recovers. He ventures west to Minnesota that spring in an effort to heal his lungs, but to no avail. By late summer he is back in Concord, and by fall it seems clear there will be no recovery. It is at this point that the seriously weakened, mostly bedridden Thoreau takes up the Kalendar project again, charting the months of October, November, and December.

## How to Use This Book

First and foremost, this book presents previously unpublished images and transcriptions of Thoreau's charts of general phenomena for April, May, June, October, November, and December. Images of the manuscript charts are followed by transcriptions. I hope these charts will interest and inspire ecologists and climate scientists, labor activists, poets, philosophers, historians,

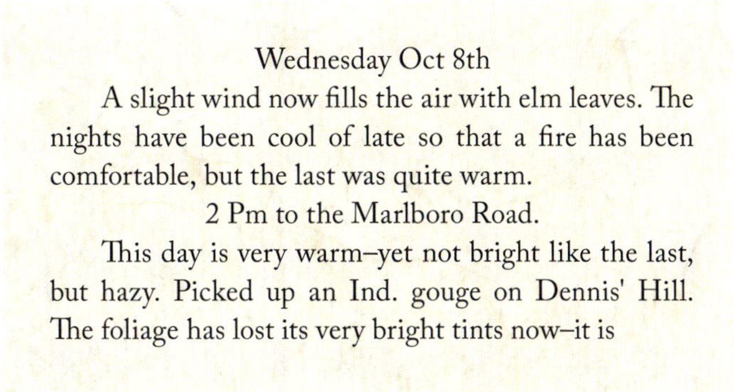

Wednesday Oct 8th

A slight wind now fills the air with elm leaves. The nights have been cool of late so that a fire has been comfortable, but the last was quite warm.

2 Pm to the Marlboro Road.

This day is very warm–yet not bright like the last, but hazy. Picked up an Ind. gouge on Dennis' Hill. The foliage has lost its very bright tints now–it is

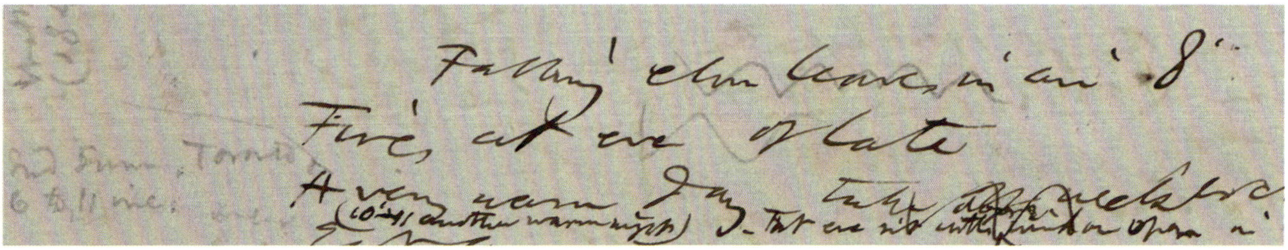

Figure 3. An ecology of texts: "Fires at Eve," October 1851, in Journal, List, and Chart.

activists and journal keepers, Thoreau scholars and time-travel enthusiasts, meteorologists and speculative fiction writers. The charts themselves are infinitely rich, both in their structure and in the particulars they present, and I believe that they can inspire readers to think differently about the ways we inhabit our times and places, and the agency we have to inhabit them differently.

Each month's set of charts is accompanied by an essay structured around a few of its key categories and the Journal passages to which they are linked. These essays seek to operate according to the logic of the Kalendar—connecting selected categories back to the descriptive particulars from which they emerged. If a chart presents the zoomed-out picture of a single month over a span of ten years, each date embedded within the chart indexes a close-up view of a given phenomenon on a particular occasion. As Michael Berger writes, in Thoreau's late natural history writings, "every phenomenon may be enhanced or intensified from elsewhere in a system of mutually glossing works, establishing various patterns of foregrounding and backgrounding in kaleidoscopic fashion." Nothing exemplifies this "foregrounding and backgrounding" effect as clearly as the Kalendar, the complex temporal scale of which "makes us more aware that our commonplace image of the world falls short, in intensity and fullness of detail, of the living reality we overlook." In an attempt to make this effect more accessible to readers, I have highlighted selected entries to which the categories are keyed, and drawn out some of the threads of Thoreau's thinking across his writings. The intention behind the structure of the essays is to demonstrate the workings of the Kalendar as technology—the way that, "with regard to any phenomenon mentioned in passing, we can recall a richness of sensuous detail expressed elsewhere within the system."

It is clear that the Kalendar project represents an aspect of Thoreau's ongoing commitment to detecting order or law in the natural world—a commitment that reflects not only Thoreau's early transcendentalist views of the relationship between nature and spirit but also speaks to a more general nineteenth-century confidence in the fundamental coherence of the universe. However, it is also evident that by 1860, Thoreau had become skeptical of ordering systems, particularly those proposed by the science of his day. Most troublesome about these systems, from Thoreau's perspective, was their tendency to hierarchize the natural world. Thoreau himself had come to understand nature as a great disrupter of hierarchy, a radically democratic order that could look like order's opposite:

In the true natural order–the order or system is not insisted on–  Each is first & each last. That nature presents itself to us this moment–occupies the whole of the present–& rests on the very top most point of the sphere–under the zenith. The species & individuals of all the natural kingdomes–ask our attention & admiration in a round robin–We make straight lines– putting a captain at their head & a lieutenant at their tails– (10/13/1860, Journal Transcript 32:163)

The "species & individuals of all the natural kingdomes"—in other words, all the diverse living beings of his world—seemed to call to Thoreau, to demand his attention, and with it, the suspension of his own previously held ideas. Moreover, this demand unfolded in a cyclical fashion: from the blooming of the first flowers in May to skating boys in December. In the structure of the Kalendar, Thoreau attempted to follow this "round robin" on its own temporal terms, and to consolidate views of each phenomenon without giving priority to any—no "captain at their head," and no "lieutenant at their tails." Any adequate representation of the life of the natural world had to reflect the basic temporal structure of that life: not linear, but cyclical, following the order of the seasons. It also had to reflect the essential equality of elements within the natural system: hence the grid, with its uniform and evenly distributed boxes. The development of the charts of general phenomena thus reflects an innovative compromise—if not a final resolution—in Thoreau's decades-long grappling with the relationship between *law* and *instance*, or *whole* and *part*.

Within its six essays, this book also contains a biographical sketch of two seasons—among the most interesting and least familiar of Thoreau's life. The first half of the book, "Synoptic Vision," borrows its title from Michael Berger's excellent account of Thoreau's natural history writings, *Thoreau's Late Career and the Dispersion of Seeds: The Saunterer's Synoptic Vision*. This portion of the book covers the spring of 1860, a season that witnesses a deeply engaged Thoreau absorbing the lessons of John Brown and Darwin, wrestling with his Emersonian philosophical inheritance, and applying the lessons of John Ruskin to the blooming and cloud-shadowed landscape. The second half of the book, "Second Nature," moves us forward in time a little more than a year, to the final autumn and winter of Thoreau's life, a period in which he is no longer able to go on long walks or keep his daily Journal, and in which he is dependent on friends to bring him news of the natural world. In this period, what had been a tool for expanded vision becomes a method for accessing what I am calling a second or virtual nature, a natural world reconstructed from his years of recordkeeping as well as from the real-time contributions of his friends. In this second season of the Kalendar, I argue, Thoreau came to use the charts not as a blueprint for a new work, but as a way to bring himself into closer relation with a natural world he could no longer directly access with his body.

The categories I've chosen to focus in and elaborate on are a reflection of my own interests and engagements with Thoreau. Another writer, with different interests, would have chosen differently. This means that the book you're reading is a self-portrait of its author at least as much as it is a portrait of Thoreau. I have tried to make this clear, rather than attempt to mitigate or obscure it, by placing myself, my own time and season, at the start of each chapter. (As Thoreau puts it in *Walden*, "In most books, the I, or first person, is omitted; in this it will be retained.") The connections I have made—between Kalendar entries and Journal entries, as well as between Thoreau's biography and his writings—necessarily reflect my own path through the massive body of written material that Thoreau left behind. The lines of meaning I have drawn can—and, I hope, will—be drawn differently by other students of the material presented here.

## How to Love the World

I first encountered the charts of general phenomena as a graduate student living in a small rural town in upstate New York. At the time, I was struggling with what felt like the meaninglessness of my academic work, which I perceived as impossibly distant from the reality of the world in which I found myself. To combat the fatigue that invariably set in during my long afternoons of reading and writing, I took walks through the woods and, returning to the desk in my small study, drew maps of the roads and fields and trails along which I had walked. These activities were immensely relieving to me. Exhausted from looking for meaning in philosophical and literary texts, I stepped out into a world in which meaning simply *was*: where every new flower or leaf that presented itself to my eyes seemed to repeat its own singular name. The names themselves were poems—*hemlock, white pine, trillium, Sawyer Pond Road*—and I began to work to know more and more of them, and to track how they changed over time. The maps I drew were not objective—they did not reflect the points of the compass. Starting in one corner I drew the way I walked: first here, to the stone wall, then left, then here, to the break in the trees, then right at the path.

When I discovered Thoreau's charts of general phenomena in H. Daniel Peck's *Thoreau's Morning Work*, I felt an immediate sense of recognition. Thoreau, too, had felt and tried to represent this way things had of showing themselves, of saying their own names, of speaking to us. And Thoreau, too, had made maps that included himself, his own way of feeling and seeing the species that surrounded him and made his world. "I think that the man of science makes this mistake–& the mass of mankind along with him," he wrote in his Journal in 1857, "that you should coolly give your chief attention to the phenomenon which excites you–as something independent on you–and not as it is related to you. . . . With regard to such objects I find that it is not they themselves–(with which the men of science deal) that concern me. The point of interest is somewhere <u>between</u> me & them (i.e. the objects)" (11/5/1857, Journal Transcript 24:610). Here was a new model of meaning, one according to which my meandering, hand-drawn path through the woods was as real, as true, as the digital map of those woods I can call up on my phone from 376 miles northeast and more than a decade in the future.

My encounter with Thoreau's charts of general phenomena reorganized my thinking, allowing me to envision a mode of scholarship from which my life—the day and its weather, the patterns and demands of domestic life, my feelings—was not excluded from the picture. Moreover, it encouraged me to understand myself as a seasonal creature, one among many who sought warmth in winter and shade in summer. I began to see the world as more-than-human, and meaning itself as a collective undertaking involving many human and nonhuman actors. I began not only to see but to feel the relationships between my being and the climate in which I lived.

In the years in which I have been working on these manuscripts, the seasons of my own life have changed the eyes through which I look at them, and the meanings they offer. In the wake of two important losses in my life, the charts began to speak to me of Thoreau's grief, and of the way mourning thickens and reorganizes time. As I suggest in the second half of this book, the Kalendar became, for Thoreau, a means of living with loss—including the impending loss of his own life. As work by Richard Primack has dramatically illustrated, Thoreau's charts of seasonal phenomena are also linked to larger, more collective losses. In March of 1856, Thoreau wrote the following Journal entry, in which he laments the "maimed & imperfect nature" with which he is intimately connected:

I spend a considerable portion of my time observing the habits of the wild animals my brute neighbors– By their various movements & migrations they fetch the year about to me– Very significant are the flight of geese & the migration of suckers &c &c– But when I consider that the nobler animals have been exterminated here–the cougar– panther–lynx–wolverine wolf–bear moose–deer the beaver, the turkey&c &c–I cannot but feel as if I lived in a tamed &, as it were, emasculated country– Would not the motions of those larger & wilder animals have been more significant still– Is it not a maimed & imperfect nature that I am conversant with? . . . –I am reminded that this my life in Nature –this particular round of natural phenomena which I call a year–is lamentably incomplete– I listen to concert–in which so many parts are wanting. . . .

I take infinite pains to know all the phenomena of the spring, for instance–thinking that I have here the entire poem–& then to my chagrin I learn that it is but an imperfect copy that I possess & have read– that my ancestors have torn out many of the first leaves & grandest passages–& mutilated it in many places. (3/23/1856, Journal Transcript 20:166–67)

As Rochelle Johnson has observed, this passage registers a haunted grief for an ecological wound that has only deepened with time: "Like many of us, Thoreau knows he walks with and among the disappeared nonetheless still there. His world is replete with ghosts—each missing mammal, each vanished species, each shrunken stream still present, apparitions felt as he moves through space and time. He walks amid them. Even through them. Presences in absence. Sounds of silence." The entry registers both grief and intimacy, both loss and love. As the realities of the climate crisis and mass extinction become ever more apparent, we find ourselves looking for ways to grieve what is lost while continuing to love the world that remains to us in the time that remains to us. Throughout his life, Thoreau was steadfast in his commitment to living a meaningful life, to remaining *awake* to his own experience, and to honoring the wonder of the world in which he lived. In his last year of life, he found ways to maintain this state of reverent alertness, even as he recognized the depth of his own losses and the losses sustained by the more-than-human community in which he lived. The Kalendar was, among other things, a tool for loving a life, and a world, riven by loss.

# Feeling Time

Chronoception—our sense of the passage of time—is both deeply internal, keyed to the operations of entropy in the cells of the body, and thoroughly collective, connected to diurnal and planetary cycles, social calendars and the shared rhythms of cultural life. As Barbara Adam writes, we experience time neither as an arrow nor as a recurrent cycle but always as both:

> There can be no un-ageing, no undying, no un-birth. We can relive past moments in our lives but we cannot reverse the processes of the living and material world. We know the unidirectionality of time from geological and historic records, from physical processes involving energy exchange, from the irreversible accumulation of knowledge, and from the fact that people and things get older and never younger. We know that the sequence of the diurnal cycle goes from dawn to midday to dusk to night and never backwards from dusk to midday to morning. These examples demonstrate that cyclicality and irreversible linearity are not, as so frequently asserted, the dominant time perceptions of traditional and modern societies respectively. Rather they are integral to all rhythmically structured phenomena.

Implicit in this understanding of the double nature of our sense of time is the complex way our individual senses of the passage of time are linked to those of other species and to physical processes of regeneration and decay that govern that material world. Recent psychological studies on the experience of awe suggests that the expansiveness associated with this state is connected to our experience of time, and in particular with a feeling of temporal expansion. The more fully we engage with our felt experience of time, it seems, the more deeply we learn both lessons: that our experience of time is surprisingly manipulable, and that we are powerless to turn the arrow. Thoreau's Kalendar, in its attempts to integrate human and more-than-human timescales and to extend moments of wonder at the abundance of the natural world, exemplifies the power of a radically expanded conception of time. As an elegy to a life lived in nature, it is also a testament to the irreversibility of time's arrow.

I hope that readers of this book will conduct their own investigations, following the Kalendar's numbers back to the Journal entries to which they point and discovering their own constellations of meaning. The transcriptions published here can also be found at the online home of Thoreau's Kalendar: Thoreauskalendar.org. Here you can follow links from each Kalendar date directly to the relevant Journal entries, walking backward in Thoreau's footsteps, and moving, as he did in his final months, between the seasons of his life. I have made such journeys myself countless times over the past decade, and doing so has taught me to think differently about my life's own seasons. The arrow of time demands that we live also in its circles, in the slow time of wonder and in the wide orbit of our planet. I hope readers will be inspired by Thoreau's slow, devoted attention to his world, and by his relentless creativity in reimagining the time in which he lived. May we find in his example the courage to reimagine our own.

# Editorial Principles and Processes

M Y  P U R P O S E  I N  P R E S E N T I N G  T H E  C H A R T S  O F  G E N E R A L phenomena in this form is to provide general readers with access to the rich world of Thoreau's late manuscripts and a lens through which to connect his work with *our own time*, in the many senses of that phrase. Though I have sought to be as accurate as possible in my transcriptions and historical interpretations, I am not trained as a textual editor and have not attempted the systematic rigor of a scholarly edition.

Each chart has been read against the original manuscript and the Journal several times and by multiple readers. However, given the age of the manuscripts and difficulty of Thoreau's hand, many uncertainties remain. The transcriptions thus represent what I believe with a reasonable degree of certainty that Thoreau has written. Where I have made an informed guess about a word or phrase, these occur in square brackets. Where this has not been possible the word has been replaced by the word "unclear" (or "uncl.") in square brackets.

For quotations of Thoreau's Journal, I have used the published volumes of the edition prepared by the *Writings of Henry D. Thoreau* under the direction of Editor-in-Chief Elizabeth Hall Witherell and published by Princeton University Press. For the later, not-yet-published volumes, I have relied on manuscript transcripts prepared by the editors. Brackets, cross-outs, and other editorial markings present in the transcripts have been omitted for ease of reading. The Princeton edition, as it is commonly known, has restored Thoreau's idiosyncratic punctuation and fluid, informal writerly gestures, many of which had been purged from the 1906 Houghton Mifflin edition of the Journal.

# *Common Abbreviations and Markings*

———————

Thoreau uses the following abbreviations and markings frequently in the charts of general phenomena:

V. – *vide*, Latin for "see." This is Thoreau's most commonly used notation, and it often signals a relation between similar phenomena occurring on different dates

Do. – ditto

Ap. – apparently

S.L. – summer level (average water depth in summer)

Ind. Sum. – Indian Summer

Consid. – considerably

Calc. – calculate

Ult. – *ultimo mense*, Latin for "last month"

F.H.P. – Fair Haven Pond

Inc. – inclusive

N.B. – *nota bene*, Latin for "note well"

N.p. – next page

The charts contain many other abbreviations that can be derived from context, e.g., T & L for "thunder and lightning," c for "chamber," etc. Many place-names and botanical names are also shortened by one or more syllable.

Thoreau's most common markings are wavy lines, arrows, circles, and underlines, which I have presented in the transcriptions as clearly as possible. These markings generally have to do with placement of text. Circles, lines, and arrows usually signify that a given entry should be moved to another square in the grid—either to a different year or to a different category. Circles and lines are also used to demarcate entries that overflow their squares, a very frequent occurrence. Carets are used to indicate additions to text. When Thoreau puts a wavy line through an entire row of the chart, this signifies that he wished to strike this category from the month in question—usually in order to include it in a different month. (There are several instances of this in November and December.)

HENRY DAVID THOREAU'S

# KALENDAR

PART I:

# *Synoptic Vision*

_____

General Phenomena for April. The Morgan Library & Museum. MA 610.

APRIL:

# *Sea Turn*

———————

THIS SPRING THE SNOWPACK HAS GONE QUICKLY, THE ONCE immovable glaciers under the eaves softened in March to an airy crystal and then gave way. We follow the news about the war. The trowels and tree limbs and broken flowerpots of a distant life reveal themselves one by one in the new light: wreckage of the past, washed up on the shore of April. If, on my hands and knees in the garden, I pulled at the pile of papery, stuck-together leaves—bleached and dry on top, black and wet underneath—I would see little green shoots fighting upwards from the still-cool earth. Who taught us this, about the palimpsest of dead leaves, and the green shoots, and the cold earth? On what calendar day did we learn it?

The first days without a fire in the stove are the coldest of the year, the yellow light pouring into the wintered-over rooms, my hands numb from typing, the cat crazed with the smells of the new season: rot and dead grass and warm wood and mud. I open the sliding glass door for her to slide inside and out, inside and out. My fourteen-year-old son's limbs assume impossible proportions. In the distance, a chainsaw, a siren, a robin. *There comes to me a melody which the air has strained.* Overhead, the geese move their collective body toward the horizon. Inside ourselves, the ache of the violence we busy ourselves against knowing spreads into our lungs. In the garden, the little green shoots root down.

\*

In the spring of 1860, Henry Thoreau's thinking was reestablishing itself in the wake of two events. These were the execution of John Brown in December of 1859, and his own reading, on New Year's Day of 1860, of an advance copy of Charles Darwin's *On the Origin of Species*. Like the dramatic, gale-like winds that make their way inland from the ocean bearing a new atmosphere, these sea turns in Thoreau's mental life changed everything.

A few months earlier, in the wake of the failed Harpers Ferry Raid, Thoreau had written in defense of the violent uprising.

> The United States have a coffle of four millions of slaves. They are determined to keep them in this condition; and Massachusetts is one of the confederated overseers to prevent their escape. Such are not all the inhabitants of Massachusetts, but such are they who rule and are obeyed here. It was Massachusetts, as well as Virginia, that put down this insurrection at Harper's Ferry. She sent the marines there, and she will have to pay the penalty of her sin.

Using the same logic that animates "Civil Disobedience," Thoreau asks in "A Plea for Captain John Brown" what it means to be a citizen in a nation constituted by slavery, a Northerner cast unwillingly in the role of overseer by "they who rule and are obeyed." In response to those who object to the violence of Brown's action, Thoreau notes Massachusetts's participation in the state violence that, in putting down the insurrection (and later in sentencing Brown to death) enforced the ongoing existence of slavery: Massachusetts "sent the marines there, and she will have to pay the penalty of her sin." The theme here, as in many of Thoreau's antislavery writings, is that slavery is *everyone's business*, that white Northerners were not absolved by geographic or even ideological distance, but bound to the crime of slavery by both material and ethical bonds.

> The slave-ship is on her way, crowded with its dying victims; new cargoes are being added in mid-ocean a small crew of slaveholders, countenanced by a large body of passengers, is smothering four millions under the hatches, and yet the politician asserts that the only proper way by which deliverance is to be obtained, is by "the quiet diffusion of the sentiments of humanity," without any "outbreak." As if the sentiments of humanity were ever found unaccompanied by its deeds, and you could disperse them, all finished to order, the pure article, as easily as water with a watering-pot, and so lay the dust. What is that that I hear cast overboard? The bodies of the dead that have found deliverance. That is the way we are "diffusing" humanity, and its sentiments with it.

In its evocation of the United States as a slave ship in which passive passengers do nothing to resist the actions of "a small crew of slaveholders," "A Plea" makes clear that, in response to such circumstances, nonaction—insistence on "the quiet diffusion of the sentiments of humanity"—in fact *constitutes* violence. The bodies that we are casting overboard are the reality behind the pious phrase.

That "we" is crucial. Make no mistake, Thoreau was saying to his white Massachusetts audience, *we* are committing the violence of slavery. Thoreau's encounter with the radical Christian, abolitionist, and insurrectionist John Brown seems to have triggered his full apprehension of the relations that bound white Northern abolitionists like Thoreau himself to slavery as an economic and political power. Thoreau's perennial question, *what does it mean to live a meaningful life?*, seemed to him to have been answered in a singularly powerful way by Brown's uncompromising life and death. At the heart of his apprehension of Brown's significance was the way it illustrated the network of relations that those who spoke of "the quiet diffusion of the sentiments of humanity" sought to obscure. This network spanned racial, geographic, and legal boundaries, bringing Thoreau into a new, felt proximity to the outlaw Brown, enslaved men and women, and the overseers who committed the outward violence of slavery.

The perception of "a web of complex relations," to use Darwin's own phrase, was equally central to Thoreau's second sea turn of 1859–60: his reading of *On the Origin of Species*. This reading occurred on New Year's Day of 1860, when Thoreau attended a dinner party at Franklin Sanborn's house with Bronson Alcott and Charles Loring Brace. Brace had come from a visit with his uncle, Harvard botany professor Asa Gray, an old friend of Darwin's, who had been sent an advance copy. As Laura Dassow Walls recounts, "Gray lent it to Brace, who showed it to Sanborn, Alcott, and Thoreau. All afternoon the four friends read *Origin of Species* aloud to one another and discussed Darwin's extraordinary principle of 'Natural Selection.'" In its description of species evolution, Darwin's book overthrew the popular picture, promoted by famed Harvard biologist Louis Agassiz, of unchanging and eternal species individually created and placed in their particular habitats by divine agency. The "special creation" argument was central to the "scientific" justification for slavery, which claimed the different races as different species, of which only whites were fully human. As Walls writes, "Darwin's revolutionary book would take on many meanings over the years, but on this New Year's Day, for the four radicals in Sanborn's parlor, *Origin of Species* was first and foremost an argument debunking the so-called scientific basis for slavery."

Darwin also confirmed what Thoreau had for some time believed, that plant generation was driven by seeds, which were in turn dispersed by wind, animals, and other environmental actors. Some seeds dropped into ponds or onto rock, but others found nourishing soil, and flourished. Thoreau's accumulated observations about the reproduction mechanisms of trees and the complex cycles of forest evolution, now informed by his reading of Darwin, would eventually become the lecture "The Succession of Forest Trees." Immediately published in the *New-York Weekly Tribune* and widely reprinted, this text was read by more people in his lifetime than anything Thoreau had ever written. It would go on to become, as Michael Berger notes, "a pioneering document in the development of forest management and of ecology."

In April of 1860, though, it was not principally the question of seed dispersal that occupied Thoreau's mind, but the dizzying holistic vision afforded by his apprehension, in two seemingly disparate spheres, of the infinite "web of complex relations" in which he was bound. The charts of general phenomena can be understood as a sketch or schematic of this vision, which, like Darwin's radical new theory, captured an unwieldy record of change and continuity over time into a single frame. Likely inspired by an assignment from Bronson Alcott in his role as superintendent of Concord schools to prepare "a small text book . . . comprising the geography, history, and antiquities of Concord," Thoreau envisioned a "Book of Concord" that would chronicle every significant natural event over the course of a typical year.

For years, Thoreau had been compelled by the prospect of multiplying perspectives in order to achieve a more holistic view of the natural world. In *Walden*, he had written, "If we knew all the laws of Nature, we should need only one fact, or the description of only one actual phenomenon to infer all the particular results at that point. . . . The particular laws are as our points of view, as, to the traveller, a mountain's outline varies with every step, and it has an infinite number of profiles, though absolutely but one form." Was he expecting such clarity of vision to emerge from the charts of general phenomena? If so, he may have been disappointed. As H. Daniel Peck writes, "The unstated assumption of the Journal is that at some future point, a point always receding before the endless work of observation, the picture will be complete. At that moment, the master perceiver will collect his views and integrate them into a coherent vision, which would be nothing less than the world as seen in the mind of God." If the Kalendar, as Peck suggests, represents an attempt to achieve this totalizing integration, it can only be considered a failure: many of the boxes remain blank, and overlapping and contradictory data confuse any single, coherent picture of an archetypal month. But it seems likely that by 1860, Thoreau was after something else. Rather than seeking a God's-eye view, Thoreau attended closer than ever to his particularly human vantage point, gathering, recording, and remembering the phenomena that marked his personal experience of the turning year. The April categories include "1st day without great coat," "first am that I sit with window open," and (inevitably) "first wear great coat again." These markers of human time, of his time, are arrayed in neighborly proximity to ripples on the lakes and the first leaves on young oaks. What the charts enabled him to see was not an ideal and harmonious vision of the months, but a wider view of the complex web of relations into which he too was woven, a truth he'd long intuited but which, in the wake of his encounters with Brown and Darwin, grasped him with the force of a revelation.

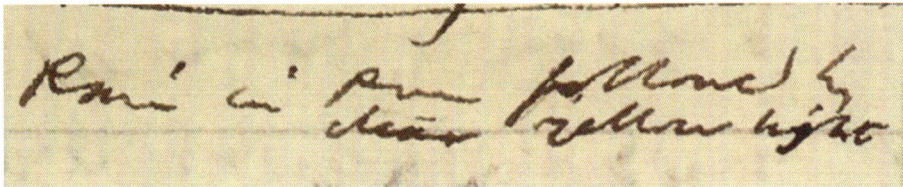

*Rain in Pm Followed by Clear Yellow Light*

The forenoon was cloudy & in the afternoon it rained–but the sun set clear lighting up the west with a yellow light.– . . . in which the frame of a new building is distinctly seen there was no green grass to reflect– while drops hang on every twig– & producing the first rain bow I have seen or heard of except one long ago in the morning. With April showers methinks come rain-bows. Why are they so rare in the winter? (4/9/1855, Journal Transcript 18:353)

Again we had this <u>Pm</u> at 2 oclock–those wild scudding wind clouds in the north–spitting cold rain or sleet with the curved lines of falling rain beneath. The wind is so strong that the thin drops fall on you in the sun shine when the cloud has drifted far to one side. The air is peculiarly clear–the light intense–& when the sun shines slanting under the dark scud–the willows &c rising above the dark flooded meadows are lit with a fine straw-colored light like the spirits of trees. (4/25/1857, Journal Transcript 23:36)

Many of the categories for April, May, and June emphasize perception: the impact of light on a landscape, the sudden appearance of rainbows, the reflective properties of water in different kinds of weather. Thoreau's interest in visual perception—its limitations and changefulness as well as the possibilities it affords—was lifelong, and the Kalendar itself can be understood as a manifestation of this interest. It was, as Walls writes, a "working tool" that allowed Thoreau to "visualize every least event in the broadest context, the grand cycle of the season in pointillist detail." The charts, she writes, "were telescopes, instruments of vision." In April of 1852 Thoreau wrote the following Journal entry, recasting, as he frequently did, the previous day's experiences in the present tense:

> From Ball's? Hill the Great Meadow looks more light–perhaps it is the medium between the dark & light above mentioned. Mem. Try this experiment again. *i.e.* look not toward nor from the sun but athwart this line. Seen from this hill in this direction–there are here and there dark-shadows spreading rapidly over the surface . . . where the wind strikes the water. The water toward the sun seen from this height–shows not the broad silvery light but a myriad fine sparkles. The sky is full of light this morning–with different shades of blue–lighter below, darker above separated perhaps by a thin strip of white vapor.– Thicker in the east . . .
>
> The aspect of the sky varies every hour   about noon I observed it in the south composed of . . . short clouds horizontal & parallel to one another, each straight & dark below with a slight cumulus resting on it. a little marsh-wise. Again, in the north, I see a light but rather watery looking flock of clouds–at mid-afternoon slight wisps & thin veils of whitish clouds also. (4/10/1852, *Journal* 4:430–32)

This entry captures the interlocking gears of time and perception that both inspired the Kalendar project and emerged from the production of the charts. On April 10, Thoreau would have made notes in pencil on small scraps of paper he carried with him while walking. These field notes he would have referred to on April 11 while writing the entry, a process that seemed to entail such vivid recollection that he slipped into—or else consciously adopted—the voice of a real-time observer. Within the entry, he addresses his future self: "Mem. Try this experiment again." The entry thus represents a nexus of past, present, and future experiences, each in some respect fed, amplified, or refracted by the others. This temporal picture would become even more complex in 1860, when a detail from the same entry, about the appearance of a cluster of dark-shadowed clouds, made its way into the list of April phenomena and then into the chart.

By 1860, Thoreau fully comprehended a principle he'd long been developing that linked time, perception, and "tracking" or writing: "A man receives only what he is ready to receive–whether physically–or intellectually or morally– as animals conceive at certain seasons their kind only," he wrote. "We hear & apprehend only what we already half know– . . . Every man thus *tracks himself*, through life–in all his hearing & reading & observation & travelling. His observations make a chain– The phenomenon or fact that cannot in any wise be linked–with the rest which he has observed, he does not observe" (1/5/1860, Journal Transcript 30:230). As early as 1852, Thoreau had been working toward this principle, making tracks for his future self to follow—"Mem. Try this experiment again."

The "clear yellow light" of April afternoons created the conditions for special perception: in this light, Thoreau could see, as if with magnified vision, "drops hang on every twig" and willows lit up as if from within, like "the spirits of trees." These were perceptive experiences to record, to remember, to seek out again in future Aprils. Embedded within the charts of general phenomena, they also represented microcosms of the whole project—instances of expanded perception that would inspire the technology of expanded perception that is the Kalendar.

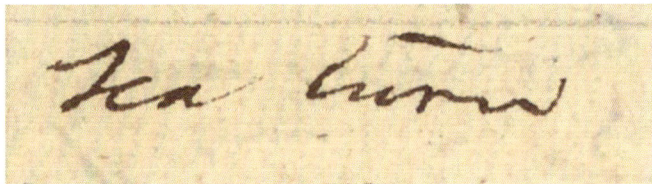

*Sea Turn*

When I reach the top of the hill–I see suddenly–all the Southern . . . horizon full of a mist–like a dust–already concealing the Lincoln hills and producing distinct wreathes of vapor– the rest of the horizon being clear  Evidently a sea turn–a wind from over the sea–condensing the moisture in our warm atmosphere–& putting another aspect on the face of things–all this I see & say long before I feel the change–while still sweltering on the rocks– for the heat was oppressive Nature cannot abide this sudden heat–but calls for her fan. In 10 minutes I hear a susurrus in the shrub oak leaves–at a distance & soon an agreeable fresh air washes these warm rocks–& some mist surrounds me. (4/18/1855, Journal Transcript 18:379)

Unlike the charts documenting bird migration patterns and the leafing out of trees, the charts of general phenomena concern themselves less with particular species and more with weather and weather-related events and activities (rain and wind, as well as plowing and glove wearing in April, for example). Thoreau understood "atmosphere" (sometimes simply "air") as a communicative medium, a channel for moods, feelings, and ideas as well as weather patterns. In Thoreau's time as in ours, *atmosphere* had both a technical, weather-related sense and an affective sense (as in "I didn't like the atmosphere of that meeting"). Atmosphere thus serves as a kind of conceptual bridge between material and immaterial registers, a way of talking about the connection between matter and spirit. Highly attendant to both of these registers, Thoreau documents atmospheric shifts and their attendant changes in visual perception and sense experience. He also writes frequently about atmosphere in terms of affect. In *Walden* he had written,

> In the midst of a gentle rain while these thoughts prevailed, I was suddenly sensible of such sweet and beneficent society in Nature, in the very pattering of the drops, and in every sound and sight around my house, an infinite and unaccountable friendliness all at once like an atmosphere sustaining me, as made the fancied advantages of human neighborhood insignificant, and I have never thought of them since. Every little pine needle expanded and swelled with sympathy and befriended me.

Here, attention to atmosphere as a living force reorients Thoreau's experience of solitude. After an initial feeling of loneliness in the woods, he comes to feel himself supported by the more-than-human forces that enable his existence: the air he breathes, the rain that gives life to the plants that in turn give life to him, the vast network of invisible connections in which he now finds himself located and held. In his most transcendental moods, Thoreau used *atmosphere* as a word suggestive of spirit: "My desire for knowledge is intermittent," he wrote, "but my desire to commune with the spirit of the universe—to be intoxicated with the fumes, call it, of that divine nectar–to bear my head through atmospheres and over heights unknown to my feet–is perennial and constant" (2/9/1851, *Journal* 3:185).

In his description of the German word *Stimmung*, Hans Urlich Gumbrecht notes that its most common English translations are "mood" and "climate." Though we typically think of mood as private and internal and climate as external and objective, the coming together of these aspects in the German concept may help us to see the way that a mood may operate like weather: both a surrounding system and a reality that colors my private experience. Etymologically linked to *stimmen*, meaning to tune an instrument, *Stimmung* also derives meaning from its association with music and hearing:

> As is well known, we do not hear with our inner and outer ear alone. Hearing is a complex form of behavior that involves the entire body. Skin and haptic modalities of perception play an important role. Every tone we perceive is, of course, a form of physical reality (if an invisible one) that "happens" to our body and at the same time, "surrounds" it. Another dimension of reality that happens to our bodies in a similar way and surrounds them is the weather. For this very reason, references to music and weather often occur when literary texts make moods and atmospheres present or begin to reflect on them.

Intensely attuned to his internal and external weather, as well as to the "web of complex relations" between them, Thoreau often invoked and created atmospheric effects in his writing. One can hear the emphasis on the subtlety of attunement in his awareness of "the very pattering of the drops" and "every little pine needle." The comprehensive phenomenon of atmosphere acts as an instrument of expanded perception, prompting an awareness of even minute details of the world around him. In this way, a new atmosphere generates a new felt relation between internal and external realities.

Thoreau was particularly interested in an atmosphere's capacity to intervene in visual perception and to carry and alter sound:

> Heard at a distance the sound of a bell acquires a certain vibratory hum, as it were from the air through which it passes– . . . It is not

the mere sound of the bell but the humming in the air that enchants me—just [as the] azure tint which much air or distance imparts delights the eye. It is not so much the object as the object clothed with an azure veil. All sound heard at a great distance thus tends to produce the same music—vibrating the strings of the universal lyre. There comes to me a melody which the air has strained.– which has conversed with every leaf and needle of the woods. It is by no means the sound of the bell as heard near at hand, and which at this distance I can plainly distinguish—but its vibrating echoes that portion of the sound which the elements take up and modulate. (10/12/1851, *Journal* 4:142–43)

Thoreau describes the sonic effects of atmosphere (an echo) in terms of a visual perception (the distant ridge) before returning to the register of sound. Both descriptions involve the effect of distance and an intervening atmosphere that produce a particular effect on the human perceiver. Atmosphere is a bridge between subject and object, or an uncertain territory between them: a place where categories of *self* and *nature* are difficult to distinguish.

Given the intensity of his interest in atmosphere and its effects, the phenomenon of the sea turn—"a wind from over the sea–condensing the moisture in our warm atmosphere–& putting another aspect on the face of things"—can only have been a source of fascination for Thoreau, for whom "putting another aspect on the face of things" was an essential function of writing.

In *Walden*, Thoreau recounts looking at prospective sites for his cabin and mentally inhabiting each spot, living in each place "in imagination . . . for an hour, a summer and a winter life." "Wherever I sat," he writes, "there I might live, and the landscape radiated from me accordingly." This link between *position* and *perception* is the crux of Thoreau's perspectivism: his understanding that the world looks, sounds, and *is* different, depending on where one sits—and what kind of atmosphere "intervenes." A sudden change in atmosphere—a sea turn—has the power to alter our perception of the world in much the same way a radical shift in position (say, moving to the woods, or climbing a mountain) does. Though only observed in 1855 and 1856, sea turns were on Thoreau's mind in 1860, no doubt in part because of changes wrought in his own internal weather by Darwin and Brown.

*Smooth Reflecting Water*

The serenity & warmth are the main thing after the windy & cool days we have had. You may even hear a fish leap in the water now. The lowing of a cow advances me many weeks toward summer. The reflections grow more distinct every moment.– At last the outline of the hill is as distinct below as above. And every object appears rhymed by reflection (4/11/1852, *Journal* 4:437)

Another still moist overcast day–without sun but all day a crescent of light as if breaking away in the north. The waters smooth & full of reflections– A still cloudy day like this is perhaps the best to be on the water– To the clouds perhaps we owe both the stillness & the reflections– for the light is in a great measure reflected from the water. Robins sing now at 10 Am as in the morning–& the Phoebe–& pig– woodpecker's caclle is heard–& many martins (with white-bel– swallows) are skimming & twittering above the water–perhaps catching the small fuzzy gnats with which the air is filled. The sound of church bells, at various distances–in Concord & the neighboring towns, sounds very sweet to us on the water–this still day– It is the song of the villages heard with the song of the birds. (4/15/1855, Journal Transcript 18:363–64)

Now we shall be recompensed for the week's confinement to shop or garden– We will spend our Sabbath exploring these smooth warm vernal waters– Up or down shall we go–to Fair Haven Bay & the Sudbury Meadows? or to Ball's Hill & Carlisle Bridge–? Along the meadows' edge–lined with willow & alders & maples–under the catkins of the early willow–and brushing those of the sweet-gale with our prow–where the sloping pasture & the ploughed ground–submerged–are fast drinking up the flood– What fair isles–what remote coast shall we explore– What San-Salvador or Bay of All Saints–arrive at? All are tempted forth like flies into the sun– All isles seem fortunate & blessed today–all capes are of Good Hope– The same sun & calm that tempts the turtles out tempts the voyagers– It is an opportunity to explore their own natures–to float along their own shores– (5/3/1857, Journal Transcript 23:48–49)

Central to Thoreau's understanding of the natural world, reflection—the phenomenon by which vision, experience, and thought bend back upon themselves, recurring, but with a difference—was associated with dazzlement, harmony, and abundance. The twinning of every object in calm water on a still day, the doubling of light produced by the reflected sun, and the more abstract mirrorings everywhere evident to Thoreau as he considered the "web of complex relations" in which he found himself—these phenomena were central to what Alan Hodder identifies as Thoreau's ecstatic vision. In Thoreau's writing, the word *ecstasy* "designates certain privileged experiences of unknown origin that from an early age fired his imagination." Like Emerson, who described nature itself as ecstatic in his 1841 lecture "The Method of Nature," Thoreau also perceived the dizzying self-reproducing logic of a world in which "every natural fact is an emanation, and that from which it emanates is an emanation also, and from every emanation is a new emanation." One senses this logic of similitude and reproduction in both the April 11, 1852, entry, in which "every object appears rhymed by reflection" and in the entry of April 15, 1855, in which reflections of sight seamlessly give way to reflections of sound.

Reflection—meaning our capacity to reproduce experience in thought or writing, as well as the optical phenomenon—was thus central to Thoreau's project as a writer and linked to some of his most frequently used strategies. Consider, for example, the effect of the bewildering reflections at the end of "Where I Lived and What I Lived For," the second chapter of *Walden*:

Time is but the stream I go a-fishing in. I drink at it; but while I drink I see the sandy bottom and detect how shallow it is. Its thin current slides away, but eternity remains. I would drink deeper; fish in the sky, whose bottom is pebbly with stars. I cannot count one. I know not the first letter of the alphabet. I have always been regretting that I was not as wise as the day I was born. The intellect is a cleaver; it discerns and rifts its way into the secret of things. I do not wish to be any more busy with my hands than is necessary. My head is hands and feet. I feel all my best faculties concentrated in it.

Here, the topsy-turvy effect of water's reflection of the sky is translated into a description that reverses other polarities: time and eternity, pebbles and stars, innocence and wisdom, head and hands/feet. The effect of this hall-of-mirrors is the kind of lostness within which, Thoreau thought, "we begin to find ourselves, and realize where we are and the infinite extent of our relations." As an optical phenomenon, reflections reveal much about those relations—between objects and surfaces and light, between what is and what is perceived, what we are and what we might become. In 1857, prompted by the "smooth warm vernal waters" and their giving back of willows and alders and maples, Thoreau asked, "What fair isles–what remote coast shall we explore– What San-Salvador or Bay of All Saints–arrive at?" This was the reflective, expansive mood of the season that above all announces the return of life. In inscribing both mood and season in the charts of general phenomena, Thoreau sought a kind of purchase on this mood unavailable in the linear experience of time. Days of smooth reflecting water, in which "all capes are of Good Hope," were fleeting—as Thoreau well knew. But as he assembled the charts that comprise his Kalendar, Thoreau could see the way such days were in fact *perennial*, part of the web of the turning year, and never fully lost, even when hidden from view.

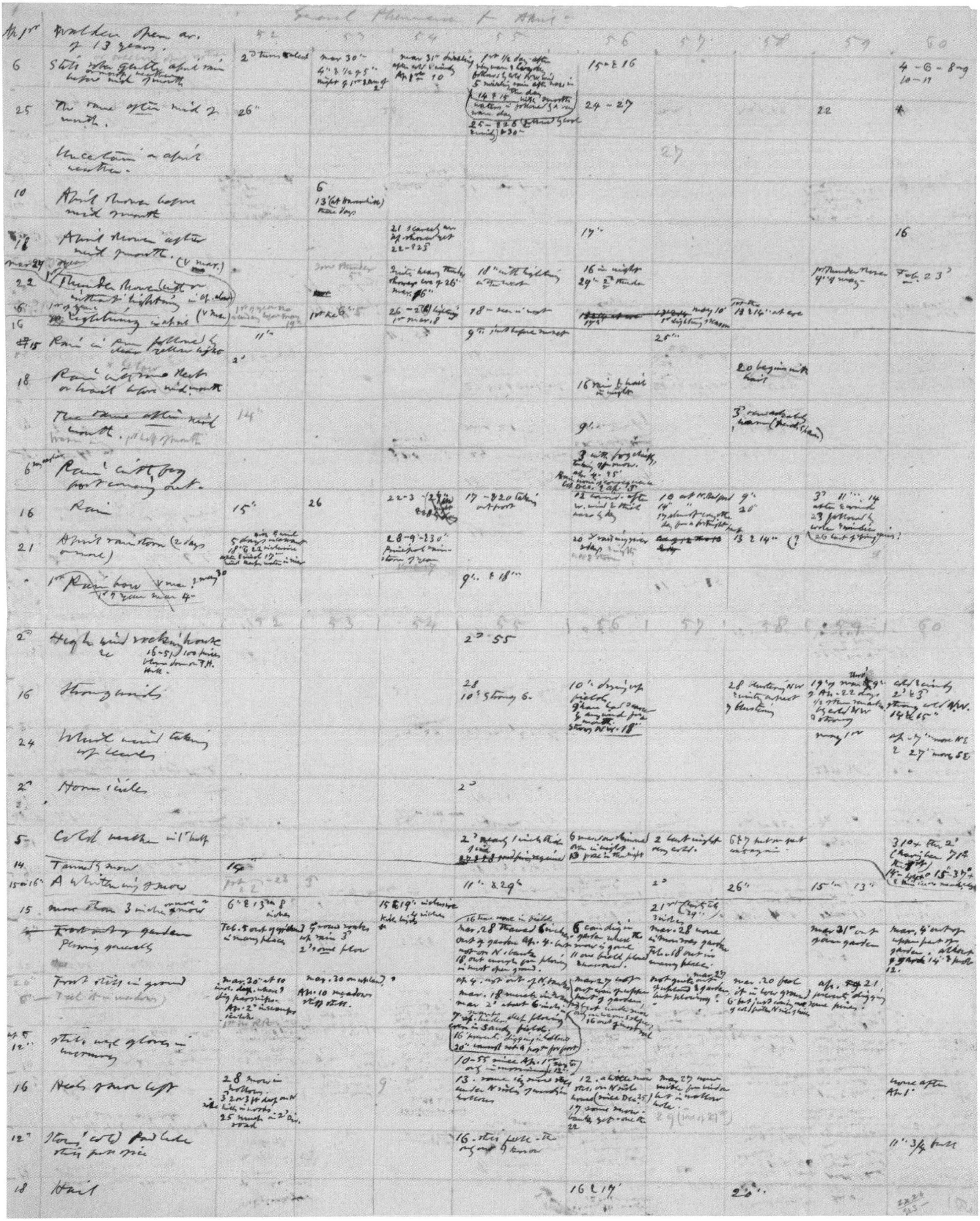
52
53
54
55
56
57
58
59
60
Rain
Strong winds
Hail

## General Phenomena for April

| | | 52 | 53 | 54 | 55 |
|---|---|---|---|---|---|
| Ap. 1st | **Walden open av. of 13 years.** | | | | |
| 6 | or overcast April weather<br>**Still sober gentle April rain<br>or moist weather<br>before mid of month** | 2nd turns to sleet | Mar 30th<br>4th & ½ or 5th<br>night of 1st & am of<br>2nd | Mar 31st drizzling<br>after cold & windy<br>Ap 1st 10 | 1st ½ day after very warm &<br>hazy day followed by cold<br>N.W. wind 5 mizzling rain<br>after haze in the day |
| 25 | **The same <u>after</u> mid of<br>month.** | 26th | | | <u>14 & 15</u> with smooth waters –<br>followed by a very warm <u>day</u><br>25 - & 26 (followed by cool<br>& windy) & 30th |
| | **Uncertain or April weather.** | | | | |
| 10 | **April shower before<br>mid of month** | | 6<br>13th (at Haverhill) three days | | |
| 18 | **April shower after<br>mid of month** | | | 21 scarcely an Ap. shower yet<br>22 - & 23rd | |
| Mar<br>24<br>22 | 1st of year (V. Mar)<br>**Thunder shower (with or with-<br>out lightning in Ap. alone)** | | Some thunder<br>5th<br>[uncl] | Quite heavy thunder<br>showers eve of 26th<br>Mar. 16th | 18th with lightning<br>in the west |
| 6? | <u>1st of year</u><br>**Lightning in April** (v. Mar) | 1st of year the Sunday<br>before May 19th | 1st the 6th 5 | 26 - 2nd(?) lightning<br>1st Mar. 8 | 18th seen in west |
| 16<br>17 15 | **Rain in pm followed by<br>clear yellow light** | 11 | | | 9th just before sunset |
| 18 | v below<br>**Rain with some sleet<br>or hail before mid month** | 2nd | | | |
| | **The same after mid month**<br>Warm in 1st half of month | 14th | | | |
| 6 Say | earlier<br>**Rain with fog<br>frost coming out.** | | | | |
| 16 | **Rain** | 15th | 26 | 22 - 3 (27th in night &<br>28 by day) | 17 - & 20 taking<br>out frost |
| ?<br>21 | **April rainstorm (2 days<br>or more)** | With E wind 5 days incessantly<br>18 – 22nd inclusive after E. wind<br>17th wind keeps water in river | | 28 - 9 - & 30th<br>Principal rain storm of year<br>16 & 17 | |
| | **1st Rainbow** v. Mar & May 30<br>1st of year Mar 4th | | | | 9th & 18th |
| | | 52 | 53 | 54 | 55 |
| 2nd | **High wind rocking house<br>&c** 16-51 100 pines<br>blown down on F.H. Hill. | | | | 2nd 55 |
| 16 | **Strong winds** | | | | 28<br>10th Strong S. |
| 24 | **Whirl wind taking<br>up leaves** | | | | |
| 2nd | **Horn icicles** | | | | 2nd |
| 5 | **Cold weather in 1st half** | | | | 2nd nearly 1 inch thick of ice<br>27 & 28 good fires required |
| 14 | **Tanned by snow** | 14th | | | |
| 15 or<br>16th | **A whitening of snow** | 1st -28<br>&2nd | 3rd | | 11th & 29th |

| 56 | 57 | 58 | 59 | 60 |
|---|---|---|---|---|
| 15 & 16 | | | | 4 - 6 - 8- 9<br>10 - 11 |
| 24-27 | | | 22 | ‡ |
| | 27 | | | |
| 17th | | | | 16 |
| 16 in night<br>29th 2nd thunder | | | 1st thunder shower<br>9th of May- | Feb. 23rd |
| 13th & 14th at eve<br>17th | 13 & 14    May 10th<br>1st lightning of season | 1st the<br>13 & 14th at eve | | |
| | 25th | | | |
| 16 rain & hail<br>in night | | 20 begins with<br>hail | | |
| 9th | | 3rd remarkably<br>warm (perch spawn) | | |
| 3 with fog chiefly, taking off<br>snow. also 4 -& 5 Rain none of<br>consequence bet Dec. & Ap. 3 | | | | |
| 12 consid. after<br>w. wind & thick<br>haze by day | 10 at N. Bedford    14th "<br>17 almost every other<br>    day for a fortnight past | 9th<br>20th | 3rd 11th 14 after E wind<br>23 followed by<br>cooler & windier<br>26 last of spring rains? | |
| 20 [?] raising river<br>2 days & nights<br>A NE storm | eve of 12 [?] 13th<br>&14th | 13 & 14th (? | | |
| 56 | 57 | 58 | 59 | 60 |
| 10th drying up fields 9th have<br>had scarcely any wind for a<br>month. Strong NW 18th | | 28 blustering NW<br>& wintry aspect<br>/ blustering | 19th of Mar thru' 5-9th of Ap. 22<br>days ½ of them remarkably<br>cold NW & strong | cold & windy<br>2nd & 3rd<br>strong cold N.W. 14 & 15th |
| | | | May 1st | Ap. 7th more NE<br>& 27th more SE |
| 6 meadow skimmed over in<br>night 13 froze in the night | 2 last night<br>very cold. | 6 & 7 put on great<br>coats again | | 31°+ the 2nd (having been 71°+<br>the 1st) 14th - 44+° 15th - 37°+ |
| | | | | & thin ice on mead. edge |
| | 2nd | 26th | 15th & 13th | |

| 15 | or more of ~~More than 3 inches of~~ snow | 6th & 13th 8 inches | | 15 to 19th inclusive 4 inches kills birds | 16 have none in fields |
|---|---|---|---|---|---|
| 4th | ~~Frost out of garden~~ **Plowing generally** | Feb. 5 Out of ground in many places | Ground soaks up rain 3rd 2nd some plow | | Mar. 28 Thawed 6 inches out of garden Ap. 4 but not on N. banks 18 out enough for plowing in most open ground. |
| 20th 6th– | **Frost still in ground** feel it in meadows | March 30th at 10 inch. deep where I dig parsnips. Ap. 2 in swamps ice-like 1st in RR | Mar. 30 on upland Ap. 10 meadows stiff still. | | Ap. 4 , not out of N banks Mar. 18 much in swamps Mar 2nd about 6 inch in swamps 7 Ap. hinders deep plowing even in sandy fields |
| up to 12th | **Still use gloves in morning** | | | | 16th prevents digging in hollows 20th cannot set a post for frost 10-55 since Ap.1st only in morning (Say to 12th) |
| 16 | **Heels of snow left** | 28 snow in hollows. 3rd 2 or 3 ft deep on N. side hills in woods 25 much in 2nd Div. road | | 9th | 13 some icy snow still under N sides of woods in hollows |
| 12th | **Stow's cold pond hole still full of ice** | | | | 16 still full - the only one I know |
| 18 | **Hail** | | | | |

*April 1852–1860 pg.2*

| 2 | 51-2 "a good solid winter" | 52 The high water year | 53 | 54 3 | 55 |
|---|---|---|---|---|---|
| 10 | **River when lowest in April & meadow** Ap 4-5 6 not yet so high by 4 or 5 feet as last winter | 4 notice marks of river May 15 (?) but still prob. up 2nd water on meadows | 1st been going down a month at least | 3rd gone down so that I have to steer carefully to avoid hummocks on meadows 23rd just left bare for blackbirds ——— 30 highest for April | May 4th generally off meads. fast & very low 29 rapidly going down shows grass on meadow Say |
| 2? 16 | **River when highest in April & how high.** (May 31-50 higher) than it has been at this season for many years - water over road below master Cheney's | 10 high, but not high for spring. 23rd highest for year 8 ½ inch above horizontal truss (i.e. 8 ft 7½ inch above SL.) 2" up but falling | 7 river raised so that I cross the great meads. Mar. 27 or 9th meads but part-ially flooded – say 7 (??) & not high. | say 29 & high owing to rain of 24 - rises a little 22 & 23 29 nearly as high as any time in this year far May 5 ^ highest in very high the year 54 as year (on ac. of rain the 3rd and 4th) arches quite concealed - highest since 23rd-52 | 14 steadily rising since 1st 19 fallen a little 21 risen again a little on ac. of rain 23 at height for this rise higher than before since winter whole of Lee Mead. covered 28 another wrack & 26th |
| 14 ? | **Smooth reflecting water** | 11 placid eve & reflecting water | | 26 - over cast | 15 still cloudy day water smooth & full of reflections 5th or 6th? |
| 12 or be-fore | **Ripples on ripple lakes** | | | | |
| 13 | **Spearing** | 8th & 30th | 1st -7th | 5th to 8th | 16 -25 |
| Mar 25 ? | **1st leave off greatcoat** v Mar.) | Mar 15 next ?) Ap. 26 | Mar 26th Ap. 13 - hear toads & take off in Haverhill | Mar 17 too warm in one Ap 25 begin to take off April 5 take off & 6 | 16 1st regret wearing great coat 17 18 - & 19th yet warmer & go without greatcoat |
| 15(?) | **Wear greatcoat again** | ~~20~~ | | | 28 – 29th & 30th 55 10th |

| | | | | |
|---|---|---|---|---|
| | 21st (lasts till 29th) 3 inches | | | |
| 6 can dig in garden where the snow is gone 11 one field plowed & harrowed. | Mar. 28 none in Monroe's garden Feb. 18 out in many places. | | Mar 31st out of our garden | Mar. 4th out of upper part of garden. all out of garden 14th & prob 12. |
| Mar 27 not out even of upper part of garden but under snow only in warm slopes 16 out of most soil | Mar. 27 not quite out of upland & garden but plowing. | Mar. 20 feel it in low ground 6 but just coming out of cold patches N side of hills | Ap. 19 21 prevents digging some pines. | |
| 12. a little snow still on N side house (since Dec 25) 17 some snow- banks yet – one the 22 | Mar. 27 none visible from window but in swallow hole. 29 (some of 27th) | | | none after Ap. 1st |
| | | | | 11th 3/4 full |
| 16 & 17 | | 20th | | |

| | 57 | 58 | 59 | 60 |
|---|---|---|---|---|
| 16 ground appears in ridges on E. Hosmer's 56 meadow 12 wrack on meadow | | 1st lowest willow bare | Say 10th | |
| 12 going down leaving its wrack May 1st water on meads rapidly going down. am confined to river for most part 3rd & quite low (14 going down rapidly Hunt's causeway just bare) | Say 1st (??) & 4 | 6 3rd Heron rock more than 1 foot out & falling to 6th at least to 9th say 9th & prob. below summer level | 10th spring freshet ends began Mar. 8 (not to mention the winter one) 17 up again so that I [unclear] further to Mantatuket's rock but already falling | Lowest for Mar. the 31st 3 ft. below H's wall or 6 ½ in above summer level Lowest ap. 30 or 3+ inches below - summer level very low lowest as yet |
| 11 at its height (v. 23rd) 23rd risen again over [unclear] mead. also 23rd begins to fall 3rd rain at last & r. rapidly rises 5 over the meads 8 higher 23 nearly as high as 11 can just get over E. Hosmer's meadow 8th cannot get under | 24 at its height - higher than before. (22 higher than be- fore & rising —— cut off great bends & fairly go over Hub B. causeway) owing to melting snow | 14 a little higher on ac. of rain but no rise of con sequence say 14? but quite low (?) | 1st to Assabet over meads in boat 10th cannot cross meads 28th Great Meadow partly over X with B & B Say 1st (?) I go to rock in boat again | rises some slightly from Ap. 7 to 14th falls from 15th to end being ½ inch above summer level the 24th at summer level 26th ... highest the 14th for Ap. but very little on meads. |
| stone bridge 15 [unclear] morning [unclear] & overcast | May 3-57 Sunday | | 17* warm & smooth & no ripple | |
| | | | 9th 5 | 15 F.H. pond |
| 25 | | | 8th | 26 |
| 7th & 8 warm enough to leave off put it on when I leave boat 9th leave it | Feb. 25 (65+° left at home - single coat too much | 7 6 & 7th put on great coat again after a week of warm weather | Mar. 17 wear but one — weather for half-thick coat 27th & 30th | Mar 31st 1st leave off & Ap.1st |
| | | 7th | | AM fire most of April |

| | | 52 | 53 | 54 | 55 |
|---|---|---|---|---|---|
| 21 | **Begin to wear one coat** <u>commonly</u> | 28 am getting great coat off | | | |
| ~~28~~ 1st | (& [unclear]) sit without fire commonly v below | ~~30~~ - 30 | | ~~26~~ 26 do with little now | ~~19th 1st time~~ 19 |
| 27 | 1st am that I sit with open window | | | | 19th 55 |
| | weather for half-thick coat | | | | |
| 20 | **Dark evening** | | | 26-54 a single cloud | 17th rainy & very dark |
| 23 | **Burning of brush** v winter Mar 30) | | | 23rd | 18 smokes in horizon |
| 25 ? | **Fires in woods late in month** a little | 28 | | | |
| 16 | **Plowing & planting going on** generally | 17th | | | 19th |
| 21 ? | **Scudding clouds** )))  ))) | | | | |
| 10th | **dark barred spring clouds** | 10th | | | |
| 18 | **Still almost sultry - with wet looking clouds hanging about - 1st time** | | | | 18th |
| 21 | **Sea Turn** | | | | 18th (a warm day warmest yet) |
| 7th | ~~1st~~ **Hazy** | 1st slight 29th | 1st & 9th | 3 1st time but not so warm as Mar. 17th | 24 cannot see distant hills |
| 17 | **Fog over river in morning** | | | | <u>some</u> 21st |
| 24 ? | **Cold in last half of month** | 28 cold & wintery | | 16 | 27 & 28 good fires required |
| 25 ? | **Mtns still spotted with snow** | 1st & 4th & 28 | | | 18th 4 - 12 |
| | **1st moon to walk by** | | | 11th 54 | |
| 19 | **Willow (alba) peels** | | 19th how long? | 27th how long? | |
| 19 (?) | **Bass peels** | | 19th how long? | | |
| 19 (?) | **S. discolor peels** | | | | |
| 20 (?) | **Tremula aspen peels** | | | | |
| 14 | **Rain after E wind** | 18 5 days storm begins after & with E wind | | | |
| 21? | **White frosts** | May 1st platforms white with 5 wets feet | 2 | 12 (after clear moon-light) | 21 saves feet a <u>wetting</u> 8th - 16 |
| 17 | **Evenings very consid. shortened** | | | | |
| 25 | **Very few leaves indeed on young oaks** | | | | |
| | **Begin to sit without fire commonly** | 30 | | 26 | 19th |
| | Warm in last half month | | | 20th - 27 | 18th - 19th |
| | Flower like scent | | | 21st-26 | |
| | Dark night | | | 26th in thunder shower <u>very</u> | |
| | Last ice [unclear] forms | | | | 16 1 foot [unclear] |

| 56 | 57 | 58 | 59 | 60 |
|---|---|---|---|---|
| | | | Say 21 (?) | 19-60 wear but 1 coat the last 10 days of Ap. |
| | May 3rd | May 1st & 2nd | ~~30~~ 30 | ~~20 beg to sit [unclear]~~ without fires more commonly |
| | | | 27 & 30th | 28th 65+ but one thickish coat is best |
| | | | | 16th rainy & very dark |
| | | | | 27 |
| | | | 21 May 4th dry leaves in woods time for fires . | 27 |
| 16-56 | | 15 many planting now | May 6 about end of very dry leaves | 12 |
| 56 | 57 | 58 | 59 | 60 |
| | 21- 24 - 25 | | | |
| | 24 | | | |
| 24th & 28 - 29 & 30th | | | | |
| 12th hazy 6th the 1st slight bluish haze | | 2nd | | |
| 28th quite a fog | | 6 pretty foggy for several mor-nings | | |
| | 28 icy cold N.W. wind | 24 cold NW wind no frogs out & for 3 or 4 days | | 18 cold with strong wind 46+ 25 -47+ |
| | 28 snow whitening the mts | | | |
| 24 peels several days | | | | 17 but not 4 or 5 days ago |
| | | | | 18 peels well |
| | | | | 18 just begun |
| | | | 13-14 snow & rain after E wind the 7th (beginning 18 March) | 11th after E wind the 10th |
| | | | following an E. wind another 22nd | 29th &9 30th melting early |
| | | | | 17th |
| | | | | 26th |
| | May 3 | May 1st & 2 | 30 | 20 |
| 30th | | | | |

General Phenomena for May. The Morgan Library & Museum. MA 610.

# MAY:

## *Washing Day*

---

In Maine, May is the month of running water. Runoff: the old season not vanished but transformed to flashing movement, running off in all directions. Streams become rivers, ditches become streams. In the woods, spring ephemerals—jack-in-the-pulpit, trillium, trout lily—grow overnight, or almost, from the watery ground. I squint at Thoreau's categories for May, tracing his tracings, move from manuscript to Journal entry to my own notes and back again. He writes, "Grass & foliage suddenly changes green" and "Cobwebs of grass in morning."

Running, my body feels alien to itself. My heart and lungs and legs revolt. It is strange to be outside with so much of myself visible. Whose legs are these? Whose forearms? January is a far-off country with quaint fireside customs and early darkness. Now all is light and atmosphere. Soon people will ask, "You get your garden in yet?" They will not ask if you've let go your despair, or if you've remembered you're alive. In the yard a sudden galaxy of tiny blue flowers—scattered, uncountable—move all together in the warm wind. When I bend down in the green, I notice the cobwebs at my feet.

※

In May of 1860, Thoreau felt the limitations of his capacities as a single and finite observer in the face of the seemingly infinite manifestations of spring. Though it had long been his practice to record "firsts" in his springtime Journal entries and to wonder how long, say, a flower has been in bloom—"*Andromeda Polifolia* - how long?"—the question appears with an almost anxious frequency in this period (5/16/1860, Journal Transcript 31:189). For some stretches of this volume of the Journal, this query appears on virtually every page. On May 5, Thoreau stops to count the individual blossoms in a mass of the ephemeral *Houstonia caerulea*, commonly called bluets:

There are some dense beds of houstonia in the yard of the Old Conantum house.

Some parts of them show of a distinctly bluer shade 2 rods off– They are most interesting now before many other flowers are out–the grass high– & they have lost their freshness– I sit down by one dense bed of them to examine it. It is about 3 feet long & 2 or more wide– The flowers not only crowd one another–but are in several tiers one above another–& completely hide the ground–a mass of white–Counting those in a small place–I find that there are about 3000 flowers in a square foot. They are all turned a little toward the sun & emit a refreshing odor. (5/5/1860, Journal Transcript 31:168–69)

Counting and measuring is a habitual practice for Thoreau, central to his work as a surveyor. But the scene illustrates the way Thoreau's observational strategies, including quantification, were overwhelmed by the magnitude and abundance of spring, which was after all happening not in *one* location but in every location at once. While some entries luxuriate in this abundance, in many one feels the enormity of the task Thoreau had set himself: to perceive and record the season in both its minute particulars—the individual bluet—and its larger recurring patterns. The tone that animates the Journal of this period is one of excitement tempered by something like overwhelm. If a single spring strained his observational capacities, how much more limited must he have felt in the face of the recurring cycles he was now committed to tracking? An exclamation point–laden entry from this period emphasizes both the feeling of power and possibility fostered by the Kalendar as instrument of perception, and the recognition of scales of time and observation utterly inaccessible to individual human perceivers.

See at Lees a Pewee (phoebe) building she has just woven in or laid on the edge a fresh sprig of saxifrage in flower. I notice that Phoebes will build in the same recess in a cliff year after year– It is a constant thing here–though they are often disturbed. Think how many pewees must have built under the eaves of this cliff–since pewees were created & this cliff itself built!! You can possibly find the crumbling relics of how many!

If you should look carefully enough. It takes us– many years to find out that nature repeats herself annually–But how perfectly regular & calculable all her phenomena must appear to a mind that has observed her for a thousand years! (5/5/1860, Journal Transcript 31:169–70)

Here, the striking image of the phoebe's nest with its sprig of blooming saxifrage sparks a meditation of the relationship between species and place over time—a relationship no doubt highlighted for him by his reading of Darwin's *On the Origin of Species* the previous December. Seasonal awareness—here, the awareness of the phoebe's nest-building habits—is thus connected to geologic timescales: the mutual creation of species and habitat. The entry refers both to how much is possible for a human observer who "look[s] carefully enough" and suggests the dream or fantasy of a timeless mind: "a mind that has observed [nature] for a thousand years." Poised between awareness of his own finitude and a drive toward an ever-fuller picture of nature-in-time, Thoreau strained at the linearity of the Journal and at the limits of his perspective. In May of 1860, this meant not only attending more closely ("look[ing] carefully enough") to individual phenomena, but also connecting his observations to those of previous years to get a sense of the larger patterns.

The May charts of general phenomena include categories pertaining to all of the senses—from the sound of crickets to the "Rank scent of Rhue." Sight, smell, sound, and haptic sensations fill the May 1860 Journal, and this intense sensory awareness informs the categories selected for the chart. A retrospective work composed at a particular moment, the Kalendar always speaks not only to the composite, multiyear perspective it was designed to illustrate but also to the particular season in which that perspective was consolidated. This May, Thoreau was awash in sensation, and it was the particularities of sense experiences his backward glance sought out.

Visually, it was the skies that drew his attention.

Thoreau's fascination with clouds, like many of his attractions, encompassed both scientific curiosity and aesthetic vision. Like many in his century, he was interested in increased knowledge about atmospheric effects as material phenomena and was aware of the categories of cloud formations (cirrus, cumulus, nimbus, etc.) developed by British meteorologist Luke Howard in his "Essay on the Modifications of Clouds" in 1803. Through his reading of John Ruskin, Thoreau was also familiar with the atmospheric and cloud-forward paintings of J. M. W. Turner. The May chart's categories involving clouds—"Summer cumuli clouds" and "Rounded clouds"—as well as horizons and sunlight—"cold slate color in horizon" and "Yellow sunlight"—reflect his long-standing interest in nineteenth-century landscape aesthetics and the philosophical categories underlying them: an interest that becomes more acute in June, as spring deepens into summer.

Smell is also prominent in the May chart, represented in five distinct categories: "Fugacious fragrance of all flowers," "Rank scent of Rhue," "scent of S. alba bloom," "Meadow fragrance," and "Peculiar fragrance in air." The latter two, which correspond to composite or unknown sources, fascinated Thoreau particularly. He seems to have first observed what he calls "the Meadow fragrance" in May of 1852 and tracked it through the next few weeks: "I still perceive that wonderful fragrance from the meadow," he writes in June of that year. Thereafter, the meadow fragrance would become one of Thoreau's significant signs of spring, a phenomenon that reflected not only the season but also the degree of his attunement to it—a measure that for him was synonymous with well-being. "I still perceive that ambrosial sweetness from the meadows in some places," he writes on June 27, 1852. "Give me the strong rank scent of ferns in the spring for vigor—just blossoming late in the spring. A healthy & refined nature would always derive pleasure from the landscape. As long as the bodily vigor lasts man sympathizes with nature" (6/27/1852, *Journal* 5:157).

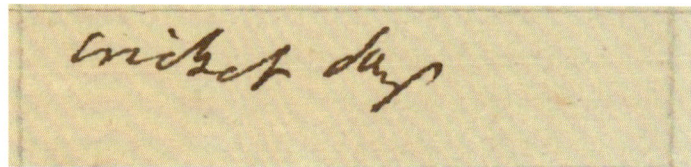

*Cricket Days*

A peculiarity of these days is the first hearing of the crickets' creak–suggesting philosophy & thought– No greater event transpires now– It is the most interesting piece of news to be communicated–yet it is not in any newspaper. (5/27/1859, Journal Transcript 29:89)

The spring of 1860 was a season of news, and the headlines sometimes included his name. In April, Thoreau's friend and fellow abolitionist, Franklin Sanborn, one of the "secret six" who knew of John Brown's plans for the raid on Harpers Ferry, had fled the US Marshals who had arrived at his door. He had refused a summons to Washington by a US Senate committee investigating the raid, and the Marshals had come to deliver him by force. Sanborn's sister Sarah alerted the neighbors, and more than a hundred townspeople rushed to his defense, enabling him to evade capture. The Boston papers reported on Thoreau's speech in Sanborn's defense at a town meeting the following day. Given the intensity of the political climate at this time, as well as the centrality of Thoreau to the main action, it is striking how little mention there is of *this* kind of news in the May Journal.

But Thoreau's impassioned response to Sanborn's arrest and his continued involvement with the abolitionist cause through the spring and summer of 1860 suggest that his immersion in the natural world during this season was not a retreat or withdrawal, but rather a consciously developed counterbalance to his involvement in politics. In "A Plea for Captain John Brown," he is candid: "I do not think it is quite sane for one to spend his whole life in talking or writing about this matter, unless he is continuously inspired, and I have not done so. A man may have other affairs to attend to." Often used as evidence of Thoreau's lack of political commitment, this statement is better understood in the context of what follows: "I do not wish to kill nor to be killed, but I can foresee circumstances in which both these things would be by me unavoidable. We preserve the so-called peace of our community by deeds of petty violence every day." Deeply aware of his own complicity with slavery, and feeling the increasing demand of conscience to participate in the fight against it, Thoreau felt that sanity demanded that he attend also to "other affairs." Throughout his writings, Thoreau uses *sanity* as an index of connection to the natural world. The "other affairs" to which he attends are those not reported by the newspapers, but by the crickets, peepers, and birds of spring. Thoreau was alert enough to realize that the other species with whom we share the planet have their own news to report, and he sought to attend to this news too—and to absorb the wordless suggestion of "philosophy & thought" announced by the new season. The more-than-human events of spring had implications for the human community, as the most memorable figure of "A Plea" suggests:

> [I]n the moral world, when good seed is planted, good fruit is inevitable, and does not depend on our watering and cultivating; that when you plant, or bury, a hero in his field, a crop of heroes is sure to spring up. This is a seed of such force and vitality, that it does not ask our leave to germinate.

Thoreau conceived of moral and political courage as *itself* a natural phenomenon, dependent not only on individual action—like Brown's campaign—but also on the ongoing vitality of a nature that produces human courage as it produces flowers. The Kalendar can be understood as an attempt to more fully realize the operations of this force.

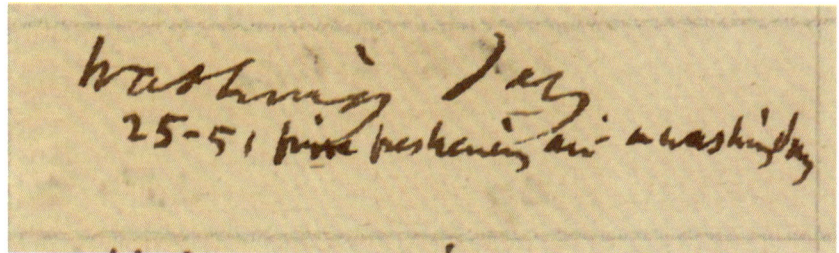

*Washing Day*

A fine freshening air a little hazy that bathes & washes everything–saving the day from extreme heat. Walked to the hills south of Wayland. by the road by Dea. Farrar's. 1ˢᵗ vista just beyond *Menans* ? looking west– down a valley with a verdant-columned elm at the extremity of the vale –& the blue hills & horizon beyond These are the resting places in a walk. We love to see any part of the earth tinged with blue– cerulean the color of the sky. The celestial color. (5/25/1851, *Journal* 3:235)

This is the third windy day–following the 2 days rain. A washing day such as we always have at this season methinks. The grass has sprung up as by magic since the rains  The birds are heard through the pleasant dashing wind which enlivens every thing. (5/22/1853, *Journal* 6:141)

There is a strong wind against which I push & paddle–but now at last I do not go seeking the warm sunny & sheltered coves– The strong wind is enlivening & agreeable. This is a *washing* day. I love the wind at last (5/10/1857, Journal Transcript 23:63)

Among the phenomena Thoreau most loved and commemorated were those that involved the feeling of being wholly surrounded. Most frequently connected to sound, this feeling entailed the self-dissolution and self-forgetting that, from the time of his brother John's death forward, had been his most reliable source of relief for feelings of grief and alienation. In an oft-cited

Journal entry from 1857, Thoreau writes of the capacity of natural sounds to produce the kind of therapeutic absorption associated with music:

> The commonest & cheapest sounds as the barking of a dog–produce the same effect on pert & healthy ears–that the rarest music does. It depends on your appetite for sound. Just as a crust is sweeter to a healthy appetite than confectionary to a pampered or diseased one. It is better that these cheap sounds be music to us than that we have the rarest ears for music in any other sense.
>
> I have lain awake at night many a time to think of the barking of a dog which I had heard long before–bathing my being again in those waves of sound, as a frequenter of the opera might lie awake remembering the music he had heard. (12/27/1857, Journal Transcript 25:24–25).

"Washing days" offered a similarly bracing experience of sensory surround: like the "cheap sounds" that provided both an immediate experience of absorption ("bathing my being") and food for future absorption ("the barking of a dog which I had heard long before") only to "healthy ears," the windy days Thoreau designated as washing days were in part determined by his receptivity to them. The bracing winds of May have a *quickening* effect, offer a kind of baptism, that the colder winds of March and April do not. The effect is both external, visible in the landscape—"the pleasant dashing wind which enlivens every thing," and a measure of his own receptivity and attunement, even of his capacity for love: "But now at last I do not go seeking the warm sunny & sheltered coves– The strong wind is enlivening & agreeable. This is a *washing* day. I love the wind at last." In the 1851 and 1853 entries, the effect of the immersive experience of this baptism by wind is like the effect of the "gentle rain" in the "Solitude" chapter of *Walden*—that of an "infinite and unaccountable friendliness all at once like an atmosphere sustaining me." Like the "Solitude" experience, washing days alter not only the environment but the perceiving subject's responsiveness to the environment, heightening the effects of color and sound: the "verdant-columned elm at the extremity of the vale –& the blue hills & horizon beyond" and the birds "heard through the pleasant dashing wind." In claiming this special, restorative, and revivifying power for the wind, Thoreau was drawing on a long-standing association between the wind and divinity in both classical and Christian thought: the etymology of inspiration (from *spiritus*—breath or wind in Latin) was well-known to both Emerson and Thoreau. As Thomas Pribeck observes in his essay on wind as metaphor in *Walden*, the trope was modified and extended by the Romantic poets.

> In the work of the English Romantics—and Thoreau later—the external wind becomes the analog of human respiration, a new use of the symbolic potential of *spiritus*. This divine breath has a human origin also; spirit can be released as well as absorbed. The wind—in *The Prelude*, for instance—is a metaphor for the poetic imagination, shaping and reshaping the world, moving its elements in order to make sense of and to show the unity of all concrete physical phenomena. In Coleridge's "Dejection: An Ode" . . . the external breeze, which strikes "upon the strings of this Aeolian lute," tells him that he is inextricably a part of the natural world and its mortality; the corresponding energy and vitality of his own respiration tells him that he has responsibility in forming his place in the world and its direction.

Similarly, the external wind with which Thoreau is washed on a washing day in spring corresponded to new *internal* energies: as the green grass springs up "as by magic" and "the celestial color" shows itself in the lakes and hills, the walker who'd so long been seeking shelter learns to love the wind at last, inspired by what he perceives—and breathes it out again in language.

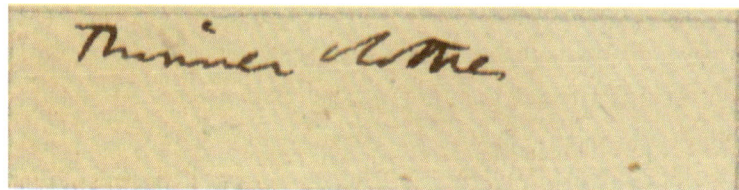

*Thinner Clothes*

The Nepeta Glechoma is out under R Browns poles– a pretty deep blue half concealed violet-like flower. It is the earliest flower of this character. Warm days when you begin to *think* of thin coats. (5/10/1853, *Journal* 6:104)

Wind suddenly changed to S this forenoon & for first time I think of a thin coat– It is very hazy in consequence of the sudden warmth after cold. & I cannot see the *mts*. . . . Just before 6 see in the N. W. the first summer clouds methought piled in cumuli with silvery edges–&

westwardward of them a dull rainy looking cloud advancing & shutting down to the horizon–later lightning in west & South––& a little rain– (5/25/1855, Journal Transcript 19:11–12)

More clearly than any other work by Thoreau, the charts of general phenomena demonstrate Thoreau's understanding of the human as a category of nature. If, for Emerson, nature was defined as the "not me,"—that which is fundamentally separate from the spiritual self—by the late 1850s Thoreau had come to see the human self as properly *part* of nature, and human health and well-being as synonymous with full, lived perception of this belonging. The Kalendar charts are studded with categories that reflect the human being as seasonal creature, and several of these are present in the May charts: "Fishing begun," "Stone heaps," "Plant my melons," "Sit with open window commonly," etc. That these categories appear alongside the meteorological and other nonhuman phenomena ("Thunder shower," "Stems of meadow saxifrage") speaks to the extent of the integration of the human and the natural in Thoreau's mature vision.

Following the April categories relating to the taking off and putting back on of his winter coat, the May chart tracks the subsequent transition to "thinner clothes." Interestingly, both the 1853 and 1855 chart entries correspond to Journal entries in which the observed phenomenon is not the first *wearing* of thinner clothes, but the first *thought* of them. It is not only visible human behavior that Thoreau tracks as characteristic signs of the changing season, but human thinking as well. In the lovely entry from May 1853, the equivalence of the seasonally determined opening of a flower—"The Nepeta Glechoma is out under R Browns poles– a pretty deep blue half concealed violet-like flower"—and the seasonally determined thought patterns of a human being—"Warm days when you begin to *think* of thin coats"—is striking.

The impulse toward ever-greater comprehensiveness that drives the integration of the human and the natural in the charts is also evident in a recurrent style in the late Journal: this is the list or catalog, a kind of inventory of the day's observations. Often list items omit articles or verbs: "Chinquapin pollen. Lupine not yet." In the 1855 entry above, these minimalist notations alternate with longer descriptive sentences: "Just before 6 see in the N. W. the first summer clouds methought piled in cumuli with silvery edges–& westwardward of them a dull rainy looking cloud advancing & shutting down to the horizon–later lightning in west & South––& a little rain." It is as if the various speeds (rapid-fire, languorous) and feelings (urgency, equanimity) associated with each observation were themselves being observed and re-corded. The catalog style brings each of these elements—mental and phys-ical, natural and human, the sudden and the slow—into comprehensive arrangement.

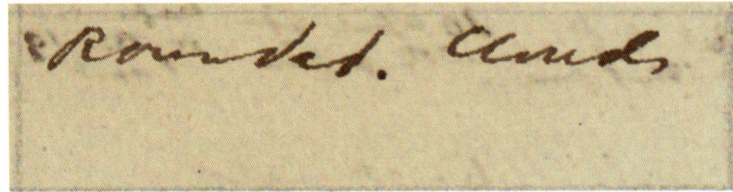

### *Rounded Clouds*

I notice this forenoon (11 ½ Am) remarkably round-tipped white clouds–just like round topped hills

on all sides of the sky–often a range of such

such as I do not remember to have seen before– There was considerable wind on the surface from the NE–& the above clouds were moving W & SW–a generally-distributed cumulus.

What added to the remarkableness of the sight–was a very fine fleecy scirrhus–like smoke–narrow but of indefinite length driving swiftly Eastward beneath the former–proving that there were 3 currents of air one above the other–

(The same form of cloud prevailed to some extent the next day) (5/2/1860, Journal Transcript 31:160)

The structure of the Kalendar provides us with a few hints as to its construc-tion: the fact that the fall and spring charts end with different years—1860 and 1861, respectively—suggests that they were drawn up close to the seasons they recorded: that they are largely, but not *wholly*, retrospective. In the fall charts, the inclusion of data from after the end date of the Journal—November 3, 1861—strongly suggests an element of more or less real-time recording. In this way, the Kalendar mediated between the present season Thoreau was experiencing—his linear progress through a given season—and the seasons of memory it evoked. Similarly, the presence of categories with few corresponding Journal entries, with rows consisting of mostly empty boxes, reflects a tension between the status of a phenomenon as a particular experience in linear time and a recurrent phenomenon of seasonal time.

"Rounded clouds" in the May chart demonstrates this effect especially well: here the category responds to only one entry, in 1860, for May 2 and 3. The cloud pattern Thoreau witnessed struck him—partly, no doubt, because of the illusion of a kind of reflection ("just like round topped hills") it evoked. The appearance of the sky in the water, or the sky on earth, was a source of fascination and delight for Thoreau: "We love to see any part of the earth tinged with blue– cerulean the color of the sky. The celestial color," he wrote in May of 1851, and the description of time as a stream whose "bottom is pebbly with stars" (5/25/1851, *Journal* 3:235) is one of the most memorable images in *Walden*. Here, hills are translated to the sky, suggesting the inner harmony or correspondence that Thoreau most delighted in. The inclusion of the category in the absence of any Journal data aside from the May 2, 1860, entry raises the question of Thoreau's criteria for characteristic phenomena. Do the blank squares in the row for "Rounded clouds" suggest that Thoreau committed this category before creating (or reviewing) the May charts he'd drawn from the Journal? Do they represent his belief that the cloud pattern *was* a characteristic phenomenon of May—just one he'd only happened to observe once? Either way, the existence of these single-entry categories dramatizes the tension between the singular and the categorical in Thoreau's imagination of time.

The entry also reflects another tension typical of Thoreau's work. As Bradley Dean observes, Thoreau likely read Howard's "Essay on the Modifications of Clouds" sometime in 1852—a copy was obtained by Harvard's library in 1851—and was certainly familiar with Howard's system of cloud classification by this year. The descriptive entry above, with its use of the classification terminology and its hypothesis that the layered effect was produced by "3 currents of air one above the other" clearly indicates Thoreau's interest in and knowledge of nineteenth-century meteorology. The comparison to rounded hills, however, is suggestive of Thoreau's ongoing poetic investment in reflection and analogy: clouds like hills, ponds like skies. One feels this familiar tension between the pull toward scientific order and a countervailing urge toward poetic vision and expression in a Journal entry on clouds from February 18, 1852: "One discovery in meteorology, one significant observation is a good deal. I am grateful to the man who introduces order among the clouds. Yet I look up into the heavens so fancy free I am almost glad not to know any law for the winds." Here, Thoreau's appreciation for the scientific order imposed by Howard is in tension with the poetic vision of "the heavens so fancy free." Interestingly, earlier in the same entry one finds one of Thoreau's most famous passages on the relationship of poetry to science, this time expressing the reconciliation of "facts" and poetry, or at least the hope of one:

> I have a common place book for facts and another for poetry–but I find it difficult always to preserve the vague distinction which I had in my mind–for the most interesting & beautiful facts are so much the more poetry and that is their success. They are *translated* from earth to heaven–  I see that if my facts were sufficiently vital & significant–perhaps transmuted more into the substance of the human mind–I should need but one book of poetry to contain them all. (2/18/1852, *Journal* 4:356)

As Dean notes, the dramatic contrast between the romantic treatment of clouds as "fleeting, mercurial, evanescent" and the meteorological view of clouds as classifiable entities emerging in the nineteenth century may have exacerbated, or at least dramatized, the tension in Thoreau's thinking about the relationship between poetic and scientific ways of understanding the natural world.

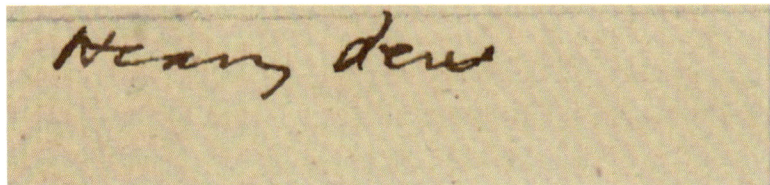

*Heavy Dew*

Sunrise–merely a segment of a circle of rich amber in the east–growing brighter and brighter at one point–  There is no rosy color at this moment–& not a speck in the sky–& now comes the sun without pomp a bright liquid gold. Dews come with the grass. . . . There is I find on examining a small clear drop at the end of each blade.– quite at the top on one side. (5/11/1852, *Journal* 5:50)

I observe this morning the dew on the grass in our yard–literally sparkling drops which thickly stud it. Each dew-drop is a beautiful crystalline sphere just below (within an 8th of an inch more or less) the tip of the blade –sometimes there are 2 or 3-one beneath the other–the lowest the largest. Each dew-drop takes the form of the planet itself.

What an advance is this from the sere withered & flattened grass–at most whitened with frost–which we have lately known–to this delicate crystalline drop trembling at the lip of a fresh green grass-blade. The surface of the globe is thus tremblingly alive. (5/13/1860, Journal Transcript 31:182)

If the dramatic cloudscapes of the season turned Thoreau's gaze skyward in May, he was equally compelled by the transformations occurring underfoot. The phenomenon of dew, and in particular the pattern of dewdrops on individual blades of glass, inspired a magnified attention to the minute particulars of the seasonal patterns. In the entries above, Thoreau shifts between planetary and microscopic scales, finding "the surface of the globe" in each "delicate crystalline drop."

The idea of the microcosm—etymologically a miniature *cosmos*—was central to Thoreau's thought and to transcendentalism more broadly. Emerson uses the dewdrop/globe figure in his essay "Compensation": "The world globes itself in a drop of dew. The microscope cannot find the animalcule which is less perfect for being little. Eyes, ears, taste, smell, motion, resistance, appetite, and organs of reproduction that take hold on eternity—all find room to consist in the small creature." As Emerson's use of "eternity" suggests, microcosms are temporal as well as spatial, and Thoreau's particular fascination was with the nested temporalities of hour, day, season, and year.

Thoreau plays with these timescales in *Walden*, reducing two lived years at the pond to one archetypal year, and framing the book itself between chanticleer's morning call in the epigraph and the "morning star" of the final sentence. In the "Spring" chapter of *Walden* he compares a single day to a year.

The phenomena of the year take place every day in a pond on a small scale. Every morning, generally speaking, the shallow water is being warmed more rapidly than the deep, though it may not be made so warm after all, and every evening it is being cooled more rapidly until the morning. The day is an epitome of the year. The night is the winter, the morning and evening are the spring and fall, and the noon is the summer.

In "Autumnal Tints," he reverses this operation, finding the hours of the day within the calendar year: "As fruits and leaves and the day itself acquire a bright tint just before they fall, so the year near its setting. October is its sunset sky; November the later twilight." This reversible temporal structure—day as year, year as day, "wheels within wheels," as Laura Dassow Walls writes—is closely related to the transcendentalist view of the individual human spirit as a microcosm of the universe. As Lawrence Buell observes,

> The basis of Transcendentalist thinking as to the role of nature in art is the idea of a metaphysical correspondence between nature and spirit, as expressed chiefly by Emerson. Man and the physical universe, Emerson says, are parallel creations of the same divine spirit; therefore natural and moral law are the same and everything in nature, rightly seen, has spiritual significance for man. The universe is thus a vast network of symbols—a Bible or revelation purer than any written scripture—which it is the chief task of the poet to study, master, and articulate. . . . A good literary work is therefore not an artificial construct, but a "second nature," growing out of the poet's mind as naturally as the leaf of a tree.

Thoreau complicates Emerson's transcendental scheme in significant ways—chiefly by decentering the human and perceiving correspondences among individual material phenomena ("horizontally," as H. Daniel Peck puts it) rather than primarily between matter and spirit ("vertically"), as Emerson does. As Peck observes, "Only in the incremental development of dozens, hundreds, finally thousands of visual relations does the writer create the full analogical framework—the fully contextualized composite view,— in which an authentic relation to the Ineffable may be achieved." However, within his own scheme of correspondence, the microcosm/macrocosm relation is as significant for Thoreau as it is for Emerson. In May of 1860, looking at the new grass, each blade adorned with a perfect reflective sphere, and contemplating the change from the "sere withered & flattened grass–at most whitened with frost–which we have lately known," Thoreau perceives nothing less than a new world, "tremblingly alive" in the morning of the year (5/13/1860, Journal Transcript 31:182).

General Phenomena for May.

| | 52 | 53 | 54 | 55 | 56 | 57 | 58 | 59 | 60 |
|---|---|---|---|---|---|---|---|---|---|
| Fragrance &c of all flowers | | | | | | | | | |
| Rank vegetation &c | | | | | | | | | |
| Heat of sultry noon | | | | | | | | | |
| May storm | | | | | | | | | |
| Rain | | | | | | | | | |
| Still cloudy, thoughtful day | | | | | | | | | |
| Summer cumuli clouds | | | | | | | | | |
| Rounded clouds | | | | | | | | | |
| Dry weather | | | | | | | | | |
| Woods fully leaving, change green | | | | | | | | | |
| Fishing begun | | | | | | | | | |
| Cobwebs on grass in morning | | | | | | | | | |
| Stems &c &c | | | | | | | | | |
| Stone breaks | | | | | | | | | |
| Clear air | | | | | | | | | |
| River when highest & lowest | | | | | | | | | |
| Rain when lowest & how low | | | | | | | | | |
| Cricket day | | | | | | | | | |
| Down from willows | | | | | | | | | |
| 1st watering tubs on walk | | | | | | | | | |
| Early potato planting | | | | | | | | | |
| Plant of my melons | | | | | | | | | |
| Rain over | | | | | | | | | |
| Larger &c all over but young white oaks | | | | | | | | | |
| Some few &c last year | | | | | | | | | |
| 1st summer shower cloud | | | | | | | | | |
| 1st with open windows | | | | | | | | | |
| Cows turned out to pasture | | | | | | | | | |

General phenomena for May

| | 52 | 53 | 54 | 55 | 56 | 57 | 58 | 59 | 60 |
|---|---|---|---|---|---|---|---|---|---|
| Cows going to country | 6 cattle going up c. 10 | 2 cattle going up c. | sell of cows expensive red 8" | 6 Road full of c. going up country | 7 C going up country per 10 cart | | | | 14 cattle red 11 going up c. Begin Ap 30 nearly the 15. 2 cool nights of late |
| Cold in 1st half | | | 6 cold enough for gloves in hand | 52 1st warm day per cart 5 cold weather for several days 8 finger cold in morning 13 cool S p in day | 2 3 cool rainy days | 11 very cold NW wind | frosty thing | about 15 a very cool part | 2 cool night of late 63 cold with much... |
| Hot in first half | more warm hazy days June R 14 | 16 the 1st sultry weather | 12 p with the windows propt | 13 warm & hazy 15 midday very warm | | 3 sit without fire 24 hazy in sun 26 very hazy | | 1st very warm | 4:70 5:76 warm... |
| Hazy (a little 25-57) 24-60 | some warm days before the 14 | 10 windows propt 28 | | 13" 24 cannot see the mts 30 much haze 26 | | | | | 5 warm... |
| Thunder clouds | 9 reduce such cloth | 10 beg. of thick g thin clouds | | 24 1st thunder g thunder coat 20-8 23 cold I warm wool cloth some | | 26 thin coat g thin hot wool | 10 will end wool a thin coat | 12-60 thun... | |
| Bathing | | 29 begins | | 13 boys bathe | | | | | 8 bathe |
| Thunder shower &c | | 16 after hail some in April very fine | thunder & rain & lightn | | 20 thunder | | | 9 the 1st thun... | 13 slight... |
| | | | | | | | | | |
| Slightly sultry in morning | | 22 slightly | 25 warm breath of fire in sultry morning | | | | | 6 at night 1st sultry even | |
| Fire again | 12-13 a rain | 27 | | 12 cold enough | | | | | 16 many stoves |
| Sleep with open window | 1st 8 sleep | | 24 sleep | 25 (last night) | | | | | 13" |
| | | | | | | | | | |
| Yellow noon light | | | | | | | | 6 & 7 in ac a haze | 14" |
| Water tepid in morning | | | 17" | | | | | | |
| Frost apprehended | 20" 52 | 31 | | | 31" | | | | |
| Frost on upland (but not in lowland) Frost on ground | 8 ground still frozen is one place | | | | | | | | 21 in sprouts 23 |
| Frost kill plants | | 26 killed grass in hollows a week since June 1 53 | | | | 19 grass black since night | 28 29 night near frost 30 hickories blackened | 22 ice many... | |
| | | | | | | | | | |
| | 52 | 53 | 54 | 55 | 56 | 57 | 58 | 59 | 60 |
| 1st shadows noticed | 11 sought but did not find Korth line | | 16 conants cliff | | | | | 4 white conspic shadow of barn | 6 shade gratified |
| 1st shadows of foliage 28-51 | 30 strong light & shadow now | | | 27 under the tree now on the road | 29 little shadow & foliage | | | | 24 oak work & hickory |
| sun red | | 28 27 | | | | | | 5 (1st red) | 4 or 5 |
| Cold in last half | 20 frost apprehended | | 31 with SE wind | 21 very cold cold from 20 to 23 strong cold wind | 25 & 26 cold 31 very cold | 19 long winter | frost the 28 & 29 | | 16 56 |
| Hot in last half | | 28 sudden heat | 28 at noon warm | 24 1st think of thin coat | 23-24 warm | 22 fail them | | | 19 SW 30 |
| Washing day | 17 after storm | 21 windy day | 19 washing | 31" | 22 washing | 10 washing | | | June 2 |
| High winds | | 30 very windy | 18 high winds | 30 strong W wind 31 windy | | 11 very cold NW wind | | | 10 winds |
| Leaves blackened by cold wind | | | | | Hickory blackened | | | | |
| Sea turn | | | 17 | | | | 31 slight 20 | | |
| Winds no rain | | | 8" | cool E wind | | | | | |
| Fog | 7 1st fog the night 29 some thick fog in the morning | 12 | 12 1st fog night 24 | | 15 fog in morning | 30 fog rising over meadow | | 6 | |
| Heavy dew | 7 which not | | 22 | | | | | | 12 very heavy |
| Meadow fragrance | 26 27 begins | 17 the first | 22 the 1st | 27 | 15 27 | 25 | | 11" | June 4 |
| Peach fragrance in air | 26 meadows | | 16 | | | | | | |

## General Phenomena for May

| | 52 | 53 | 54 | 55 |
|---|---|---|---|---|
| **Fugacious fragrance of all flowers** | 9th - 16 | | | 6th (& [unclear] 1st of May) |
| **Rank scent of rhue** | | | | |
| **Scent of s. alba bloom** | | | | |
| | Not cold | | April 28 - 9 - 30 | |
| **May Storm** June 2-60 past week several rainy or cloudy days - esp. rainy - 30th & 31st & night of June 1st | 14 3 or 4 day <u>about</u> this 12 - 13 - 14 - 15 | 18 & 19 gentle May storm 27 principal May storm ends   (2 ½ days) | 1st & 4 3 days since Principal rain of spring 3 & 4th esp. hard the night of 4th These two storms settled | 8th at noon beg. cold May storm with E wind & thro 9th <br> <s>June</s> |
| **Rain** | 10th 27th a wet day | | 3rd    the spring <br> 10 early & then rain threatening | 1st some last night & <u>am</u> 4th a shower 20th a little June 3rd rains at last 1st of consequence for some time |
| **Still, cloudy, thoughtful day** | | | | |
| **Summer cumuli clouds** | | | 16 Rhomboidal masses | 24 1st summer cumuli |
| **Rounded clouds** | | | | |
| **Dry Weather** | | | | |
| **& foliage** Grass ^ suddenly changes green | 10th shoots up | 19 foliage of maples shows darker after rain 25 many shades darker within a week past | | |
| **Fishing begun** | | 7th | 18 one man caught a few | |
| **Cobwebs on grass in morning** | | | 21 & 1st I have witnessed | |
| **Stems of meadow saxifrage** | | | | |
| **Stone heaps** | | 7 already | | |
| **Clear air** | | | | |
| Corner [unclear] [unclear] | the 20th 30th 52 | 53 | 54 | 55 |
| **River when highest & how high** | 18 - still high 20 still high over meadows 25 subsided as to show the pads | | 5 water higher than before this year (1st higher than before after 3 days rain) 5 higher I think | 4th now generally off the meadows <u>25</u> |
| | | | than anytime since the greatest of all rises - the arches are quite concealed 8 fallen off about a foot but cannot get under arch | |
| **River when lowest & how low -** | | | 17 getting shallow on meads 21 going rapidly down 28 still have to take down mast at Br. | 25-4 inch below long stone i.e 4 inch below <u>S.L.</u> 1st gone down very fast & grass sprang up |
| | | | | 4th now generally off the meadows |
| **Cricket day** | | | | |
| **tender** Down from ^ foliage | 20 23rd at Plymouth | 27. 53 - v June 3rd up to June 21 | 26 begins to come off | |

| 56 | 57 | 58 | 59 | 60 |
|---|---|---|---|---|
| | | 14 air suddenly full of fragrance | | |
| 28  leaf [unclear] June 10 flower buds | | | | |
| | 8 | | | Ap. 10th |
| 2 & 3rd cool rainy days 8 - 9 - 10th & 11th rain 17 rain or lowering 28 - rainy | 19 - 20 - 21    rotting seeds    in ground | 20 cloudy & rainy    for 4 or 5 days past 22 much rainy weather about a week past Rain in night 11 - 12 | | 30 - 31st perhaps 21-& 22nd Anniversary week (& end of May) said to be commonly rainy |
| | 4th 28 rain again June 1 weather less re- liable for weeks past    or before | 12 1st summer shower in pm. 17th soothing rain | 19 warm muggy rainy eve 22 warm drizzling day | 19 gentle & warm 1st since Ap. 16 after a remarkable drought clears up in afternoons 21 pm & in night chiefly |
| | | | | 9th |
| | | | | 13th |
| | | | | 2 & 3rd round hill like |
| | | | 4 quite dry leaves in woods time for fires 6 about last of very dry leaves in woods | Remarkable drought - no rain from Apr. 16 to May 19 |
| | | | 9th after the 1st thundershower | |
| | | | | 5th |
| | | | 26 tender white conspic. toward sun at eve | 30 |
| | 29 after rain or cloud | | | |

| 56 | 57 | 58 | 59 | 60 |
|---|---|---|---|---|
| 10 goes over meads again after they were almost bare 12th as high as before this spring 17 fallen a foot | 23 still generally over meads can cross (Hubs mead. 3 still high - 20 rising | | 25 quite high for season on ac. of late rains | 31 highest 1/2 inch below S.L. & rising |
| | 25 still high | | | |
| 1st w on meadows rapidly going down confined to River for most part | 23 | | | 2nd 3 5/16 below S.L. 6th not essentially lower than Ap. 29th (with no rain 13 6 15/16 below S.L. |
| | | | | 17th lowest 7⅛ in below                    S.L. |
| | | | 27 | 13 commonly heard at Lee's cliff |
| | | | 28 sticks to clothes | |

| | | | | |
|---|---|---|---|---|
| 1st notice linty dust on water | | | | |
| Early potatoe planting | | | | |
| Plant my melons | | | 9th | |
| Rainbow | | | 11th | April 9 & 18 55 |
| Leaves off all oaks but young white os | | | 7th | |
| Some front yard grass is mowed | | | | |
| 1st summer shower cloud slate color in horizon or- falling rain in warm day | | | | |
| Sit with open window commonly | May 1st & 8 at least | | | |
| Cows turned out to pasture | | | 7th | |

## General Phenomena for May

| | 52 | 53 | 54 | 55 |
|---|---|---|---|---|
| Cows go up country | 6 cattle going up c. 10th | 2nd cattle going up c. | First of consequence the 8th | 6 Road full of c. going up country.  12 1st warm day for a week or 2 |
| Cold in 1st half | | 16th the 1st sultry weather 1st cold NW wind 8 cold SW wind | 6 cold enough for gloves in wind. | 5 cold weather for several days 8 finger-cold in morning 13 cool E wind in pm 12 cold enough for fire this many |
| Hot in last half | some warm hazy days before the 14th 5th really warm 11th Kossuth here | 16 the 1st sultry weather | 12 sit with open window & forget fire 11 warm night 15 suddenly very warm | 12 warm  a day 13 warm & hazy 15 suddenly very warm |
| Hazy (a little 25 -51) 24 -60 some | some warm hazy days before the 14 7th thick W. wind =8th very thick | 10—divides west 28 | | 13th 24 cannot see the Mts. 30 much haze 26 |
| Thinner clothes | 9 reduce neck cloth | 10 beg. to think of thin coats | | 24 1st think of thin coat 20-& 23 cold & wear great coat some |
| Bathing | | 29th begins | | 13 boys bathe |
| Thundershower &c | 1st lightning of year the Sunday before 19th | 16th also had some in April when I was in Haverhill -18th at night | 11 Thunder shower & rain bow - christen - ing of Summer | |
| Open window & no fire v April | Open all day the 5th | | 20th in N.  before/ 29 Thunder & Lightning rain | April 19th 1st am [unclear] sit with open window |
| Slightly sultryish morning | | | 22 slightly | 25 Hear buzz of flies in sultryish morning |
| Fire again | 12 -13 in rain | | 27 | 27 12 cold enough for a fire this many a day 20 to 23rd inclusive |
| Slept with open window | 1st & 8 at least | | 24 last night | 25th (last night) |
| Yellow sun light | | | | |

| | | | | |
|---|---|---|---|---|
| | | | 27 | 23 after rain |
| | | | | May 1st midst yet |
| | | 7 too early for this year | | 10th |
| 30 slight | | | | |

| | | | | |
|---|---|---|---|---|
| | | | | 30 |
| | | 12th | | 25 |
| | | | | say mid. of May? |
| | | | | |

| 56 | 57 | 58 | 59 | 60 |
|---|---|---|---|---|
| 7  c. going up country for a week | | | | 14  cattle still going up c. Begins Ap. 30 most the 7th gen cease the 15th |
| 2  & 3  cool rainy days | 11  very cold NW wind | [unclear] | about 15th  a very severe frost | 2nd  cool nights of late 63+ with wind makes a cool day 14  Pm cooler 60+ |
| | 3  sit without fire (11 a very cold NW very warm      wind. with smooth water      2 pm 78+ 6 -7 –8 remarkably warm | 1st a ^ warm & pleasant day - 2nd  no fire today nor yesterday 14 1st summer-like day. | 1st  very warm 4 - 4th warm day 6 suddenly op- pressively hot in woods 7 hotter 88+ 8 - 90 & more | 4th  70+ 5 - 76 warm & hazy 6  chamber too hot at eve 11  very warm 77+ 12 - 81 - 13 - 82 - 14 |
| | 24  hazy in pm 26  very hazy | | 4th  & 5th 6 - smoky ? meads 7 do. [unclear] | Sultry evening 5th  warm & hazy 6th "" & 7th &c 14  remarkably hazy 15  hazy -16-17 |
| | 26  thin coats & straw hats worn | 10th  wish I had worn a thinner coat | 12-60 thinner neck cloth & coat 12- remarkably warm - 60 | 5th  thick coat too much v Ap. 28  No outside c. Ap 19 & May 15 at least & no fire in c. |
| | 8  some boys have bathed 25  I bathe | | Ap. 27-& 30 weather for half thick coat      59 | 12  I bathe |
| 20 - Thunder | 10  some thunder & L (the first) 29 - 1st reg. summer | | 9 The 1st T & L shower this Pm | 13 lightning seen in N. - 30 a succession of moderate T& L showers in Pm |
| | Thunder shower 3rd sit without fire | 1st  & 2nd  58 without fire | 30 April sit without fire | no fire in chamber from Ap. 19 - May 15 at least |
| | | | 6  at night 1st sultry buzz of a fly in chamber | |
| | | | | 16  many have 21  I have it & 22 27th |
| | | | | 13th |
| | | | 6  & 7  on ac.of haze | 14th |

| | | | 17th | |
|---|---|---|---|---|
| **Water tepid in morning.** | | | 17th | |
| **Frosts apprehended** | 20th 52 | 31 | | |
| **Frost on upland** NB (last frost on lowland in June) | | | | |
| **Frost in ground** | 8 ground still frozen in some places | | | |
| severe ^ **Frosts kill plants** | | | 26 kills oaks &c in hollows a week since v. June 1st 53 | |
| | **52** | **53** | **54** | **55** |
| **1st shadows noticed** | 11 sought but did not find — —Kossuth here | | 16 Conant. Cliff | |
| **1st shadows of foliage** 28 51 trees beg. to shade the streets | 30 strong lights & shades now | | | 27 - casting darker shadows over the meads Elm tree tops thicken |
| **sun sets red** | | 28 & 27 & warm weather | | |
| **Cold** in last half | 20 - frost apprehended | | 31 cold SE wind | 21 very cold— cold from 20 to 23rd incl. wear great coat some stormy cold wind from NW. |
| **Hot in last half** haze saves from extreme heat 25 -51 | | 28 sudden heat | 28 oppressively warm | 24 1st think of thin coat 25 warm night the last 28 oppressively warm |
| **Washing day** 25 -51 fine freshening air - a washing day | 17 after storm 30th & shadows of clouds— | 21 windy day after May rains - washing days (19 -20 -21 -2 -3 ) | 19th washing day 20 blowing off some apple bloom | 31st 27th 26 strong cold NW ^wind |
| **High winds** | | 30th very windy | 18 high winds racking young trees & blowing off blossoms 5 very windy NW cking wind (8 sma | 30 ^ strong W. wind 31 windy washing day June 1 & 2 very windy making 4 days |
| **Leaves blackened by cold wind** | | | | |
| **Sea turn** | | | 17 | |
| **E winds & no rain?** | | | | Cool & wind in Pm 13th |
| **Fog** | 7th 1st fog very slight 29 some slight fog in the morning. | 12th 1st considerable one June 1st quite a fog principle fogs begin | 12 1st fog slight 24th consid fog at 4 ½ am | |
| **Heavy dew** | 7 - which wets feet 11 observe it | | 22 now wets completely 12 grass high enough to be wet | |
| **meadow fragrance** | 26 & 27 begins much as ever June 24 & still June 27 16 | 17 the first | 22 the 1st | 27 |
| **Peculiar fragrance in air** | 26 meadows smell most at night | | 16 sweet scent from expand. leafets or other cause | |

| 56 | 57 | 58 | 59 | 60 |
|---|---|---|---|---|
| 31st | | | | 21 on squashes in garden & in woods (v 22 & 25) 29th |
| | 19 ferns blackened within a night or 2 ) | .28 & 29th nights severe frosts 30 hickories blackened by | 22 see many leaves killed about 15th v. late for birds | |
| | | | 4 notice conspic shadow of Conant. Cliff warm SW wind | 6 shade grateful 11 notice on ac. of warmth - before leaves of apple trees 20th v. 24th 23rd on meadows |
| | 29 little shadows produced by expanding foliage | | | 24 openwork shadow of hickories |
| | | | 5 (1st time) followed by very hot & hazy day. | 4th or 5th 15 & 14th & 16th |
| 25 & 26 cold 31 very cold for 2 or 3 days past | 19 frost within a night or 2 past ) | Frost the 28 & 29th | | 4th or 5th 16 - 56+ & fires again 20 strong cold W wind 60+ at 2pm 21 colder & fire 22 being wet |
| & 23 -24th warm summer-like evening. 24 suddenly melting hot 94+ at 1 Pm. | 22 - fair & warm at last 70+ 24 very warm morn 3Pm 88+ 25 3 ½ pm 87+ | | | SW |
| 12 - washing day after rains | 10th a washing day | | | 19th 30th & June 2nd |
| | 11th (?very cold NW wind?) | | | 10th winds may be said to have died away with April. 20 strong cold W. wind |
| Hickory blackened by blowing in cold wind 31st | | | | |
| | | 31st slight in Am 20 perhaps a little | | |
| | | | | Prevailing wind NE (& Early) from mid April to mid of May 19 at least cool rains cool E wind 14 & 15th |
| 15 fog in morning 19 thick fog in morn till late forenoon) | | 30 fog rising over meadow at evening — | | 6 mists these mornings & for a week after. 17 quite a fog till 8am 28 low solid white by noon high + on meadow |
| | | | | 12 very heavy dew & mist plowed ground black with it 13 beautiful dew drops |
| 15th & 27 | 25 | 25 | 11th | June 4 |
| | | | 4 a peculiar fr. in air - not meadow fragrance 26 air full of terabinthine o sweet fern &c. | June 4 arbor vitae &c |

General Phenomena for June. The Morgan Library & Museum. MA 610.

# JUNE:

## *Shadows of Clouds*

————————————

THESE MORNINGS THE LIGHT THROUGH THE TREES MAKES SO many places of shadowed brightness the yard seems full of secrets. June is the season of dandelions and then, very soon after, the season of dandelion seeds, which catch in the cobwebs that, every morning, connect everything to everything else—porch railing, broken flowerpot, old chair. Every leaf of the maple tree is silvered by sun on one side, blue shadowed on the other, so that what seems a lush green when you look glancingly is a quick flashing blue-silver when you look closer. I am thinking about the almost-nothing quality of dandelion and gossamer and milkweed seeds and pollen of various kinds and other elements whose power is to be airborne and close to nothing—almost without body, barely there at all. Dickinson's "certain Slant of light" has this winking quality—not even light, but a slant of it. If you are reading this sentence, you are reading the words that followed the thought of silk thread so delicate it barely even was, and then was not. I think, for the minute or two I can stand to think of it, of the physical pain borne by people I love, and then of the physical pain borne by the people I don't know. My daughter, who once pressed her whole tiny body against the glass doors and repeated the word *outside outside outside* with an animal desperation now comes and goes as she will, drives a car, has flown alone in airplanes. She paints the green-blue landscapes of imagined worlds.

❖

If, for Thoreau, May was the season of flowering, June was the season of light and shadow—the dramatic unfurling of leaves, the lengthening of days, the arrival of hazy afternoons and the transformation of landscape. In June of 1860, Thoreau was particularly attentive to landscape effects present and past: rainbows, fog, blue-tinted air, the "glaucous sheen of bent sedge" in the fields.

Though Thoreau seems to have had little interest in looking at pictures, he often characterized his desire to represent nature in pictorial terms. In January of 1852, articulating the aims of his mature Journal, he announces the aesthetic and epistemological principles that animate both his Journal practices and the eventual development of the Kalendar.

> To set down such choice experiences that my own writings may inspire me.– and at last I may make wholes of parts.
>
> Certainly it is a distinct profession to rescue from oblivion & to fix the sentiments & thoughts which visit all men more or less generally. That the contemplation of the unfinished picture may suggest its harmonious completion. Associate reverently, and as much as you can with your loftiest thoughts. Each thought that is welcomed and recorded is a nest egg–by the side of which more will be laid. Thoughts accidentally thrown together become a frame–in which more may be developed & exhibited. Perhaps this is the main value of a habit of writing–of keeping a journal. That so we remember our best hours –& stimulate ourselves. My thoughts are my company– They have a certain individuality and separate existence–aye personality. Having by chance recorded a few disconnected thoughts and then brought them into juxtaposition–they suggest a whole new field in which it was possible to labor & to think. Thought begat thought. (1/22/1852, *Journal* 4:277–78)

As H. Daniel Peck observes, the language here—particularly "unfinished picture," "frame," and "exhibited"—suggests that Thoreau thought of the Journal as a repository of *views* as much as a collection of *facts*. The entry articulates Thoreau's perspectivism: the belief that only by consolidating multiple views can one arrive at an adequate representation of the world—in his terms, a finished picture, or "harmonious completion." This orientation toward the pictorial deepened with his exposure to works by the travel writer William Gilpin, whose work he began reading in 1852, and the English art critic John Ruskin, whose *Elements of Drawing* he read shortly after its publication in 1857. A year after discovering Gilpin, Thoreau wrote the following entry, which both captures the pictorial quality of the landscape—its color, form, and perspective—while also conveying, as pictures cannot, the unfolding of time:

> Seen from this point now the pitch pines on Bear Garden Hill– The fresh green foliage of the deciduous trees now so prevails–the pitch pines which lately looked–green–are of a dark-brownish or mulberry color–by contrast & the white pines almost as dark but bluer– In this haziness no doubt they are a *little* darker than usual. The grass on pretty high grounds is wet with dew an hour before sun set. White weed now & cotton grass. For $^3/_4$ of an hour the sun is a great round red ball in the west–reflected in the water–at first a scarlet but as it descends growing more purple & crimson–& larger with a blue bar of a cloud across it– still reflected in the water, 2 suns one above the other, below the hilly bank–as if it were a round hole in the cope of heaven through which we looked into a crimson atmosphere– If such scenes were painted faithfully they would be pronounced unNatural. (5/28/1853, *Journal* 6:157)

The entry conveys something of Thoreau's skepticism of the conventions of landscape painting and the limits of naturalistic representation, which, as the last sentence argues, often implies a regularizing view of the highly irregular natural world: His own perspective-gathering endeavor, the charts of general phenomena, would attempt to capture both the regular, recurrent patterns, and the idiosyncratic particulars of nature.

Aesthetic theory was of interest to Thoreau in part because it offered a new way of framing, and to some extent challenging, the legacy of Emersonian idealism. As early as 1851, Thoreau was complicating the Emersonian formula "Nature is the symbol of spirit." "Let me not be in haste to detect the *universal law*," Thoreau directs himself in December of 1851, "let me see more clearly a particular instance" (12/25/1851, *Journal* 4:223). Thoreau would have found support in Ruskin for his growing determination to stay with the particulars of perception rather than allowing these to be subsumed by symbolic signification. While it is easy for any inheritor of a romantic imagination to invest objects in the visual field with spiritual meanings, staying with appearance requires discipline. Ruskin writes,

> The perception of solid Form is entirely a matter of experience. We *see* nothing but flat colors. . . . The whole technical power of painting depends on our recovery of what may be called *the innocence of the eye*: that

is to say, a sort of childish perception of those flat stains of color, merely as such, without consciousness of what they signify.

Thoreau's attention to color as it appeared within a given landscape is a key feature of the spring 1860 Journal and corresponds to his increasing interest in allowing individual material phenomena to disclose themselves without making an immediate leap to poetic or spiritual meaning. Far from impoverishing his sight, Thoreau's increased attentiveness to "the particular instance" of natural phenomena in the later years of the Journal deepened his experience of perception. By 1860, just *seeing* the landscape was a kind of drama.

> Land at the first angle of the Holt–  Looking across the Peninsula–toward Balls Hill–I am struck by the bright blue of the river (a deeper blue than the sky) contrasting with the fresh yellow-green of the meadow (ie of coarse sedges just starting) & between them a darker or greener green next the edge of the river–esp. where that small sand bar island is–the green of that early rank river grass This is the first painting or coloring in the meadows. These several colors are as it were daubed on–as on china ware–or as distinct & simple as a child's painted. I am struck by the amount & variety of color–after so much brown. (5/4/1860, Journal Transcript 31:165–66)

The use of the present tense in this passage, combined with the repetition of the phrase "I am struck," creates the sense of the vista as aesthetic event—not the static picture of a landscape but an unfolding act of creation: "the first painting or coloring in the meadows." The starkness and flatness of the colors suggested by the phrase "daubed on" and the evocation of a child's painting suggest the defamiliarization techniques urged by Ruskin. At the same time, the recognition of the relativity of colors and the impact of their intensity in springtime ("after so much brown") speaks to Thoreau's deeply relational epistemology, his sense that "the point of interest is somewhere between" ourselves and the objects we perceive (11/5/1857, Journal Transcript 24:610).

Ruskin's emphasis on the separation of what one knows objectively or abstractly from what one perceives from one's actual, subjective position likely contributed to the relational stance that informed the charts of general phenomena. As Peck notes, *phenomena* is "the term Thoreau most often uses to reconcile the power of the creative eye with the independent status of the world . . . an entity that bridges the gap between subject and object."

Developed at the height of Thoreau's creative and intellectual power, in the wake of his exposure to Ruskin and Darwin, the spring Kalendar charts seek not only to "make wholes of parts" but also to unite the power of scientific observation with the power of aesthetic vision, to do justice not only to each observed particular, but also to the wonder of perception itself.

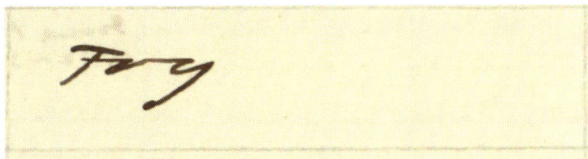

### Fog

A low fog on the meadows, but not so much as last night–a low incense frosting them. The cloud scattered wisps in the sky like a squadron thrown into disorder at the approach of the sun. The sun now gilds an eastern cloud a broad bright coppery-golden edge–fiery bright–notwithstanding which the protuberances of the cloud cast dark shadows ray-like up into the day. The curled dock rumex crispus– & the Malva   the cheese mallows. A new season. The earth looks like a debauchee after the sultry night. Birds sing at this hour as in the spring. (6/16/1852, *Journal* 5:102)

A prevalent fog though not quite so thick as the last described–it is a little more local–for it is so thin SW of this hill that I can see the earth through it–but as thick as before NE. Yet here & there deep valleys are excavated in it–as painters imagine the red sea for the passage of Pharaoh's host–wherein trees and houses appear as it were at the bottom of the sea. (6/9/1853, *Journal* 6:187)

A cold fog– These mornings those who walk in grass are thoroughly wetted above mid-leg. All the earth is dripping wet– I am surprised to feel how warm the water is–by contrast with the cold foggy air. The frogs seem glad to bury themselves in it. The dewy cobwebs are very thick this morning little napkins of the fairies spread on the grass. Whorled utricularias. . . . A potamogeton off Dodd's with fine grassy thread-like leaves & stem (somewhat flattish) & small globular spikes–maybe some time? Ranunculus reptans maybe a day or more. A duck–prob. wood duck which is breeding here. From the hill–I am reminded of more youthful mornings–seeing the dark forms of the trees eastward in the low grounds–partly within & against the shining white fog–the sun just risen over it– The mist fast rolling away eastward from them. –their tops at last streaking the mist & dividing it into vales–All beyond them a submerged & unknown country as if they grew on the seashore– Why does the fog go off always toward the sun– is seen in the E when it has disappeared in the W? The waves of the foggy ocean divide & flow back for us Israelites of a day to march through– I hear the half-suppressed guttural sounds of a red squirrel on a tree–at length he breaks out into a sharp bark.

Slavery has produced no sweet scented flower like the water-lily–for its flower must smell like itself. It will be a carrion-flower. (6/17/1854, *Journal* 8:202–3)

Among the many atmospheric effects Thoreau recorded in the June chart, fog was a particular catalyst for the imagination, inspiring both metaphor and reverie. In 1852, the fog over the meadows is "a low incense frosting them"—a composite image that speaks to both the ephemerality and the materiality of the phenomenon. Fleeting as smoke, fog nevertheless transforms the meadows like a frost, imparting a whole new color to the world. Characteristic of summer heat, the arrival of this fog signals "a new season," in which "the earth looks like a debauchee after the sultry night." "Debauched look of streets in morn" is also a June category, with only this one entry filled in for 1852—a fact that speaks to the resonance of the image for Thoreau, in spite of its apparent uniqueness as a descriptor of June.

Associated with pleasure and indulgence, "debauched" is derived from the French *débaucher*—meaning to turn away from duty. Coupled with this word, "sultry" takes on its secondary meaning—eliciting sexual desire—in addition to simply signifying heat. This may seem strange territory for the famously abstemious Thoreau, and it is significant that the object of this evocative description is not a person but the earth itself. Thoreau's experience of his own sexuality was complex: though he seemed to have been physically attracted to men, there is no evidence that he acted on those attractions. He had several intense relationships with women—Lidian Emerson, Lucy Jackson Brown, and Ellen Sewall, for example—but these attractions generally seemed to be platonic and spiritual rather than sexual in nature. In her compelling essay "Chastity and Vegetality: On Thoreau's Eco-erotics," Cristin Ellis argues that to understand Thoreau as simply closeted or repressed in his sexuality fails to account for the rich eroticism of his descriptions of his experience in nature.

> Thoreau conceives of chastity as a discipline not of mastery but of sensuous self-surrender, a practice that involves attending to the subtle inclinations of the body which can only arise when we are alone in nature and which urge us—through tugs of attraction, threads of affection, and bursts of sexual exhilaration—toward the gratifying expression of a libidinal economy Thoreau associates with vegetal sexuality.

In other words, for Thoreau, chastity itself involved a kind of sexual expression. In the "Higher Laws" chapter of *Walden*, Thoreau articulates a Victorian division between our higher, spiritual nature and the "animal in us, which awakens in proportion as our higher nature slumbers." This aspect of our nature is "reptile and sensual, and perhaps cannot be wholly expelled; like the worms which, even in life and health, occupy our bodies." While Thoreau's belief that the goal of moral life was for "spirit" to "pervade and control every member and function of the body, and transmute what in form is the grossest sensuality into purity and devotion," which seems characteristically Victorian, in the following sentence one senses the way this transmutation itself contained a sensual aspect: "The generative energy, which, when we are loose, dissipates and makes us unclean, when we are continent invigorates and inspires us." The distinction between looseness and continence here aligns with the idea of debauchery as a turning away from duty: a relaxing of spring energies into the sultry dissipation of midsummer. In June of 1854, he writes, "It is dry hazy June weather. We are more of the earth–farther from heaven these days– We live in a grosser element" (6/17/1854, *Journal* 8:204). The rhythms of the seasons were, for Thoreau, significantly connected to the bodily rhythms of desire and its transmutation.

Fog also seems to prompt a kind of imaginative freedom—perhaps related to the sensual looseness he associates with debauchery. In 1853 he describes the fog as looking like paintings of the parting of the Red Sea—an image he takes up again the following June. Interestingly, in the 1853 entry he describes the passage of "Pharaoh's host" through the excavated valleys in the fog—a surprising formulation, since in the biblical story, Pharaoh's army did not successfully pass through the parted sea after the Israelites but were drowned by it. In 1854, the same image is used, but this time with reference to the Israelites rather than the Egyptian army: "The waves of the foggy ocean divide & flow back for us Israelites of a day to march through." In both instances, the presence of the fog speaks to the miraculous power of the unseen to radically transform landscape, and to act in ways that preserve and destroy human life.

It is perhaps the reference to the Israelites, slaves to the Egyptians, that prompts the reflection on slavery in the 1854 entry—a passage that would later become part of his speech (and, still later, essay) "Slavery in Massachusetts." The speech was a direct response to the re-enslavement of Anthony Burns, who escaped slavery in Virginia and was tried in Massachusetts under the Fugitive Slave Act. In another June 1854 Journal entry imported into the essay, he writes,

> But what signifies the beauty of nature when men are base? We walk to lakes to see our serenity reflected in them– When we are not serene we go not to them. Who can be serene in a country where both rulers & ruled are without principle? The remembrance of the baseness of politicians spoils my walks–my thoughts are murder to the state– I endeavor in vain to observe Nature–my thoughts involuntarily go plotting against the state– (6/16/1854, *Journal* 8:200)

Though it's possible to read in this passage Thoreau's frustrated desire to retreat from a political reality that "spoils [his] walks," more often his comments on slavery *connect* his environmental observations to his commitment to abolition. As James Finley argues, "for Thoreau, the landscapes of the slave state are not ahistorical pastoral spaces beyond the reach of social processes but rather landscapes radically integrated with, and infernally corrupted by, the slave system." This understanding of slavery as an environmental, rather than merely a social and political crisis, is another instance of Thoreau's reintegration of the human into a more-than-human world.

The water lily passage from the June 1854 Journal also makes its way into "Slavery in Massachusetts," where it is elaborated into an extended metaphor. Describing the scent of the flower, he writes, "If Nature can compound this fragrance still annually, I shall believe her still young and full of vigor, her integrity and genius unimpaired. It reminds me that nature has been partner to no Missouri Compromise." Ultimately, as Finley writes, he suggests "that both the slave system and the environmental degradation that results are unnatural."

Though it would seem we have come a long way from Thoreau's observations of June fog, it is a measure of Thoreau's habit of ecological thinking that the fog, debauchery, the water lily, and slavery must ultimately be understood not as isolated phenomena but as interconnected parts of a single system: one that, in June of 1860, Thoreau was hard at work endeavoring to comprehend in all of its complexity and detail.

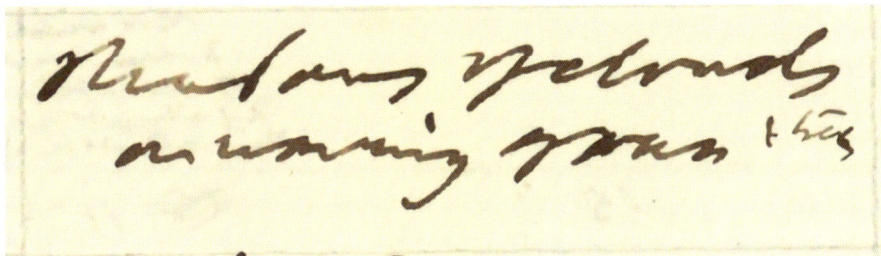

*Shadows of Clouds on Waving Grass*

It has just cleared off after this first rain of consequence for a long time & now I observe the shadows of massive clouds still floating here & there in the peculiarly blue sky–which dark shadows on field & wood– are the more remarkable by contrast with the light yellow-green foliage–now–& when they rest on evergreens they are doubly dark–like dark rings about the eyes of June. Great white bosomed clouds darker beneath . . . . float through the cleared sky–& are seen against the deliciously blue sky–such a sky as we have not had before– Thus it is after the first important rain at this season. The song of birds is more lively and seems to have a new character–a new season has commenced. (6/4/1855, Journal Transcript 19:29–30)

*June 7.* <u>Pm</u>.–To Walden.
Warm weather has suddenly come–beginning yesterday–today it is yet warmer–87°+ at 3 pm compelling me to put on a thin coat–& I see that a new season has arrived– June shadows are moving over waving grass fields. The crickets chirp uninterruptedly–& I perceive the agreeable acid scent of high blueberry bushes in bloom–The trees having leaved out you notice their rounded tops suggesting shade–the night hawk sparks & booms over arid hill sides & sproutlands. (6/6/1858, Journal Transcript 26:335–36)

Thoreau was especially attentive to the skies of June, and to the relationship between sky and earth that resulted from the new atmospheric conditions of the season. The sunny days and blue skies of summer rendered both the clouds and their shadows highly visible, and Thoreau delighted in the drama of their simultaneous movement across the landscape. As Bradley Dean notes, Thoreau inherited the Romantic view of clouds as evanescent and moody—he saw them, as he saw wind and gossamer, as phenomena at once material and spiritual. In the conclusion of *Walden*, he had written, "If you have built castles in the air, your work need not be lost; that is where they should be. Now put the foundations under them." The sentiment encapsulates Thoreau's lifelong interest in the airy and the earthly, a dichotomy he more fully explicates in "Spring," where he ecstatically traces the relationship between the word *lobe* and its meaning:

> The radicals of lobe are *lb*, the soft mass of the *b* (single lobed, or B, double lobed,) with the liquid *l* behind it pressing it forward. In globe, *glb*, the guttural *g* adds to the meaning the capacity of the throat. The feathers and wings of birds are still drier and thinner leaves. Thus, also, you pass from the lumpish grub in the earth to the airy and fluttering butterfly. The very globe continually transcends and translates itself, and becomes winged in its orbit.

Here, sound, language, flora, and fauna are described in terms of a progression, from "the lumpish grub in the earth" to the leaves and wings and letters that inhabit and partake of the air. While the surreal, kaleidoscopic vision of "Spring" may be Thoreau's most elaborate articulation of the earth-air relation, it is one of many. The dichotomy itself represents a kind of naturalized transcendentalism, a version of the relation between animal and spiritual life he traces in "Brute Neighbors" and "Higher Laws."

By 1860, Thoreau had significantly modified the idealism he'd inherited from Emerson. As Peck observes, he was more apt, by this point, to trace relations horizontally between material phenomena than to seek symbolic equivalences vertically—between "natural" and "spiritual facts," to use Emerson's terms. And he was attentive to the living, changing qualities of the natural world that complicated the static, one-to-one picture of natural objects and spiritual laws sketched by Emerson's *Nature*. Both of the Journal passages keyed to the category "Shadows of clouds on waving grass" unfold in the present tense, and both emphasize the movement of the landscape:

the shadows "float," "rest," and are "moving over waving grass fields," while "crickets chirp uninterruptedly," and "the night hawk sparks & booms over arid hill sides & sproutlands." This is a landscape not of objects but of changing and unfolding perceptions, and even those elements most aligned with the old dualism of spirit and matter—the clouds and the earth—are united by the light of June, through which the shadows move.

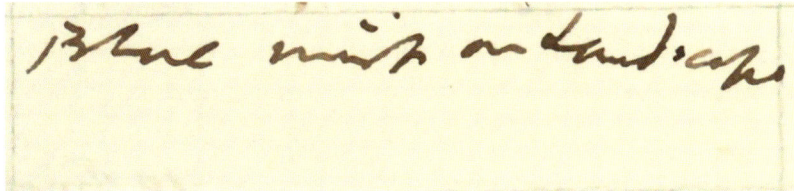

*Blue Mist on Landscape*

While waiting for Mother & Sophia I look now from the yard to the waving & slightly glaucous tinged June meadows–edged by the cool shade– (gelid)–of shrubs & trees–a waving shore of shady bays & promontories– Yet different from the August shades– It is beautiful & elysian. The air has now begun to be filled with a bluish haze– These virgin shades of the year–when everything is tender fresh & green– – how full of promise– promising bowers of shade in which heroes may repose themselves–  I would fain be present at the birth of shadow– – It takes place with the first expansion of the leaves. (6/2/1854, *Journal* 8:171)

This is a decidedly dog-dayish day & the 24th also–foretold by the red-moon of last evening.
  The sun light, even this forenoon, was peculiarly yellow–passing thro' misty clouds–& this afternoon the atmosphere is decidedly blue. I see it in the street within 30 rods– & perceive a distinct–musty odor.–
  First *bluish misty* dog-day–& sultry. (6/23/1860, Journal Transcript 31:274)

In January of 1854, Thoreau copied the following passage from Gilpin's "On Sketching Landscape" into his Journal: "When you have finished your sketch therefore with India ink, as far as you propose, tinge the whole thing over with some light horizon hue. It may be the rosy tint of morning; or the more ruddy one of evening; or it may incline more to a yellowish, or a greyish cast. . . . By washing this tint over your *whole drawing*, you lay a foundation for harmony" (1/8/1854, *Journal* 7:227). Thoreau registered "bluish" atmospheres in June before encountering this passage, but the articulation of a phenomenon he'd already begun to observe himself seems to have intensified his noticing. A few months later, he notes both the "glaucous-tinged meadows" and the "bluish haze" pervading the June landscape. It is no wonder Thoreau responds to Gilpin, who seeks, on the one hand, to attend ever more faithfully to the external reality of nature's particulars, and, on the other, to seek "a foundation for harmony" in his own unifying vision.

Despite—or perhaps in part because of—their provisional, unfinished nature, the charts of general phenomena Thoreau created in the spring of 1860 provide us with unique insight into Thoreau's mature aesthetic, ecological, and philosophical thought. In these charts, the transformative quality of perception, the role of the human in a more-than-human world, and the relationships between the categories of *spirit* and *matter* (as well as those of *general* and *particular*) are elaborated, charted, and worked out, all in a form that also allows us to picture the cosmos in its temporal dimension. As Peck observes, by the early 1850s Thoreau's Journal had become "what might be called a material memory, a book deliberately conceived to 'keep' time by enlarging the temporal view of reality through a process of cross-reference." In 1860, Thoreau modified this basic, linear design to capture the cyclical qualities of seasonal time, an innovation that enables an exponentially—almost infinitely—fuller picture: "When the past is viewed in this way—and *viewing* is indeed the right word—it becomes possible to 'see' time, and to see it whole, as a full matrix of past, present, and future."

No completed work speaks to the fullness of Thoreau's vision in all of its interrelated facets as do these charts—in part because they are not a discrete literary, political, or scientific work, but rather a sketch of a life lived in time, a map of experience itself. They give us—both in their overall structure and in the particular detail of the entries—an extraordinary picture of the mature Thoreau, the Thoreau who had absorbed the lessons of Darwin, Ruskin, and John Brown as thoroughly as he once had the early lessons of Emerson. Though it is likely that the Kalendar was initially intended as a blueprint for a major work, it seems clear that the purpose it finally served was a more personal one: a consolidation of perspectives that made possible a more integrated life in nature and time. In an 1851 Journal entry, Thoreau describes a remembered state of identification with the more-than-human world: "Formerly methought nature developed as I developed and grew up with me.

My life was ecstasy. In youth before I lost any of my senses– I can remember that I was all alive–and inhabited my body with inexpressible satisfaction" (7/16/1951, *Journal* 3:305–6). For the whole of his adult life, this ideal of growing *with* nature—of being keyed to the seasons as they unfold—was Thoreau's definition of happiness, sanity, and health. In his final spring of full health and mobility, Thoreau devised a technology for more fully perceiving and experiencing seasonal time. In *Walden*, he had written, "To affect the quality of the day, that is the highest of arts. Every man is tasked to make his life, even in its details, worthy of the contemplation of his most elevated and critical hour." The great work for which the Kalendar would finally serve as index and outline was not a book, but a life of multiplied perspectives, lived in fuller time.

Grand Phenomena for June

| | 52 | 53 | 54 | 55 | 56 | 57 | 58 | 59 | 60 |
|---|---|---|---|---|---|---|---|---|---|
| River Lowest | | | | | | | | | |
| River highest | | | | | | | | | |
| Haze | | | | | | | | | |
| Fog | | | | | | | | | |
| our light yellow | | | | | | | | | |
| great Fog | | | | | | | | | |
| misling weather | | | | | | | | | |
| Rain | | | | | | | | | |
| Dog days | | | | | | | | | |
| Thunder Shower | | | | | | | | | |
| Succession of Thunder Showers | | | | | | | | | |

General Phenomena for June

| | '52 | '53 | '54 | '55 | '56 | '57 | '58 | '59 | '60 |
|---|---|---|---|---|---|---|---|---|---|
| Hot in 1st half | 3' sultry 19 hot weather | 14 warm above 64 FS set 16 warmer for past night past | | | 4' very warm 11' very hot | 2 very warm this 3 PM | 5' swimming in Thomas Pool 6 warm in middle sun 7 89° at 3 PM | 15 sultry hot 90° after very cool | 4'' uncomfortably warm in nothing day 15 '' warmer nite PM 12 85° at 2 PM |
| Hot in last half 30 = 5? afternoon warm 25-60 89 at PM | Before 24 a week of more of warm days & nights 19 & 18 sultry nights | 20 hot weather 21 warmest day, yet 30 hot again | | 22 warmest days Jun 30 95° 2 PM | 21-2 PM 98- 210'' | | 24 very hot = 25' hottest this summer before 93° at 1 PM | 29 very hot | 16 85°+ 2 PM this is hot for morning 29 67° 91° warm most nite 85° at 2 PM PM 89° |
| cold in 1st half sultry nights | | 20 21 hottest warmest 22 & 23 warm 24' ahead of mid 27 hot yet 21-8 excessively | | | | | | | |
| It banched leaks on sheets in room. | 16 | | | | | | | | 4'' |
| Sense of flannel Beg. to sleep with two windows constantly | | | | | | | | | 10 |
| Beg. to wear thin sack | 18 now PM a thin coat | 14'' | | | | | 7'' | | June 1st 15'' 2 or 3 days past |
| Rain needs a ribbon | | 20 have week for a few days (my 2) | | | | | | | 15 ribbon or 3 days past |
| Bring umbrella | | | | | | | | | |
| cold in 1st half | 10'' some cold wind till 10 past days | | 1st | | 6 cold immediately | | | 13 very cold days | 10 thing & cold & jar wild 58° at PM |
| cold in last half | 24 uncommonly cold after a week or more of warm days & nights | 26 very cold (34 day is cool) | | | | 29 '' with & wind & blue mist in air | | 30 cooler with northerly wind | 21½'' 12 PM 54° |
| Warm again | 15 parts of the past week | | 23 parts of time all days past | | | | | | 6 on ac. grain 21 cooler & rain not day – not cool play |
| Thick coat again | | | 1st | | | | | | 22 cold wind 60° at 12½ PM |
| cool eve | | | | | | | | | 2'' & white frost ½ PM |

MA 610

| | 52 | 53 | 54 | 55 | 56 | 57 | 58 | 59 | 60 |
|---|---|---|---|---|---|---|---|---|---|
| Thunder showers around Summer showers in P.M. | | | 13-14-15-16 high in E. part of watches | | | 2" above | | | 5 much of forenoon 8 another hot day uncertain weather (showers around may 25) 15-16 19 |
| Violent showers or Thunder showers. not violent since the 29-60-19th. no cattle here this month. | | | 19 a great thunder shower. strikes near | | | | | | 29 at 6 p.m. a short deluge with very strong gusts after it 91° 2 very much 9 another shower |
| Hail | | 26 slight in P.M. | | | | | | | 9" a little |
| Rainbow | 22 25" morning | 30 in moon | | | | | | | 7" p.m. 8" very slight |
| Birds killed by wet & cold | | | | | | | 20" | | |
| Rank weeds, trees | | | | | | | | 22 | |
| Clearer air | | 5 comparatively clear 26 wonderful clear after rain | 23 clear after 1 or 2 wet & rainy days 26 & 28" | | | | | | 5" 27 cool |
| Breezy days | 16 has been quite hazy more or less the morning 9 a week past, very light washing days for 9 a week past, very drying through just begun 10 quite settled in day past 23-24 rough day, not washing days | 6 | 4" | | | 2" in P.M. | | | 1 quite windy 2 a week, was very NW wind 3 clear windy days 2 windy after raining much last month very dry 11 to 14 |
| Glaucous green of bent ridge | 14' | 6 | 26 2nd | | | | | 15 " | 11" part of it |
| Light under sides of leaves in wind | 14' 26 | 6 | 4" beg. & then | | | | | 18 very white 11" and single & leaves, leaves a slight dimness | |
| Red bark turned up | 29' | 6 | | | | | | 30 | 11 |
| Very windy | | | | 9 or the 3 one 2' window then began shutter hours, unsettled 10 SW for morning = howling | | | | | 10 strong cold air 11 in quite strong wind |
| E wind in P.M. | | | 16 cool & wind forenoon & P.M. 3' cools the air | | | 29" | | | 23' cooler |

General Phenomena of June

| | 52 | 53 | 54 | 55 | 56 | 57 | 58 | 59 | 60 |
|---|---|---|---|---|---|---|---|---|---|
| Tear in grass | | | 1st last mile | | | | | | |
| Water cooled grain | | | | | | | | | 6 |
| Effect of recent frost in hollows | 6" | 8 of last winter readits / 14 great show goods not of some autmgs70 | 1st of this mo | | | | 14 a tangled fans killed by frost 9 28 & 29 primary | 11 does see a fans killed last month | |
| Leaves torn & blacked by cold wind. / 15-51 hickory blackened by north lately | 6 | | | 4" | | | | | 10 5 a very thin & cold N.W. wind |
| Frost on low ground | | 1st | | | | | | | 22 thin air killed flowering fern in this meadows |
| Fresh shade or gloom / June 21 – 60 1st this about full of dark shadow at last. | 2 hill a good deal of shade with heavy gloom / 19 dark gloomful this 9 at last. | 6 thick heavy cool shadow shade gloom may & y boom with shadow | 11 admire form | 11 observe the dark even now of June | 9 black about the shadow of June | | | | 16 hazy & white darkening cloudy billows 9 from S. dense & heavy already |
| Observe shadows of trees &c | | 6 of trees & pligs remark shift | 2 very in shade along meadow edge June / 26 peculiar dark shade of June | 6 dark eye shadow | | | 7 deeper & rounder tops suggest shade | | |
| Shadows of clouds on waving grass &c | | | | 4 in feel shadow of y cloud on village foliage – a new day | | | 7 | | |
| Bluish glimmering air over water | 15" & 23 & 24 | | | | | 7" | | 15 fume & leaf with greener heat over this a bright haze | |
| Bubbles on the quick river | | | | | | 7" | | | |
| Blue mist on landscape | | | 1 & 2 | | | 29 in form with a wind & cold | | | 28 air blue without any afternoon wind & cooler |
| Summer aspect June | | 19 rain long a June late | 5 rich cool wet light & fresh weeds grain in | 9 with about rich grain in rainly | | | | | 24 hazy show summer aspect |
| Summer begins June | | | | | | | | | 30 wet drive in 9 fresh month & rippled meadows |

MA 610

## 29

## General Phenomena for June

| | 52 | 53 | 54 | 55 | 56 | 57 | 58 | 59 | 60 |
|---|---|---|---|---|---|---|---|---|---|
| Potamogetons beg. to prevail | | | | | | | 9" | | |
| Dust on River | | | 40' snow & days 9" | 6 | | 3" | | | 8 on all things - next rain |
| Dust comes off leaves | | 21 this may 27 (3 June 3" 6 1" muddy white 21) milk at this 12" | may 26-& 28 | 4" | | | | | 8 |
| Methihania washed off | | 24 Wheat leaf | | 28 | | | | | |
| Pollen on road | 15" | 1st - & 14" | | | 21 much | 3" perhaps | 7" & 20" | | 4" this morning Poll: & June 18 roads washed up |
| 1st hoe corn & potatoes | 19 hoein corn & potatoes | 1st hoeing corn commencd | | | | | | | roads & meadow Aug 1" 5 " potatoes this |
| Cut grass in front yard | | 10 | | | | | | | |
| Upland haying begins 30-31 | | 21 haying comn — cutting today | 20 begin — ning | | | | | | 30" cutting clover |
| Freshness of barn leaves & vines (?) | | 27 nearly passed generally in heat & middle & more green | 11 upland less green from approach & dire grass | | | | | | |
| Hellebore turns yellow | | 19 turning yellow | | | | | | | |
| Dun (or moon) days | | | 16' sun set 17 misty 17 & 18 sun set | | | | | | 22 new moon at eve |
| Drought | | (raining) 21 est & sprinkling since may 26 14 ground getting dry 16 dur, hot & dry 20 continued to 25 | 4' & 7 1" dry today 16 drier for last fortn water low & dry 19 1st rain of summer 5 fairly begin | 3 very dry June springs low &c | | | | |
| Longest days | 18" | 22 | | | | | | | 6 " |

| | 52 | 53 | 54 | 55 | 56 | 57 | 58 | 59 | 60 |
|---|---|---|---|---|---|---|---|---|---|
| Fragrance in air | 10 mead. frag since this also 24 & 27" then unusual 15 perfume around | | | | | | | | 3" mead. fragr - ance |
| Scent of Pine | | | 7" | | 10 | | | | 24 |
| Scent of arbor vitae | | | | | | | | | 3 |
| Peculiar stillness summer | | | | | 11" | | | | |
| Summer Cumuli | | | | | 11" | | | | |
| Birds keep quiet | | | | | 21" (may 27) | | | | |
| Fresh mackerel | 16 | 17 some days | | | | | | | |

| General Phenomena for June | | | | |
|---|---|---|---|---|
| | 52 | 53 | 54 | 55 |
| **River Lowest** | 1st down at last<br>11 shrunk to sum-<br>mer width | 16 stone heaps partly exposed<br>21 quite low shores<br>covered with confervæ paper | 7 summer width | |
| **River highest** | | | | |
| **Haze**　v blue mist [unclear]<br>28-51 Thick fog like haze<br>　tempering the heat. | 2nd<br>15 | | 17 dry hazy June weather<br>16 thick fog or haze with E.<br>wind for several Pms past<br>17th very | |
| **Fog** | 16 low on meads<br>　early | 9 prevalent in Am<br>11th | 17 consid. | |
| sun light yellow | | | | |
| **Great Fog** | | 1st quite a fog<br>great fogs beg. & mid<br>June & more or less in July<br>2nd great fog<br>6 considerable | 7th thick fog<br>21 thick " & rain<br>through it | |
| mizzling weather | | 10th great fog<br>15　"　" | 1st changeable weather | 7 |
| **Rain**<br>June 7 51 a gentle straight down<br>　rainy day - a fishing day | 25 heavy rain<br>after rainbow in<br>morn. | 22 smart shower<br>for 15 min first since<br>May 26<br>24 a little last night | 7th [unclear] & 8th gentle<br>steady rain storm<br>19th 1st of conseq. for 3<br>weeks - with a gust & big<br>drops -  21 | 3rd rainy day at last clears<br>up Am of 4th 1st important rain<br>of season<br>14 sudden heavy rain |
| **Dogdayish** | | 23 first time misty<br>　low clouds hanging<br>about. | 23 Foggy haze<br>dog day like - more or<br>less 10 days past<br>& cold | |
| **Thunder Shower** | 3rd slight (sultry)<br>v 22nd & lightning<br>17 slight | 22 1st Thunder<br>since May 26 | 28 Pm (v 19th | |
| **Succession of Thunder-<br>　Showers** | 22nd | | | |

| General Phenomena for June | | | | |
|---|---|---|---|---|
| | 52 | 53 | 54 | 55 |
| **Hot in 1st half** | 3rd sultry<br>15 hot weather | 14 warm - warm-est Pm yet<br>16 warmer for fort-<br>night past | | |

| 56 | 57 | 58 | 59 | 60 |
|---|---|---|---|---|
| | | 14 raised surprisingly by rain of 12th Mill brook has been over T. pike | 29 river falls several inches | 1st 1 $^3/_8$ above S.L. |
| | | 15 remarkably high -far higher than before this year & rising - can paddle all about Mantatuket <u>willowy</u> meadow | 18 river raised by rain last night 20 some 2 ft. above summer level ? | 23rd 15 $^3/_4$ above S.L. |
| | | 25 & see no Mts. <u>very hot</u> | | 4 <u>Mts</u>. concealed |
| | | | | 12 a very low solid <u>local</u> fog (or dew) at eve 17 quite a fog |
| | | | | 23rd |
| | 8th | | | |
| 6 drizzling 26 at N. Bedford | 18 drizzling on C. Cod | | night of 1st | 1st season of cold storms of 2 or more days past? |
| 8 have had 6 days either rain- threatening or rainy | 1st less reliable for a few weeks past than at any other season, have unexpected showers | 4th on RR in Win- chendon 12 all day - much water falls - 15 rain again no clear weather since 11th | 18 heavy rain raining since last night 18 more rain [unclear] under bridge 24 in spite of cobwebs | 5 NE wind steady rains 6 rain still - clears up before night 20 heavy rain most of day & part of night next 2 $^1/_8$ inches beats down crops & no dew <u>in morn.</u> |
| | 30th & cold. | | 23 ~~23~~ foggy day with E.<u>ly</u> wind - Cape- coddish 24 another & rain | 18 & not rain threatening & 19th 2 $^1/_2$ days then the heavy rains of 20th [unclear] 23 decidedly [uncl.] <u>musty</u> & bluish 24th & 26th & 29th |
| | | | | 17 the 3 day of in <u>Pm</u> (here or around) preventing walks |
| | | | | 9th half a dozen from W & NE 10 showery |

| 56 | 57 | 58 | 59 | 60 |
|---|---|---|---|---|
| 4th very warm 11th very hot | 2 very warm till 3 <u>Pm</u> | 5 surveying for Thomas Brooks 6 warm w. suddenly come 7 87° at 3 <u>Pm.</u> | 15 suddenly hot 90° after very cool days | 4th uncomfortably warm in walking 15th warmer since the 12 85+ at 2 Pm |

| | | | | |
|---|---|---|---|---|
| **Hot in last half**<br>30 - 51 oppressively warm<br>25 - 60 85 2 <u>Pm</u> | Before 24 a week or more of warm days & nights<br>15 -16 sultry night<br>16 very hot | 20 hot weather<br>21 warmest day yet<br>30 hot again | | 22 warmest day yet<br>30 95°+ 2 <u>Pm</u> |
| ~~Cold in 1st half~~<br>**Sultry night** | | 20<br>21 perhaps warmest night of year up to 29th at least— some sit in their yards<br>21 -2 exceedingly | | |
| **Debauched look of**<br>streets in morn. | 16 | | | |
| **Leave off flannel** | | | | |
| **Beg. to sleep with open**<br>window commonly | | | | |
| **Beg. to wear thin sack** | 15 now <u>for</u><br>a thin coat | 14th | | |
| **Have sack or ribbon** | | 20 have sack for<br>a few days (say <u>2</u>) | | |
| **Bring [unclear]** | | | | |
| **Cold in 1st half** | 10th some cold wind<br>in 10 past days | | 1st | |
| **Cold in last half** | 24 uncommonly cold<br>after a week or more<br>of warm days & nights | 26 very cool<br>(24 to 27 inc. cool) | | |
| **Have a fire** | 15 part of the<br>past week | | 23 part of time<br>for 10 days past | |
| **Thick coat again** | | | 1st | |
| **Cool eve** | | | | |

| | 52 | 53 | 54 | 55 |
|---|---|---|---|---|
| **Thunder showers around**<br>Summer showers in P<u>m</u> | | | 13 - 14 - 15 - 16 high<br>in E fail to reach us | |
| **Violent Showers**<br>or Thunder showers<br>most violent shower the<br>29 - 60 after<br>the hottest hour of the month | | | 19 a gusty thunder-<br>shower strikes near — | |
| **Hail** | | 26 slight in <u>pm</u> | | |
| **Rain bow** | 22<br>25 in morning | 30 in morn | | |
| **Birds killed by wet**<br>& cold | | | | |
| **Rank weeds droop** | | | | |
| **Clear air** | | 5 comparatively clear<br>26 wonderfully clear<br>after hail | 23 clearer after<br>1 or 2 cool rainy days<br>26 & 28th | |
| | 16 has been quite breezy | | | |

| | | | | |
|---|---|---|---|---|
| 21 - 2 Pm 98<br>& 20th | | 24 very hot - 25th<br>hotter still — & muggy<br>& close 93°- at<br>1 Pm | 29 very hot | 16 85+ 2 Pm<br>this is hot for June<br>29 6 Pm 91° warm-<br>est of month |
| | | | | .85° at 2 Pm<br>the 23rd |
| | | | | 4th |
| | | | | 10 |
| | | 7th | | June 1st<br>15th 2 or 3 days past |
| | | | | 15 ribbon 2 or 3 days<br>past |
| 6 cold drizzling weather | | | 13 very cool days | 10 strong & cold<br>N.W. wind 58° at 6 Pm |
| | 29th with E wind<br>& blue mist in pm | | 30 cooler with<br>northerly wind | 21 - 12 Pm. 59°+ |
| | | | | 6 on ac. of rain<br>21 cooled by rain yester<br>day - must have fires |
| | | | | 22 cold wind 60° at 12 ½ pm |
| | | | | 2nd & white twi-light |

| 56 | 57 | 58 | 59 | 60 |
|---|---|---|---|---|
| | | | | 8 season of Pm showers<br>is for a day or 2 had |
| | 2nd at eve | | | 8 [uncl] within a day or   2<br>uncertain walking —<br>(1st summer shower<br>May 25 )   15 — & 16<br>29 |
| | | | | 29 at 6 Pm<br>a short deluge<br>with very strong gusts<br>after at 5 Pm 91°+<br>injuring [unclear] and buildings |
| | | | | 9th a little |
| | | | | 7th Pm<br>9 at eve [unclear] |
| | | 20th | | |
| | | | 22 | |
| | | | | 3rd<br>27 & cool<br>29th quite windy |

| | 52 | 53 | 54 | 55 |
|---|---|---|---|---|
| **Breezy days**                         ever | windy this month<br>9th washing days for a week past<br>waving of boughs just leafed<br>10 quite windy 10 days past<br>23 -24 agreeably cool | 6 | 4th | |
| **Glaucous sheen of bent sedge** | washing days<br>14th | 6 | 26<br>2nd | |
| **Light undersides of leaves in wind** | 14<br>26 | 6 | 4th beg. to show | |
| **Red pads turned up** | 29th | 6 | | |
| **very windy** | | | | 1st the 3rd one<br>2nd windier than before<br>shakes home night & day<br>10 SW for season wracking trees |
| **E wind in Pm** | | | 16 cool E wind<br>for several Pms past<br>3rd cools the air | |

## General Phenomena for June

| | 52 | 53 | 54 | 55 |
|---|---|---|---|---|
| **Fear a frost** | | | 1st/last night | |
| **Water cooled by rain** | | | | |
| **Effects of recent frost in hollows**<br>15- 5 | 6th | 1st of last night & earlier<br>14 great show of oaks<br>cut off some weeks ago | 1st of this am | |
| **Leaves torn & blackened by cold wind.**<br>15 - 51 hickory blackened by frosts lately | 6 | | | 4th |
| **Frost in Low ground** | | | 1st | |
| **Dark shadow of Elms**<br>June 21 - 60 1st within days full of dark shadows at dusk. | 2nd hold a good deal<br>of shade rich & heavy<br>19 dark grateful shade of at dist. | 10 streets beautiful<br>with verdure & shade of elms<br>May 27 heavy with shade | 11 admire forms | 11 observe the dark<br>ever green of June |
| **Observe shadows of trees &c** | | 6 of trees & foliage<br>& Conant. cliff | 2nd virgin shades<br>along meadow edge<br>26 peculiar dark shade of June | 6 dark eye - shade of June |
| **Shadows of clouds on waving grass   & trees** | | | | 4th dark shade of in clear<br>air after rain - on light green<br>foliage - a new sky<br>6 |
| **Bluish filmy air over water** | 15th & 23 -&24 | | | |
| **Bubbles on sluggish river** | | | | |
| **Blue mist on Landscape** | | | 1 & 2nd | |
| **Summer aspect of river** | 19 river has a June<br>look | 5th pick weed 1 foot<br>high -  & other weeds | 9th with Utric. vul-<br>garis as yesterday | |
| **Summer regime of river** | | | | |

|  | 2nd in Pm |  |  | 2 a windy washing N.W. wind<br>3 clear breezy days<br>7 ap. after rains<br>21 almost in constant breeze<br>this month — so far (& all of it &<br>into July |
|---|---|---|---|---|
|  |  |  | 15th | —<br>15=11th first of it |
|  |  |  | 18 swamp wht o. red maple -<br>willows &c. beg. to show<br>a slight silveriness | 11th |
|  |  |  | 30 | 3 11 |
|  |  |  |  | 10 strong cold wind<br>NW<br>11 - pretty strong still |
|  | 29th |  |  | 23rd & cooler |

| 56 | 57 | 58 | 59 | 60 |
|---|---|---|---|---|
|  |  |  |  | 6 |
|  |  | 14 interrupted ferns<br>killed by frost of 28th —<br>& 29th of May | 11 some scent of<br>ferns killed last<br>month |  |
|  |  |  |  | 10 by a very strong<br>& cold N.W. wind |
|  |  |  |  | 22 this am killed flowering<br>ferns in river meads |
| 9 black elm tops<br>& shadows of June |  |  |  | 2 6 beg. to mature<br>darkening along highway<br>4 comp. dense & heavy already |
|  |  | 7 leafed & rounded<br>tops suggest shade |  |  |
|  |  | 7th |  |  |
|  |  |  | 15 fumes of lead with 1st June<br>heat seen thru a slight haze |  |
|  | 7th |  |  |  |
|  | 29 in pm with<br>E wind & cold |  |  | 23rd air blue in street eves &<br>afterward E wind & cooler - |
|  |  |  |  | 24 begs. to wear<br>summer aspect |
|  |  |  |  | 30 with divisions of pads -<br>smooth & rippled surface |

## General Phenomena for June

| | 52 | 53 | 54 | 55 |
|---|---|---|---|---|
| Potamogetons beg. to prevail | | | | |
| Lint on River | | | 4th now a-days<br>9th | 6 |
| Lint comes off leaves | | 21 still<br>May 27-(& June 3d to 21)<br>1st makes white as a<br>    miller - & the 12th | May 26-& 28 | 4th |
| Vallisnaria washed up- | | 24 & heartleaf | | 28 |
| pollen on pond | 15th | 1st-& 14th | | |
| 1st hoe corn & potatoes | 19 hoeing corn<br>& potatoes | 1st hoeing corn<br>commences | | |
| cut grass in front yard | | 10 | | |
| upland haying begins<br>    30-51 | | 21 haying & sum-<br>mer culminates | 21st 20 begin-<br>ning | |
| Freshness of year begs<br>    to wane (?) | 27 nearly passed!<br>generally inclined<br>to a reddish brown<br>green | 11 appears less<br>green from ripening<br>of June grass | | |
| Hellebore turns<br>    yellow | | 19 turning yellow | | |
| Sun (or moon) sets <sup>or rises</sup> ^ red | | | 16th sun sets<br>17 rises<br>17 & 18 sun sets | |
| Drought | (the night of | 21 only 1 sprinkling<br>17) since May 26,<br>14 ground getting dry<br>18 Lees Cliff & Island<br>[late] [&] dry by mid June<br>2 0 continues - to 22nd | 4th & 7 1st dry spell<br>16 drier for last fort-<br>night & yet not very-<br>19th 1st rain of conseq.<br>  for 3 weeks<br>18 fairly begun. | 16 drier 2 very dry some<br>springs dried up. |
| Longest days | 18th | 22 | | |
| | 52 | 53 | 54 | 55 |
| Fragrance in air | 10 meadow fra-<br>grance still<br>also 27 & 27th<br>[unclear] unaccountable<br>perfume-sweet | | | |
| | 15 | | | |
| Scent of Rhue | | | 7th | |
| scent of arbor vitae | | | | |
| Peculiar stillness<br>    of summer | | | | |
| Summer Cumuli | | | | |
| Birch sap good | | | | |
| Fresh mackerel | 16 | 17 some days | | |

| 56 | 57 | 58 | 59 | 60 |
|---|---|---|---|---|
|  |  | 9th |  |  |
|  | 3rd |  |  | 8 on all stagnant water |
|  |  |  |  | 8th |
|  |  |  |  |  |
| 21 much | 3rd perhaps | 7th V 20th |  | 4th flies readily of p. pine 18 most washed up<br><br>visible at Walden July 11 |
|  |  |  |  | 5th potatoes            mine |
|  |  |  |  |  |
|  |  |  |  | 30th cutting clover |
|  |  |  |  |  |
|  |  |  |  |  |
|  |  |  |  | 22 new moon at eve |
|  |  |  |  |  |
| 56 | 57 | 58 | 59 | 60 |
|  |  |  |  | 3rd mead. fragrance |
| 10 |  |  |  | 24 |
|  |  |  |  | 3 |
| 11 |  |  |  |  |
| 11th |  |  |  |  |
| 21st 27 & May 27 |  |  |  |  |
|  |  |  |  |  |

PART II:

*Second Nature*

_____

General Phenomena for October. Henry David Thoreau Collection.
Yale Collection of American Literature, Beinecke Rare Book & Manuscript Library.

# OCTOBER:

## *Gossamer Days*

---

*PERENNIAL*, MEANING LASTING THROUGH THE YEAR. MEANING, can be counted on to return. In October, the leaves cease their miraculous transformation of light into food, begin their spectacular decline. Decline meaning a bending down, a letting go, a setting, like the sun. Emerson wrote, "the way of life is wonderful. It is by abandonment." I can still feel summer on a warm afternoon, heat trapped in the pavement, sun on the back of my head, though the first frosts were weeks ago. I make a fire in the dark most mornings, watch the sun hit the red-gold maple leaves, then the still-green leaves further down. Still green, still green. The way of life is wonderful. In Maine, people talk about the turning leaves the way farmers talk about crops, shake their heads about the inches of rain and the timing of the inches, compare this year's harvest to last. We all feel it: the tightening economy of light, the sudden abundance of color. We photograph this ungatherable surplus as though a photograph were a kind of holding.

I am trying to remember that our declines are perennial, our deaths perennial. Perennially, we decay. My hair is becoming white. At odd moments waves of heat overtake me, a function of my body no longer readying itself to reproduce. The chlorophyll breaks down in the leaves. Our eyes are keyed to it. In his decline, my father's body shook. He could not remember. Still, we laughed and were alive together in the hospital room. I wrote a poem called "Decay," remembering. We cover the grills, bring in the flowerpots, ready ourselves. A flash of light on the retinas, wonderful, wonderful. A flash of gold.

\*

By the fall of 1861, Thoreau's health was failing. He had returned from his trip to Minnesota, which his friends had hoped would improve his health, but his decline was evident, and no longer reversible. Though Thoreau had "set off still hopeful, still venturing, still planning future work," by his return in late July, he knew he had little time left, and that nearly all of it would be spent indoors.

Housebound, cut off from the long daily walks that had anchored his writing and his life for a decade, he all but abandoned his Journal, writing his final entry in early November. The work now was retrospective: with the devoted help of his sister Sophia, who, Walls notes, "added amanuensis to her other roles as caretaker, companion, and eventually literary executor," Thoreau prepared manuscripts for publication and corresponded with publishers. He was putting his literary affairs in order.

Given the clear indications that Thoreau knew there could be no new work, why did he resume the Kalendar project, on hiatus since June of 1860, in the fall of 1861? The most important indication that he did so at this time—the existence of a column and a smattering of observations for October, November, and December of 1861—also suggests a reason. Despite his inability to participate in them as he had in the past, the seasons continued their unfolding. If he could not minutely track their changes by walking out into the woods and fields of Concord, he could witness the broader strokes of seasonal change through the windows of his family's Main Street house. From the west-facing windows of his attic room he could see the river and its reflections of seasonal phenomena. As Robert Thorson writes, "views from this frame–of mists, sunsets, reflections, colors, ice, plant growth, autumnal tints, and moving boats, were like time-lapse photographs taken from a stationary camera." The front parlor, where Sophia would move his bed in December to save him the effort of climbing the stairs, also overlooked the river, a central focus of the charts for these months, along with other weather-related phenomena—temperature, for instance—that he could track from indoors. Facing the end of his own life, Thoreau took comfort in the continuity and regularity of seasonal change, which would proceed without him. The Kalendar, with its picture of time as cyclical and ongoing, replaced the linear temporality of the Journal.

And windows were not his only access to the seasons. Thoreau's friends brought nature to him. Ellery Channing, on whose property sat the notched willow tree from which Thoreau measured the height of the river, now took measurements on his behalf. Horace Mann brought him specimens of animals and plants.

If in the spring of 1860 the Kalendar project represented a tool for new discovery and expanded vision, by the fall of 1861 it represented a technology for reinhabiting the natural world, a way back into the experience of the seasons that his illness deprived him of. In October of 1861, Thoreau took up the technology he'd developed as a new way of navigating and comprehending seasonal time and adapted it for use as a kind of perceptual extension: a way of extending the agency of his own body, allowing him to participate in the life of the season in an entirely new way. This technology was crafted from two sources: Thoreau's own copious and meticulous observations, collected and recorded for a decade in his Journal, and the real-time observations made on his behalf by his friends.

Thoreau was nothing if not willing to continually reimagine his way of living. "This is the only way, we say," he wrote in *Walden*, "but there are as many ways as there can be drawn radii from one centre." Thoreau's finding of *another way* in his last months may well have constituted a reimagining as profound as any he underwent in his life. Instead of walking out into nature, he would mentally travel back into his own extensive record of the season through which he was living, gathering the key experiences of that season, and transcribing them again, live them again, with their particulars intact. He describes this idea in "October, or Autumnal Tints," one of the manuscripts he and Sophia would prepare for publication during his final winter:

> I formerly thought it would be worth the while to get a specimen leaf from each changing tree, shrub, and herbaceous plant, when it had acquired its brightest, characteristic color, in its transition from the green to the brown state, outline it and copy its color exactly with paint in a book, which should be titled October, or Autumnal Tints. Beginning with the earliest reddening–woodbine, and the lake of radical leaves, and coming down through the maples, hickories and sumacs, and many beautifully freckled leaves less generally known, to the latest oaks and aspens. What a memento such a book would be! You would need only to turn over its leaves to take a ramble through the Autumn woods whenever you pleased. Or if I could preserve the leaves themselves unfaded it would be better still. I have made little progress toward such a book, but I have endeavored instead to describe all these bright tints in the order in which they present themselves.

The method described here matches that of the Kalendar project: Thoreau seeks to preserve the "characteristic" phenomena of each month "in the order in which they present themselves." More importantly, Thoreau's description of his ideal, unrealized book of autumnal tints provides a clue to the appeal of chart keeping at this late season of his own life. In tracking seasonal phenomena through the pages (or "leaves") of his Journal, Thoreau is able to take a ramble through the woods of the given season, even while bedridden. What gratitude he must have felt for the precise observations he'd painstakingly compiled for a decade without knowing the end they would serve: to act for him as a virtual world, a second nature, in his final, bedridden months.

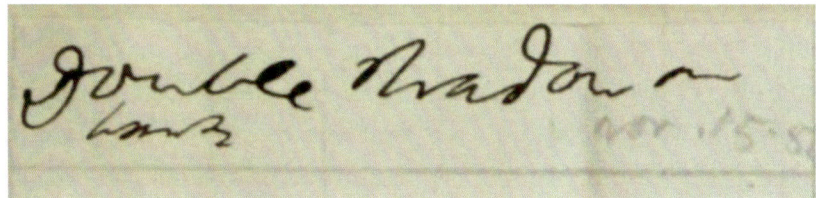

*Double Shadow*

PM with Sophia boated to Fair-Haven, where she made a sketch. . . . Returning late we see a double shadow of ourselves & boat one the true quite black– the other directly above it & very faint on the willows & high bank– (10/18/1853, *Journal* 7:103–4)

Just after sundown–though it had been windy before–the waters came suddenly smooth–& the clear yellow light of the western sky was handsomely reflected in the water making it doubly light to me on the water. diffusing light from below as well as above. (11/15/1853, *Journal* 7:163)

Sailing past the bank above the RR just before a clear sundown– Close to the shore on the E side I see a 2nd fainter shadow of the boat sail myself & paddle &c directly above & upon the first– on the bank. What makes the 2nd? . . . At length I discovered that it was the reflected sun which cast a higher shadow like the true one– As I moved to the west side–the upper shad. rose grew larger & less perceptible. & at last when I was so near the W shore that I could not see the reflected sun–it disappeared– but then there appeared one upside down in its place! (11/2/1854, Journal Transcript 18:75)

Thoreau's interest in shadows and reflections was long-standing. In *Walden* he describes the double-shadow effect when standing on the ice: "Sometimes, also, when the ice was covered with shallow puddles, I saw a double shadow of myself, one standing on the head of the other, one on the ice, the other on the trees or hillside." In a double shadow, the reflected light acts as a second source, and the primary shadow acts as a shadow-casting body. The phenomenon speaks to a porousness between actual experience and its double, echo, or representation—the complex way in which every re-presentation extends but also alters its original. Like the echo of a bell, which he describes in the "Sounds" chapter of *Walden* as "an original sound . . . not merely a repetition of what was worth repeating in the bell, but partly the voice of the wood; the same trivial words and notes sung by a wood-nymph," the shadow is of interest in part because of the distance effect it entails: the second shadow, an image of an image. In the echo, distance alters the decaying sound, a phenomenon Thoreau imagines as the intervening woods *entering into* its tone. Like the echo or double shadow, the fall charts, now cut off from the ongoing "original" experience of walking in nature, are second-level representations, rich in temporal distance effects.

In reading through his own accounts of the seasonal phenomena he can no longer directly experience, Thoreau attunes himself to the ways in which these experiences echoed or reflected themselves through the years of his Journal, each iteration colored by local effects. If in the fall of 1861 Thoreau was bereft of the active bodily experience of the natural world that was his principal source of solace and joy, the charts offered a new source of experience: the accumulated echoes or double shadows of his own carefully observed experiences of the natural world.

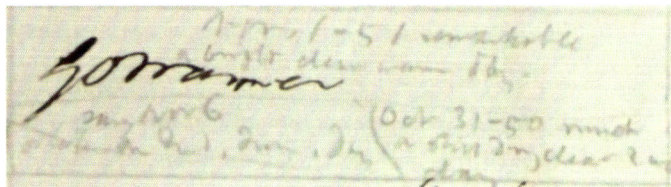

*Gossamer*

It is a remarkable day for fine gossamer cob-webs. Here on the causeway as I walk toward the sun I perceive the air is full of them streaming from off the willows & spanning the road–all stretching across the road–and yet I cannot see them in any other direction– and feel not one  It looks as if the birds would be incommoded. They have the effect of a shimmer in the air. This shimmer moving along them as they are waved by the wind gives the effect of a drifting storm of light. It is more like a fine snow storm which drifts athwart your path than anything else. What is the peculiar condition of the atmosphere to call forth this activity. If there were no sunshine I should never find out that they existed– I should not know that I was bursting a myriad barriers. Though you break them with your person you feel not one. Why should this day be so distinguished. (11/1/1851, *Journal* 4:159–60)

I slowly discover that this is a gossamer day. I first see the fine lines stretching from one weed or grass stem or rush to another sometimes 7 or 8 feet distant–horizontally & only 4 or 5 inches above the water– – When I look further I find that they are everywhere & on everything– sometimes forming conspicuous fine white gossamer webs on the heads of grasses. . . . They are so abundant that they seem to have been suddenly produced in the atmosphere by some chemistry–spun out of air– I know not for what purpose– . . . These gossamer lines are not visible unless between you and the sun. We pass some Black willows now of course quite leafless–& when they are between us and the sun they are so completely covered with these fine cobwebs or lines– mainly parallel to one another that they make one solid woof–a misty roof. against the sun. They are not drawn taut but curved downward in the middle like the rigging of a vessel–the ropes which stretch from mast to mast.–as if the fleets of a thousand Lilliputian nations were collected one behind another under bare poles. But when we have floated a few feet further–& thrown the willow out of the sun's range not a thread can be seen on it– I landed & walked up & down the causeway–and found it the same there–the gossamer reaching across the causeway–though not necessarily supported on the other side. They streamed southward with the slight zephyr– As if the year were weaving her shroud out of light. . . . And yet one with his back to the sun walking the other way would observe nothing of all this. . . . Methinks it is only on these very finest days late in the autumn that this phenomenon is seen–as if that fine vapor of the morning were spun into these webs. According to Kirby & Spence "In Germany these flights of gossamer appear so constantly in Autumn that they are there metaphorically called 'Der fliegender Sommer' (The flying or departing Summer)." What can possess these spiders thus to run all at once to even the least elevation & let off this wonderful stream. . . . Sophia thought that thus at last they emptied themselves & wound up– or, I suggested, unwound themselves. cast off their mortal coil  It looks like a mere frolic spending & wasting of themselves–of their vigor–now that there is no further use for it (10/31/1853, *Journal* 7:127–30)

A fine Ind. summer afternoon– There is much gossamer on the button bushes now bare of leaves and on the sere meadow grass looking toward the sun–in countless parallel lines–like the ropes which connect the masts of a vessel. (10/17/1855, Journal Transcript 19:119–20)

Very much gossamer on the withered grass is shimmering in the fields–& flocks of it are sailing in the air (11/1/1860, Journal Transcript 32:264)

The sudden appearance, in mid-autumn, of delicate lines of spider silk between objects, visible only in direct sunlight, appealed to Thoreau the poet, as well as Thoreau the naturalist. "Let us not underrate the value of a fact," he had written in "A Natural History of Massachusetts," "it will one day flower in a truth." Though Thoreau increasingly adapted this early, transcendental view of nature as a storehouse of symbols for "higher" moral and spiritual truths into a more horizontal sense of interconnectedness, he never stopped seeking and perceiving connections—both between natural phenomena and between mental and physical experience.

Recalling the gossamer days he carefully recorded in his Journal, the Henry Thoreau of 1861 would have found an image for many of the aspects of the natural world that most delighted and amazed him: its tendency toward reproductive superabundance, or what Emerson called "ecstasy"; its multidirectional interconnections; its penchant for hiding in plain sight. "They are everywhere & on everything," he writes, with an uncharacteristic vagueness that suggests the dizzying ubiquity of the phenomenon, an almost-magical plenty: "They are so abundant that they seem to have been suddenly produced in the atmosphere by some chemistry– spun out of air." This capacity of the natural world to stun and overwhelm the senses, to enchant, is part of nature's restorative power for Thoreau.

The phenomenon of gossamer—not only the spider's web into which it is spun, but the delicate, silky, visible-invisible matter itself—was the kind of liminal phenomenon that captivated Thoreau. In 1853 he had written in his Journal, "Ever and anon something will occur which my philosophy has not dreamed of. The limits of the actual are set some thoughts further off. That which had seemed a rigid wall of vast thickness unexpectedly proves a thin and undulating drapery–the boundaries of the actual are no more fixed & rigid–than the elasticity of our imaginations" (5/31/1853, *Journal* 6:153). The "thin and undulating drapery" he pictures here as the boundary of the actual is reminiscent of the gossamer described in the entries above, a hybrid of matter and spirit, "as if that fine vapor of the morning were spun into these webs." That gossamer is visible only when illuminated by direct sunlight—"If there were no sunshine I should never find out that they existed"—speaks to the partiality of human perception and its necessary involvement in the observed phenomenon. Gossamer is produced by human vision and sunlight, as well as by spiders.

Gossamer was also associated for Thoreau with comfort, order, and absorption in the natural world. In 1857 he wrote,

> *There*, in that Well meadow Field perhaps–I feel in my element again, as when a fish is put back into the water. I wash off all my chagrins–all things go smoothly as the axel of the universe. I can remember that when I was very young I used to have a dream night after night over & over again–which might have been named Rough & Smooth. All existence–all satisfaction & dissatisfaction–all event–was symbolized in this way–Now I seemed to be lying & tossing perchance on a horrible–a fatal–rough surface–which must soon indeed put an end to my existence–though even in the dream I knew it to be the symbol merely of my misery– – then again suddenly–I was lying on a delicious smooth surface–as of a summer sea–as of gossamer or down–or softest plush–& life was such a luxury to live–
>
> My waking experience *always* has been and is–such an alternate Rough & Smooth–In other words it is Insanity & Sanity. (1/7/1857, Journal Transcript 22:180–81)

Thoreau frequently uses the word *sane* in the Journal to refer to a condition or feeling of connectedness to the natural world. This feeling of beneficent absorption is often described in response to sound. Of the music of the telegraph harp, he writes, "it always intoxicates me– makes me sane–reverses my view of things" (1/9/1853, *Journal* 5:437). The same feeling of wonder and revised perspective is evident in the descriptions of gossamer days—a kind of bewilderment that results from the special vision afforded by the calm and sunny conditions—and it is telling that gossamer is among the elements associated with smoothness or "sanity" in the dream. These qualities are connected for Thoreau with "the axel of the universe," which, like the seasons, turns perpetually, without regard for the frictions and losses of individual lives. To feel this turning—and his own connectedness to it—is Thoreau's definition of sanity.

Like Indian Summer, gossamer evokes the special fecundity and splendor he connects with the onset of the end of life. The unattached strands, he writes, "streamed southward with the slight zephyr– as if the year were weaving her shroud out of light." Later in the same entry he speculates that the rapid production of the spiders "looks like a mere frolic spending and wasting of themselves–of their vigor–now that there is no further use for it, their July, perchance, being killed or banished by the frost." The proliferation of fanciful metaphors in these entries reflects the spirit of "frolic spending" Thoreau perceives in the phenomenon, which he compares not only to a shroud of light but also to "the rigging of a vessel– the ropes which stretch from mast to mast. – as if the fleets of a thousand Lilliputian nations were collected one behind another under bare poles." These imaginative flourishes are shed when Thoreau transfers his seasonal data from discursive Journal entries to the tight economy of the charts, but in selecting the categories for representation in his Kalendar, Thoreau draws upon the detailed descriptions he has stored away over the many Octobers he has faithfully recorded. Taken together, these gossamer days must have returned him, in the rough days of his disability, to the smooth turning of the axle.

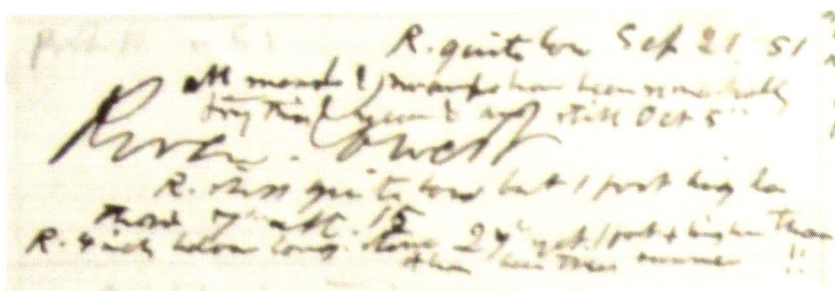

*River Lowest*

The river is 8 and $^{1}/_{12}$ feet below top of truss add 8 ½ inches for its greatest height this year you have 8 feet 9 ½ inches for the difference. It is ap.

as low now as in the first week in July. That is Those are the limits of our river's expansibility– so much it may swell. (8/23/1852, *Journal* 5:307)

The river is as low within an inch or two as when I made my mark. (10/2/1852, *Journal* 5:364)

Much of Thoreau's recordkeeping in the Journal of the 1850s involved the height of the river. By 1852, if not earlier, he had begun systematic measurements through which he was able to compare the height of the river across both seasons and years. On August 23, 1852, Thoreau noted in his Journal "The river is 8 and $\frac{1}{12}$ feet below top of truss" of the railroad bridge, from where he measured an annual low point. He then calculated, "add 8 ½ inches for its greatest height this year you have 8 feet 9 ½ inches for the difference." This comparison gave him a picture of the annual range of the river's volume: "Those are the limits of our river's expansibility– so much it may swell."

The October chart refers to this key entry in the column for 1852: "Oct 2$^{nd}$ as low 'within an inch or 2 as when I made my mark' Aug. 23 8 9 ½ /12$^{ths}$ ft lower than in April or (as I cacl. In '61) 2 inch lower s.l. 59." This highly condensed entry makes reference to five dates: October 2 of 1852 (this is where we are "located" in the Kalendar schema, according to the logic of its month/year/date system); August 23, 1852, the date on which Thoreau "made [his] mark" on the railroad truss for future measurements; April 23, 1852, the high-water mark for the river that year; summer 1859; and the present moment of the composition of the chart—"as I calc[ulate] in '61." Unpacking the entry and cross-referencing it to his Journal entries, we can make sense of this dense knot of observation spread over multiple temporal points: On October 2, 1852, the river was quite low, "within an inch or two" of the level of August 23 of that year, when Thoreau marked the railroad truss. This level is in turn two inches lower than the "summer level" of 1859. So Thoreau calculates now, in the fall of 1861. This entry points to the dizzying intertextuality of the Kalendar charts, and the way Thoreau made use of its multiplication of perspectives to arrive at a zoomed-out picture of the river's complex patterns of behavior.

Thoreau's interest in the river intensified in the late 1850s. In the summer of 1859 he had been hired by a group of farmers seeking state intervention against the owners of the Billerica dam, which, the farmers argued, was causing ruinous floods each year. As Daegan Miler writes, Thoreau's task was to "measure and catalog the width of each bridge that crossed the Concord between Sudbury and Billerica, the characteristics of every pier that might jut its obstructing pylons into the water, the history of each bridge's construction and improvement, and the character of the falls at Billerica itself."

Though in the end Thoreau never testified in the case—Robert Thorson suggests that the evidence he collected was too complex to fully support either side in the dispute—the assignment prompted thirty-three pages of notes, which Thoreau compiled into a single chart entitled *Statistics of the Bridges over Concord River, between Heard's Bridge and Billerica Dam, Obtained June 22nd, 23rd, & 24th 1859; The Level of the Water at Concord in the Meantime, not having Varied One Inch from about 3 Feet Above Summer Level.* The collection of this data deepened Thoreau's lifelong interest in the behavior of the river. In an early Journal entry he'd written, "For the first time it occurred to me this afternoon what a piece of wonder a river is – A huge volume of matter ceaselessly rolling through the fields and meadows of this substantial earth making haste from the high places, by stable dwellings of men and Egyptian pyramids, to its restless reservoir" (9/5/1838, *Journal* 1:55).

Thoreau's minute observations of the river also convinced him of the influence of the upstream mills on its periodic rise and fall, lending support to Robert Thorson's claim that through his river forays, Thoreau came to recognize the pervasiveness of human impact on the natural world and the erosion of the boundary between human and nonhuman.

Thoreau's data gathering for the farmers overlapped with his creation of a seven-and-a-half-foot-long scroll map, copied from a map drawn in 1834 by B. F. Perham and filled in with Thoreau's personal notations. These include not only descriptions of the river's current in various places but also more subjective data: the good swimming holes, as well as the location of his "boat place." Finally, the map identifies "what plants grow where: individual oak and ash trees, polygonum, bulrush, and many others." In this way, the river survey is analogous to the charts of general phenomena. Both projects seek to unite the methods of science with personal, subjective experience—to attain the double perspective of the poet-naturalist. The map's key reads as follows:

> Soundings, in feet, so much below summer level – which is 3 ft 6 ½ inches below
> The wall at Hoar's steps –or 2 ft + 8 inch. Below the notch in my willow at my boat.
> Breadth on right bank in rods, as paced. Meadows & some hills &c. by me, in black.

"My boat" refers to Thoreau's "boat place," located on Channing's property; the notched willow tree nearby was his convenient local datum for river measurements. It seems highly probable that the data included in the October and November charts of general phenomena were in fact supplied by Channing, companion on so many of his boating excursions and constant at his bedside in the fall of 1861, who would have understood not only Thoreau's idiosyncratic system of measurement but also the importance for his friend of gathering such data. In February of 1860, Thoreau had written,

> It excites me to see early in the spring that black artery leaping once more through the snow-clad town– All is tumult & life there, not to mention the rails & cranberries that are drifting in it. Where this artery is shallowest, comes nearest to the surface & runs swiftest–there it shows itself soonest–& you may see its pulse best.
>
> These are the wrists—temples of this earth where I feel its pulse with my eye. The living waters not the dead earth. It is as if the dormant earth opened its dark & liquid eye upon us. (2/12/1860, Journal Transcript 30:308–9)

By October 1861, Thoreau could no longer register the living river's "pulse" with his own eyes. But by this time his years of data collection had translated the immediate sensory experience of the river's ever-changing body to a precise internal representation. "Our river's expansibility" was now a reality both known and felt, his awareness of it derived from his countless river excursions, careful measurements, and observations. Even when he could behold the river itself only through a window and at a distance, Channing's data was enough to help him feel its still-beating heart.

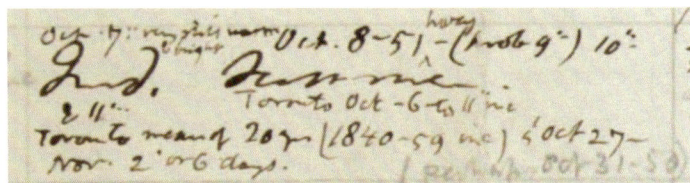

*Indian Summer*

The air this morning is full of blue-birds–and again it is spring. There are many things to indicate the renewing of spring at this season.

The blossoming of spring flowers–not to mention witch-hazel–the notes of spring birds–the springing of grain & grass and other plants. (10/10/1851, *Journal* 4:136–7)

It is a beautiful warm & calm Indian summer afternoon– The river is so high over the meadows & the pads and other low weeds so deeply buried–& the water is so smooth and glassy withal that I am reminded of a calm April day during the freshets. (10/31/1853, *Journal* 7:126)

After a rain-threatening morning it is a beautiful Indian summer day–the most remarkable hitherto–& equal to any of the kind. Yet we kept fires in the forenoon–the warmth not having got into the house– It is akin to sin to spend such a day in the house– The air is still & warm– This too is the *recovery* of the year– As if the year having nearly or quite accomplished its work–and abandoned all design were in a more favorable and poetic mood–and thought rushed in to fill the vacuum– . . . . The wool-grass with its drooping head & the slender withered leaves dangling about its stem–stands in little sheaves upon its tussucks–clean dry straw–and is thus reflected in the water– This is the november shore– (11/1/1855, Journal Transcript 19:163–64)

Thoreau's interest in Indian Summer corresponds to his interest in gossamer days—both reflect a particular late-life brilliance or extravagance, the same kind of final flowering represented by the October leaves: "Every fruit on ripening, & just before its fall, acquires a bright tint– So do the leaves–so the sky before the end of the day–& the *year* near its setting–October is the red sunset sky–" (10/24/1858, Journal Transcript 27:257). The little spring-within-autumn that typically occurs at the end of October or the beginning of November was for Thoreau a phenomenon that linked the days, seasons, and the lifespans of human and nonhuman organisms: a law of late flourishing. In October of 1861, Thoreau must have considered what might flower for him in this "*recovery* of the year," a period in which we may briefly *get again* (the etymological meaning of *re-cover*) the apparent losses of our spent or "accomplished" seasons. Intriguingly, this formulation personifies the year, assigning it both a mood and "thought," which "fill the vacuum" left by the accomplished work. The year's harvest of thought, in this complex figure, is the bright, still, warm day: a season within a season, generated by and for *recovery*. In Thoreau's life, too, the ongoingness of thought—informed by years of walking, boating, observing, and writing—would recuperate some measure of the monumental loss.

Of special interest within this category are the accompanying notes, for the years 1851–1859, for Indian Summer in Toronto. These dates are taken from a table reprinted from a record titled "North-West Territory" by Henry Youle Hind. Thoreau copied the dates into a notebook titled "Extracts, mostly upon Natural History" and later copied them from this notebook onto the October chart. Thoreau's interest in comparing the mean dates for Indian Summer in Concord and Toronto suggests that even if, as Robert Richardson has argued, he had by this time abandoned the "Book of Concord," he remained interested in the project of deriving average dates for individual phenomena. The leftmost column, present in the October chart, is further evidence of Thoreau's continued interest in deriving mean dates for phenomena even after the initial structural purpose of these dates—as the ordering mechanism for an eventual book—had almost certainly become moot. Why did these averages retain their interest for Thoreau?

Years earlier, in the wake of the back-to-back deaths of his brother John and Emerson's beloved five-year-old son Waldo, Thoreau had written to Emerson:

> Nature is not ruffled by the rudest blast. The hurricane only snaps a few live twigs in some nook of the forest. The snow attains its average depth each winter, and the chic-adee lisps the same notes. The old laws prevail in spite of pestilence and famine. No genius or virtue so rare and revolutionary appears in town or village, that the pine ceases to exude resin in the wood, or the beast or bird lays aside its habits.
>
> How plain that death is only the phenomenon of the individual or class. Nature does not recognize it, she finds her own again under new forms, without loss.

Having long been comforted by the idea that the snow "attains its average depth each winter" in spite of the myriad individual losses every winter must represent, Thoreau in the fall of 1861 sought further comfort through ever-finer apprehension of "the old laws." By the fall of 1861—nearly twenty years after his initial formulation of seasonal time as a means of contextualizing and living with loss—Thoreau had fine-tuned his method for perceiving and realizing these laws. The patterns he perceived in the charts—the average height of the river, the average dates of the "recovery of the year" in Indian Summer—reassured him that death, even his own, was "only the phenomenon of the individual." The old laws still held.

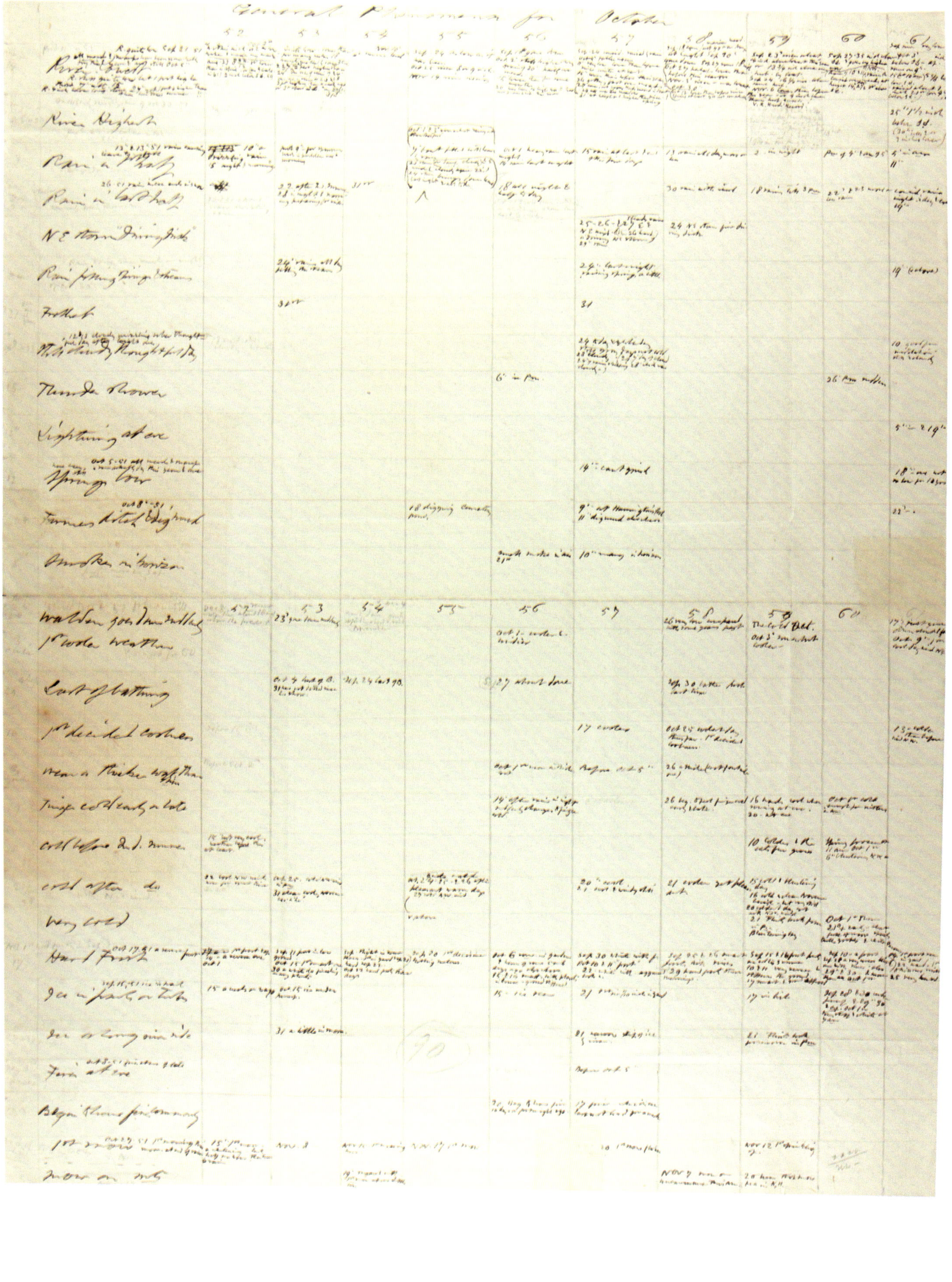

General Phenomena for October

52 | 53 | 54 | 55 | 56 | 57 | 58 | 59 | 60 | 61

River Lowest

River Highest

Rain in 1st half

Rain in last half

NE storm driving mist

Rain filling springs & streams

Freshet

Thunder Shower

Lightning at eve

Springs low

Smoke in horizon

1st cold weather

Last of bathing

1st decided coolness

very cold

Hard Frost

Ice in pails or tubs

Fire at eve

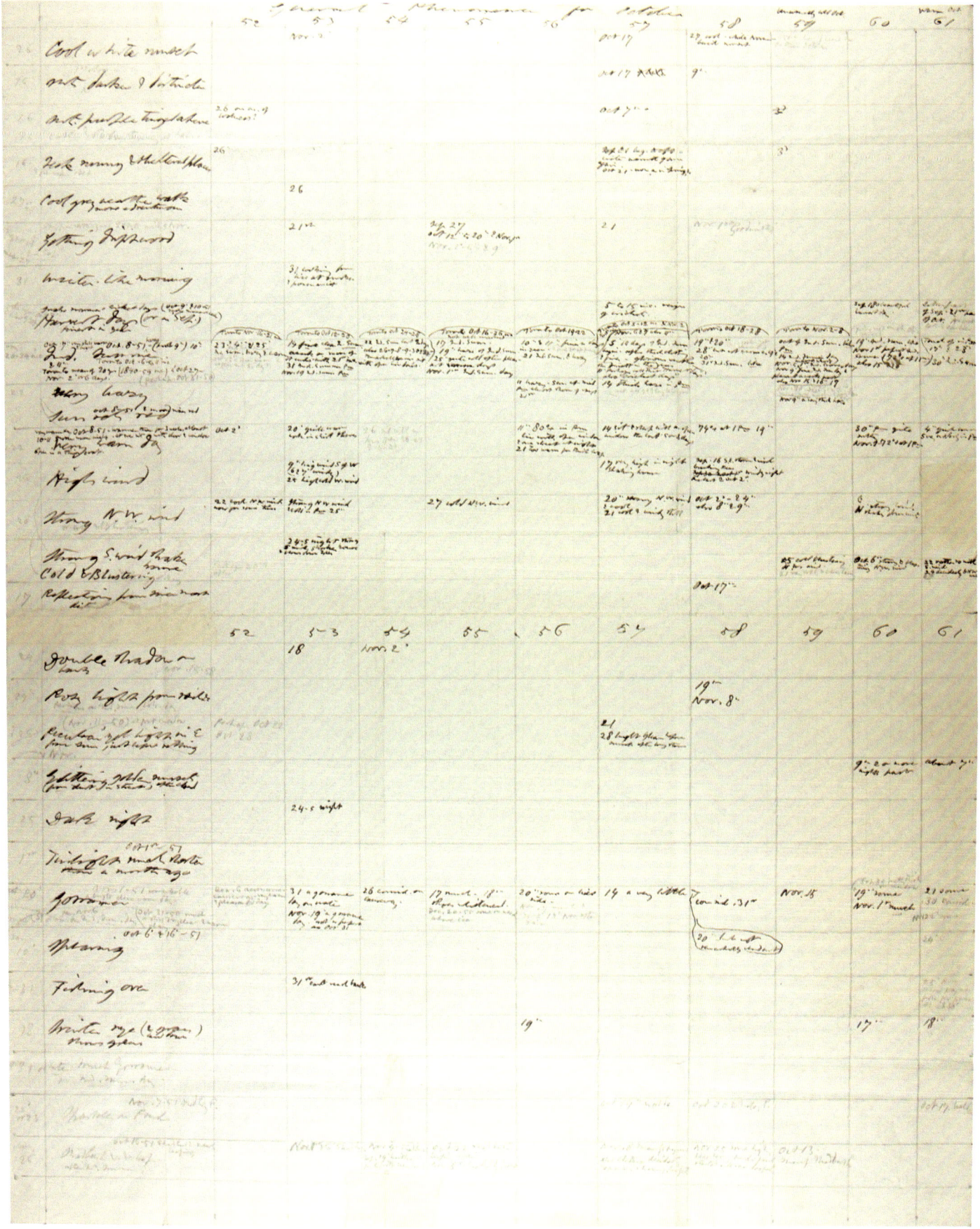

## General Phenomena for October

| | | 52 | 53 | 54 | 55 |
|---|---|---|---|---|---|
| 19 | prob. 11 in 51    R. quite low Sep 21-51 all meads & swamps have been remarkably dry this year & are still Oct. 5th<br><br>**River Lowest**<br>R. still quite low but 1 foot higher than 7th on 15th<br>R. 4 inch below long stone 27th yet 1 foot higher than it has been this summer!! | Oct 2nd "within an inch or 2 as low as when I made my mark." Aug. 23 8 $\frac{9\frac{1}{2}}{12}$ ft lower than in April or (as I calc. in 61) 2 inch lower s.l. 59 say 9 or 11 | Quite low, lower than for <u>many weeks</u> 18 much swelled by <u>rain</u> 25- 6 & 27 2 feet higher than on 24th <u>on ac. of rain of 24th</u> on ac. of rain of 23 & 28 3 feet higher than a week ago or 3 feet above 28th on ~~27th~~ 31st | Nov. 10th "at summer level" | Sep. 24 as low as it has been Oct 25 risen 8 or 9 inch. Nov 14 river rising |
| Say 26 (or 27) | [unclear][unclear] of Oct 30-51<br>**River Highest**<br>prob 27th or earlier in 51 31st-51 | say 31st yet | say ~~say~~ <u>31st</u> 3 ft above S.L. | | Prob. about 27th<br><br>Oct 1st & 3 somewhat rainy at [unclear] |
| 9 | 12th & 13th 51 rain causing leaves to fall<br>**Rain in 1st half**<br>bringing down leaves | ~~12 & 13th~~ -10th a drizzling rain 15th night & morning | prob. 9th- for sparrows wash in puddles next morning. | | 7th boat filled with leaves 1st rain 21 rain (or damp cloudy) & E wind (cloudy again 22nd) 24 rain brings down leaves last night & all today |
| 24 v 25 | below   26-51 rain in eve ends in snow<br>**Rain in last half**<br>commonly following [unclear] | ~~22~~ 30 & 31 & Nov 1st warm mizzling rain | 22 after Ind. summer 28 in night & morn- ing preparing for winter | 31st     warm rain | , ^ |
| 25 | **N.E. storm "driving drisk"** | | | | |
| ~~24~~ 25 | Rain raises river much in night<br>**Rain filling spring streams**<br>of Oct 30th | | 24th rains all day filling the stream | | |
| ? 21 [uncl] 11 yrs | **Freshet** | | 31st | | |
| ~~15th~~ or 13 | 12 &13 cloudy mizzling sober thought- ful day after bright one<br>**Still cloudy thoughtful day** | 18 mild still cloudy + rain | | | |
| 15 | **Thunder shower** | | | | |

| 56 | 57 [unclear] 15th | 30th    58         mania mead | [unclear][unclear][unclear] in last half  59 Say 8 | 60 | Say 15    61 Sept river very low |
|---|---|---|---|---|---|
| Sep 18- gone down Oct. 2 still higher owing to rain of 30th partly cover meads. 15th lower than for some months 20th has been so high no B.Beckii nor p. amphib. this season | Sep. 24 consid. raised by rain Oct 4 fallen again 11th very low lower than before since winter at least 15th lower than before this year 26 getting fast over meads 27 can just cross Hub's mead. in boat 29 all over the meadow 31st at highest + higher than since spring | Sep 18 can just go over the Am^ at height Sep 20th gone down Sep 27th some 18 inch Oct 27 perhaps lower than before this season Nov 3rd risen - was lowest Oct 30th Oct. 12 lower than before since spring at least yet not remarkably | Sep 23rd risen about 14 inch above lowest this year or 13 ¾ inch above my mark by boat Sep 24 16 ¾ inch above same mark. Nov 6 lower than before this year about 4 inch lower than mark I made! | Sep 27- 35 inch    above S.L. & goes no higher now.          of Nov. Rain of 10th & 11th raises R. consid. over meads, at Nov height 14th^ 2 ⅓ ft. above s.l. | Oct 3rd    inch below S. L. - at same on 9th 15 (at 10 Am.) 5 ⅝ be-low S. L. raised about 1 inch (or 4 ⅝ below S.L.) |
| Say 20th or later | 31st | say Oct 1st | V.R. Hurd's Record [unclear] Oct 8 [uncl.] 10 ½ inch higher than Aug 22    River lowest for Oct (when I was here Aug 22 below SL.) + Oct 11 19th 4 in. above Aug 22    say 11??' | 22/3rd | 25th 1 ½ inch below S.L. (30th wells 2 or 3 inches lower) |
| Oct 1 heavy rain last night 14 rain last night | 15 rain at last & end of the fine days | 13 rain all day more or less | 2 – in night | Pm of 4th and Am of 5th | 5th in am 11th |
| 18 all night & half today Oct 10 [unclear] [un-clear] to abundance of rain these last 6 weeks | | 30 rain with wind | 18 rains till 3 Pm | 22nd and 23rd more or less rain | consid. rain night & day begin 19th |
| | 25-26 -& 27 E & NE wind (the 26 hard) a driving NE storm) 29th rain | 24 NE storm fine dri-ving drisk | | | |
| | 24th Last night raising springs a little | | | | 19 (v. above) |
| | 31 | | | | |
| | 24 today + yesterday still gray days not cold 28th cloudy -(29th 7th day of cloud & 4th of rain skipping 28th which was cloudy -) | | | | 10 good for ventilation still & cloudy |
| 6 in Pm | | | | 26 Pm sudden | |

steady rain

| | | | | | |
|---|---|---|---|---|---|
| 12th | Lightning at eve | | | | |
| 12 | Oct 5-51 all mead & swamp have been remarkably dry this year & are still<br>Springs low | | | | |
| | Oct 8th-51<br>Farmers ditch & dig pond | | | | 18 digging cemetery pond. |
| 8 | Smokes in horizon<br>prob. more in Sep | | | | |
| 25<br>20 | About Nov. 8 50 fallen a little<br>Walden goes down suddenly | Dec 8　52　recent winter time about 18 inch above the present | 53<br>23rd gone down suddenly | 54　v. Dec. 4 went down quite swiftly around mid- | 55 |
| 3 or earlier | 1st cooler weather<br>v. very cool for 50 | | | November | |
| of Sep 29 | Last of bathing | | Oct 4 last of B.  31 have not bathed since C. show. | Sept 24 Last of B. | |
| 16 | 1st decided coolness | before 15 (?) | | | |
| 3 or earlier | wear a thicker coat than thin | before Oct 2nd | | | |
| 14 | Finger cold early or late | | | | |
| 10 | cold before Ind. summer | 15 isn't very cool weather before this at least | | | |
| 27 or 28 | cold after do.<br>with NW wind | 22 cool NW winds now for some time [unclear] 20th | Oct 25 cold NW wind in Pm<br>31 clear, cool, November-like! | | Quite cold<br>Oct. 24- 25-& 26 after pleasant warm day<br>27 cold N.W. wind |
| | very cold | | | | v. above |
| NB<br>17 | 1st hard frost is in Sep Oct 17-51 a severe frost<br>Hard Frost | 17a 1st frost Sep 14 - a severe one Oct 1 | Sept 11 frost in low ground<br>Oct 15 1st smart one<br>30 a white [uncl.] finishing many plants | Sep. slight in some places.  1st in yard. Sep.  21 hard Sept 22.<br>Oct 22 hard frosts these days | Sep 20 1st decisive killing melons. |
| 8 | Sep 15-51 ice in pail<br>Ice in ponds or tubs | 15 a week or 2 ago | Oct 15 ice under pump. | | |
| 27 or 28 or before | Ice along river side | | 31 a little in morn. | | |
| say 3rd or earlier | Oct 8-51 fires at eve of late<br>Fires at eve | | | | |
| say 16th | Begin to have fire commonly | | | | |
| 19 | Oct 27-51 1st snowing this morn. at end of rain<br>1st snow<br>NB in Nov.　V. Nov. | 15 1st snow - a whitening - but half an hour, then turns to rain | Nov. 8 | Nov 15 1st sugaring here. | Nov 17 1st snow |
| 25 | snow on mtns<br>v. Nov　Nov.13-51 | | | 19th sugared with - 1st snow above Little-ton | |

| 56 | 57 | 58 | 59 | 60 | 61 |
|---|---|---|---|---|---|
| | | | | | 5th—& 19th |
| | 14th - can't grind | | | | 18th- one not so low for 10 years |
| | 9th at Harrington's pool 11th dig mud elsewhere | | | | 22nd—. |
| smell smoke in air 21st | 10th many in horizon | | | | |
| **56** | **57** | **58** 26 very low compared with some years past | **59** The cold Oct. | **60** | **61** 17th first came down around 1ft |
| Oct 1 – cooler & windier | | | Oct 3rd somewhat cooler | | Oct 9th 1st cool day wind NE |
| Sep. 27 about done | | Sep 30 bathe prob. last time | | | |
| | 17 cooler | Oct 25 coolest day thus far - 1st decided coolness - | | | 13 colder than before wind NW |
| Oct 1st wear a thicker coat | before Oct 5th | 26 a thicker (best outside one) | | | |
| 14 after rain in night suddenly changes to finger-cold | 21st at least | 26 beg. to feel finger cold early & late | 16 hands cool when rowing at eve. 20– at eve | Oct 1st cold enough for mittens in am. | |
| | | | 10 colder & the cat's fur grows | Spring frozen at 11 am Oct 1st 6th blustering N.W. w | |
| | 20th cool 21 cool & windy still | 21 cooler yet pleasant | 15 cold and blustering day 16 Cold and clear November-ish - but very still 20 coldest day yet with N.W. wind | | |
| | | | 21 Flint's brook frozen in Pm. Blustering day. | Oct 1st I hear 21 degrees + early about full of moon spoils Bull's grapes & white  o. acorns | |
| Oct 6 some in garden I hear of some 5 or 6 days ago elsewhere 15 & 16 smart kills plants in house - ground stiffened | Sep 30 white with fr Oct 10 & 11 "frost" 22 white with - aggravated look | Sep 25 & 26 smart frost kills vines 29 hard frosts other mornings. | Sep 15 & 16 frost puts an end to summer 10 & 11 very severe & stiffens the ground 17 smart & ground stiffened | Sep 10- a frost Sep 28 a very severe black one kills vines also 29th & 30th & more than on Oct 1st | 14   1st frost seen in yard 22 hard. 1st skim over night 25 very hard |
| 15- ice seen | 21 1st ice 1/10th inch in yard | | 17 in tub | Sep 28 & 30 under pump & 29th 30 & esp Oct 1st trees still white at 7 am | |
| | 21 narrow strip of ice by river. | | 21 Flint's brook frozen over in Pm. | | |
| v. below say 6 | before Oct 5th | | | | |
| 20 Beg to have fire 10 days or fortnight ago. | 17 fire which we have not had for a week | | | | |
| | Nov 20 1st snow flakes in air. | | Nov 12 1st sprinkling of. | | |
| | | Nov 7. Snow on Uncannanuc this am | 20 hear that snow fell in N.H. | | |

| | | General Phenomena for October | | | |
|---|---|---|---|---|---|
| | | 52 | 53 | 54 | 55 |
| 26 | **Cool white sunset** | | Nov. 2nd | | |
| 16 | 1st [unclear] **Mts ^ darker & distincter** | | | | |
| 16 / 16th | **Mts. purple tinged above** cold & Blustering v below | 26 on ac. of coolness? | | | |
| 16 | **Seek sunny & sheltered places** & perhaps Sep. | 26th | | | |
| 27 & 8 | **Cool grey weather walk** more adventurous | | 26 | | |
| ? / 21 or 19 / perhaps / 27 | say from the start of Sep to mid of Nov. **Gathering driftwood** and in Sep. | | 21st | | Sep 27 / Oct 12th to 20th & Nov. 1st / Nov. 1st-6th- & 9th |
| 31 | **Winter-like morning** | | 31 looking from hill at smokes & frozen mist | | |
| Say before Oct 8 [?] & last of Sep. | snake summer cricket days (Oct 9 & 10 - 51 snake summer or week) H. **Harvest days** (or in Sep.) finest in year | Toronto Nov. 16-21 inc | Toronto Oct 12-20 | Toronto Oct 24-28 | Toronto Oct 16-26 inc not well marked |
| say 20-24 inc | Oct 7th very still warm & bright hazy / Oct 8 - 51 ^- (prob 9th) 10th **Ind. Summer** & 11th  Toronto Oct - 6 to 11th inc / Toronto mean of 20 yrs (1840-59 inc) is Oct 27 - Nov 2 or 6 days. (perhaps Oct 31 – 50) | 23rd-4th & 25th Ind. sum. hazy & warm Oct 13th a clear warm & rather Ind. S. day [uncl] | 14 fine clear In. Sum. a week or more of it ends - with 21st inc. 31 Ind. Summer Pm Nov. 19 Ind. sum. Pm | 22 Ind. Sum last 2 days also 26-7-8-9-30 & 31st remarkably warm, sit with open windows. | 17 Ind. Sum. 19th haze of Ind. sum. 25th quite cold after pleasant warm days Nov. 1st Ind. Sum. day |
| 22 | **Very hazy** | | | | |
| | oct 8 - 51 & moon rises red **Sun sets red** | | | | |
| 22 | very warm day Oct 8 – 51- warmer than for 3 weeks at least 10-11 another warm night - at eve sit with door & window **Very warm day** open in a thin coat | Oct 2nd | 20th quite warm work in shirt sleeves | 26 sit with windows open 26-27 8-9-30 | |
| 26 | **High wind** | | 9th [unclear] wind S of W (6 & 7windy) 25 high cold W. wind | | |
| 28 | **Strong N.W. wind** or cold & Blustering | 22 cool N.W. winds now for some time | strong NW wind & cold in Pm 25th | | 27 cold N.W. wind |

| 56 | 57 | 58 | unusually cold Oct. 59 | 60 | warm Oct. 61 |
|---|---|---|---|---|---|
| | Oct 17 | 27 cool - white Novem-berish sunset | November pleasant-er than October | | |
| | Oct 17 ~~of late~~ | 9th | | | |
| | Oct 7th<br>Nov 4 decidedly | | 3rd | | |
| | Sep 21 beg. to appre-ciate warmth of sun again. Oct 21 now, as in spring &c | | 3rd | | |
| | | | | | |
| | 21 | Nov 1st Goodwin [unclear] | | | |
| | | | | | |
| | 5 to 15 inc. reign of crickets | | | Sep 18 beautiful harvest day | Latter part of Sep. - & 1st part of Oct. As Oct 4th & 8 earlier |
| Toronto Oct 19-22 add 12th | Toronto Oct 5-12 inc & Nov. 2 to 8 inc Nov. 6 & 7 also 11th | Toronto Oct 18-28 | Toronto Nov. 2-8 | prob. not much ob-served | |
| 10th & 11th finest days in year - ^& prob 2 days preceding<br>21 Ind. Sum. & hazy | 5th 10 days of Ind. sum. begin. after thick clothing & fires - glorious weather the finest in the year<br>11th Perhaps call these "Harvest days"<br>also "cricket days" | 19th & 20th (21-cooler yet pleasant)<br>28th but not as warm as 19th & 20th<br>31st Ind. Sum. like | Oct 4 Ind. sum. like Pm<br>14 Ind. Summer day on Long Wharf<br>Nov. 5 ^ 1st Ind. Summer day<br>Nov 9 fine Ind. Sum day & pleasant a week past | 19th Ind. sum. like Nov 1st perfect Ind. Summer (72°+ at 1 Pm) also 15 & 16 | Touch of in Pm 17th & 23rd 30th Ind. sum. |
| 11 hazy - sun at mid pm almost shorn of rays 21st | 14 thick haze in Pm (Oct 24 getting [unclear] | | also Nov 15 & 16th 17<br>Nov 30-Dec. 1st & 2nd remarkably warm spring like days<br>Nov 9th a very thick haze | | |
| 11th 80° + in pm lie with open window & one sheet at night 21 too warm for thick coat | 14 sit & sleep with an open window the last 5 or 6 days | 74° + at 1 Pm 19th | | 30th pm quite sultry Nov 1 - 72°+ at 1 Pm | 4th quite warm 5 very suddenly in Pm |
| | 17 very high in night shaking house | Sep. 16 S.E. storm & wind breaking trees<br>~~Sep 30 & Oct 1st~~ windy night the last 2 Oct 2nd | | | |
| | 20th strong N.W. wind & cool 21 cool & windy still | Oct 2nd - & 4th also 8th & 9th | | 6 strong wind N shakes down limbs | |

| | | 52 | 53 | 54 | 55 |
|---|---|---|---|---|---|
| | **Strong S. wind shakes** house | | 24-5 night strong S wind shakes house & blows down trees | | |
| | **Cold & blustering** day | Perhaps 20th & after | | | |
| 17 | **Reflections from river most distinct** | | | | |
| 24 | **Double shadow on** banks    Nov. 15-58 | | 18 | Nov. 2nd | |
| 29th | **Rosy light from rails** Perhaps an Ind. Sum. like day | | | | |
| ?~~26~~ | (Nov 11 – 50) at Nut Meadow **Peculiar yel light in E from sun just before setting** v Nov. | Perhaps Oct 22 Oct 28 | | | |
| 8th | **Glittering golden sunset** (from dust in street) after clouds | | | | |
| 25 | **Dark night** | | 24- 5 night | | |
| 1st | Oct 1st-51 **Twilight much shorter than a month ago** | | | | |
| Oct 20th  much 31 | Nov. 1 - 51 remarkable a bright clear warm day – **Gossamer** say Nov 6 an Ind. Sum. day or later Oct 31 - 50 much a still dry clear & warm day | Dec. 6 across corner causeway - very warm & pleasant day | 31 a gossamer day on water Nov. 19th a gossamer day. not as perfect as Oct 31 | 26 consid. on causeway | 17 much - 18th shoes whitened Dec. 20 - 55 some on weeds above ice |
| say 10th | Oct. 6th &16th - 51 **Spearing** | | | | |
| ? - 31 | **Fishing over** | | 31st can't reach banks | | |
| 18 | **Winter rye** shows green   (& grass laid down) | | | | |
| 31 or | later **Much Gossamer** on Ind. sum. day | | | | |
| 22nd or 23 | Nov. 7 - 51 Dudley P. **Sparkle on ponds** | | | | |
| say 26 | Oct 16 - 51 Shadbush newly leafing **Shadbush &c. leaf** after Ind. summer? | | Nov 1st & 6th Shadbush | Nov 4th Shadbush Sep. 19 hardhack puts forth new leaves | Oct 22 Shadbush leafing again Nov. 5 checked by frost |

| 56 | 57 | 58 | 59 | 60 | 61 |
|---|---|---|---|---|---|
| | | | 15 cold blustering N.W. wind / 21 very cold & blustering | Oct 6th strong & blustering N.W. wind | 22 rather south E. wind / 24 decidedly & N.W. / 28      wind |
| | | Oct 17th | | | |
| | | 19th / Nov. 8th | | | |
| | 21 / 28 bright gleam before sunset after long storm | | | | |
| | | | | 9th 2 or more nights past | about 7th |
| | | | | Sep 30 pretty thick on meadow / 19th some / Nov. 1st _much_ | |
| 20th some on hill side - / Nov. 7 much & some 13th Nov. after rain | 14 a very little | consid. 31st | Nov. 15 | | 21 some / 30 consid. / Nov. 22nd some |
| | | 20th look not remarkably abundant | | | 24th |
| | | | | | 25th River so low Haynes fishes for pickerel & 30th |
| 19th | | | | 17th | 18th |
| | Oct 14 Walden | Oct 20 White P. | | | Oct 17 Walden |
| | Nov. 8 swamp pyrus also clethra decidedly expanded showing leafets | Nov. 25 some high blueberry bushes fairly started into red leafets | Oct 13 swamp shadbush | | |

General Phenomena for November. The Morgan Library & Museum. MA 610.

# NOVEMBER:

## *Seek Sheltered Places*

---

BY NOVEMBER FIRES ARE REGULAR: THE OLD IRON AUGER CHURNING
the pellets I pour each morning from forty-pound bags hauled in from the
garage, the little chamber filling with smoke, then the flickering light.
Unlanguaged, I feel alien to myself, cut off. The landscape contracts to
quieter colors, opens to a larger sky. On the news, children are killed
when soldiers open fire. Language is always threatening with a kind of
easy sense.

Mist rises from the little pond I pass walking to work. The bare trees are
bathed in it. On the ground, the oak leaves are edged in frost, the intricate arc
of each absence made plain. It will be gone in an hour, this crystal articulation, these perfect lines. Each blade of grass repeats itself in a white shadow. The
milkweed pods are empty, the two-chambered hollows hardened into a graceful
depletion. It is difficult to witness. I stop in a pocket of yellow light that shimmers
like a little fire on the pond's surface. Little warmth of November, little shelter.

Later, I trace the tracings of November: chart to notes to Journal. I read
about the "very pale brown bleaching–almost hoary fine grass or hay in the
fields–akin to the frost which has killed it–& flakes of clear yellow sunlight
falling on it here & there." Here and there. In this time, in another time,
the layered time of our living and dying. Winter will be wet this year, di-
sastrously. I know because I am writing this later, after it has all happened.

⁎

In November of 1861, as the days grew shorter and the season stilled in antic-
ipation of winter, Henry Thoreau's health continued its downward slide. On

November 3, he writes what will be the final entry in his Journal. Venturing out of the house, he observes that the gravel surface of the railroad causeway is marked with parallel lines like the striations in a rock, caused by the morning's hard rain hitting the surface at an angle. "All this is perfectly distinct to an observant eye," he writes, "– Yet could easily pass unnoticed by most– Thus each wind is self-registering" (11/3/1861, Journal Transcript 33:109). A fitting note on which to close his own "great monument to self-registering."

Back in January of 1860, he had written:

> A man receives only what he is *ready* to receive–whether physically–or intellectually or morally–as animals conceive at certain seasons their kind only.
>
> We hear & apprehend only what we already half know– If there is something which does not concern me–which is out of my line– which by experience or by genius my attention is not drawn to–however novel & remarkable it may be–if it is spoken, we *hear* it not–if it is written we read it not–or if we read it–it does not detain us.
>
> Every man thus *tracks himself*, through life–in all his hearing & reading & observation & travelling. His observations make a chain– The phenomenon or fact that cannot in any wise be linked–with the rest which he has observed, he does not observe. (1/5/1860, Journal Transcript 30:230)

Thoreau's Journal had made him aware of the normally invisible process by which his mind made sense of the world: each day's new observations fitted into his store of previous observations, filling in the picture a little more. Knowledge was dependent upon prior knowledge, attention upon previous attention. In the pages of his Journal he had left material tracks, traces of past experience as legible as striations in gravel left by the rain and wind. As he felt the future close ahead of him, Thoreau turned backward, toward his faithfully documented past. The new work would be to follow his own tracks: stitching together the composite picture of the season they suggested in order to hear the individual notes he'd transcribed over the years played together in their complex symphonic order. Encountering the season, he would encounter himself.

As the winter of his life began in earnest, Thoreau's thoughts lingered on memories of warmth and light: the emergence of new buds on skunk cabbage and pitch pines, the particular yellow light of November, which he'd long experienced as richer, somehow *warmer* than the heat of summer—its scarcity and contrasting context heightening our perception of and gratitude for it. In "A Winter Walk," one of his earliest essays, he'd written of the "slumbering subterranean fire in nature which never goes out, and which no cold can chill," a warmth that lingers in memory as it does through the change of season. "We resort in thought to a trickling rill, with its bare stones shining in the sun, and to warm springs in the woods, with as much eagerness as rabbits and robins." The special warmth of winter days, he wrote, "comes directly from the sun, and is not radiated from the earth, as in summer; and when we feel his beams on our backs as we are treading some snowy dell, we are grateful as for a special kindness, and bless the sun which has followed us into that by-place." The November charts are especially replete with light-related phenomena: Thoreau tracks "Thin yellow sunlight," "Sparkle," "Cool silvery light in white pines," and "sparkling windows at sunset." In the 1857 entry for "Seek sheltered places" he writes "rejoice in."

But not all of Thoreau's thoughts this November were retrospective: Ellery Channing came daily, and brought news.

Back in the spring of 1861, before leaving for Minnesota with Horace Mann, Thoreau had written a Journal entry reflecting on the rapidly melting ice on Walden Pond, the height of the water on the meadows, and evidence of mice gnawing on pitch pines. What makes this entry stand out from the thousands like it in the last decade of the Journal is that the observations on which it is based were not made by Henry Thoreau. Channing had come to visit his bedridden friend and brought with him evidence of the season: "The water is now high on the meadows & there is no ice there–owing to the recent heavy rains– Yet C. thinks it has been higher a few weeks since." Later he writes, "C. observes where mice (?) have gnawed the p. pines the past winter. Is not this a phenomenon of a winter of deep snow only?" (3/11/1861, Journal Transcript 33:82).

Thoreau and Channing's friendship had been decades in the making: cultivated over hundreds of walks and conversations and letters and boat rides. Channing is often the unnamed other half of the *we* that alternates with the *I* of Thoreau's Journal, appearing particularly in passages describing walks and boating excursions. "At the Hubbard bridge we hear the incessant note of the Phoebe–" Thoreau writes in one characteristic entry in April of 1856. Later in the same entry he notes "By rocking our boat & using our paddles can make our way through the softened ice 6 inches or more in thickness" (4/7/1856, Journal Transcript 20:210–11). The unnamed companion was no doubt Channing, who, like his friend, was attuned to the sounds of birds and interested enough in the character of ice to venture out by boat onto the still partially frozen river. Interestingly, this entry occurs only a few weeks after Thoreau complains about Channing's insensitivity: he was a famously difficult friend. Thoreau once declared him "the moodiest person perhaps that I ever saw." His marriage to Margaret Fuller's sister Ellen was a disaster, and his family suffered from Channing's irresponsibility and dark moods.

Whatever inward difficulties Thoreau felt, however, Channing was his steadfast companion, their observations and excursions more and more often fusing into that unmarked *we*. Their togetherness was so habitual it felt almost like inhabiting a shared self—so much so that Channing joked when he was sick with a cold that Thoreau could replicate their walking together by taking twice as long a walk by himself, effectively taking Channing's part of the walk for him:

> A rainy day. Called to C. from the outside of his house the other <u>Pm</u> in the rain. At length he put his head out the attic window & I inquired if he didn't want to take a walk–but he excused himself saying that he had a cold but added he, you can take so much the longer walk–double it. (11/4/1858, Journal Transcript 27:301)

During his river investigation in 1859 Thoreau was often assisted by Channing, and Thoreau's boat place and local point for river measurements was in his old friend's backyard. Channing's long and deep connection to Thoreau's habits of observation and in particular his detailed knowledge of the river project and the surveying techniques it involved allowed him to help his friend keep feeding his charts with present-tense observations. He was Thoreau's link to the still-living season.

*River Lowest/River Highest*

6 ½ Pm to Baker Farm by boat
It is a full moon–& a clear night–with a strong northwest wind–so C and I must have a sail by moonlight. The river has risen surprisingly

to a spring height owing to yesterday's rain–higher than before since spring  We sail rapidly upward– The river apparently almost actually as broad as the Hudson–Venus remarkably bright just ready to set–not a cloud in the sky–only the moon & a few faint unobtrusive stars here & there & from time to time a meteor– The water washes against our bows with the same sound that one hears against a vessel's prow by night on the ocean– The shore lines are concealed– You look seemingly over an almost boundless waste of waters on either hand– the hills are dark vast lumpish–some near familiar hill appears as a distant bold mountain.– for its base is infinitely removed. It is very pleasant to make our way thus rapidly–but mysteriously over the black waters–now black as ink & dotted with round foam spots with a long moonlight sheen on one side– to make one's way upward thus over the water of waters not knowing where you are exactly only avoiding shores– The stars are few & faint in this bright light– How well they wear. C. thought a man could still get along with *them* who was considerably reduced in his circumstances– that they were a kind of bread & cheese that never failed. (11/14/1853, *Journal* 7:161–62)

The water on the meadows–which are rapidly becoming bare–is skimmed over–and reflects a whitish light like silver plating–while the unfrozen river is a dark blue–

In plowed fields I see the asbestos like ice crystals–more or less mixed with earth–frequently curled & curved like crisped locks, where the wet ground has frozen dry– By the spring under Fair Haven Hill I see the frost about the cistus– now at 11 AM in the sun. For some weeks I have heard occasionally the hounding of hounds like a distant natural horn in the clear resonant air– (11/25/1853, *Journal* 7:174–5)

The water is falling fast–& I push *direct* over the meadow this evening prob. for the last time this fall–scraping the cranberry vines & the hummocks from time to time with my flatbottomed boat. (11/2/1857, Journal Transcript 24:599)

Often the river entries give us a key to the Kalendar's telescopic logic: zoom in on an entry in the chart, and a detail or data point opens out to the more inclusive picture captured in the Journal. Michael Berger describes the way the field notes, lists, Journal, charts, and essays in Thoreau's late work together composed a vast network of interrelated projects that were also interrelated *perspectives* on the natural world, ways of multiplying what a single observer could see: "This composite picture makes us more aware that our commonplace image of the world falls short, in intensity and fullness of detail, of the living reality we overlook. With respect to any phenomenon mentioned in passing, we can recall a richness of sensuous detail expressed elsewhere within the system."

Thus the note "Meadows rapidly becoming bare" in 1853 (across from the category "River Highest") can be traced back from this data point in the sweeping, decade-wide overview of the November chart to the Journal entry above, and witnessed again on the scale of the single day, restored to the unfrozen river, the whitish light, and the ice crystals, "curled & curved like crisped locks."

Interestingly, the categories "River Lowest" and "River Highest" each include entries referring to the opposite phenomenon, as if to illustrate the uncontainable flux of the river itself. The entry for "River Lowest" on November 14, 1853, for example, details the surprising height of the river on a moonlit night, while an entry for "River Highest" on November 25 of the same year points to the water level's relative decline, the meadows "rapidly becoming bare." As H. Daniel Peck writes, when studying the Kalendar, one can't fail to notice the ways that "the seasons . . . were always drifting one into the next, and at every turn the categories were sliding out of focus." As Peck convincingly argues, such contradictions, complications, and spillings-over were an inherent feature of the collision between Thoreau's subjective, perception-oriented approach to the charts and his "great nineteenth-century dream" of a totalizing vision, a dream he perhaps came closest to fulfilling in his long study of the Concord River.

The river data for November of 1861 is astonishingly replete, given Thoreau's health, with measurements on five different dates. On the 5th, the 14th, the 17th, the 20th, and the 28th, Channing crossed his yard to Thoreau's boat place, and probably using a marked stick Thoreau had left nearby for this purpose, measured the height of the river against the notch in the willow tree before walking the short distance down Main Street to visit with his friend, numbers in hand. Thoreau would scrawl the day's seasonal news, often including these measurements, in a running list of general phenomena for the month divided into years. On the November list he notes,

"Nov 14 -61, river at 11 am 2 ½ inches above S.L." These lists were the intermediate step between the Journal and the seasonal charts. Now, however, Channing's news was added directly to the list, and the once-complex chain of transcription from field notes to Journal to lists and finally into the charts has collapsed into a meager two-step process: data points were entered into the list, list entries were transcribed onto the chart. Unlike all other entries in the charts, these final observations are not linked to longer and more detailed descriptions placing the phenomenon in its lived context. It is as if we can witness, in the thinning out of the observational stream, the encroaching horizon of remaining time—the diminishment of the present.

But we also witness, in these final observations, a new chapter in a long-evolving friendship. In a Journal entry from 1853 he revisited for the compiling of his November lists and charts, Thoreau writes with a tone of exuberant camaraderie, "It is a full moon–& a clear night– with a strong northwest wind–so C and I must have a sail by moonlight." This emphatic compound subject "C and I" is forged by a joint imperative: the two "must have a sail by moonlight." Recorded in the same entry, Channing's description of the stars as "a kind of bread & cheese that never failed"—a steady source of nourishment that can always be relied upon, even in the worst times—speaks to the extent to which Channing shared, or at least understood, Thoreau's dependence on and attunement to the natural world. Channing recognized that Thoreau's friendship with the seasons was the essential nourishment that sustained him through the "reduced circumstances" of grief, alienation, and, eventually, illness. It was for this reason that he tended to his friend the way he did, walking, as he had once jokingly suggested to Thoreau, on his friend's behalf, and taking up his measuring stick.

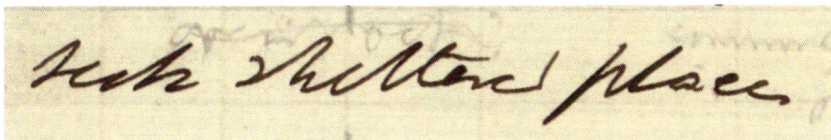

*Seek Sheltered Places*

The sunlight is a peculiarly thin & clear yellow falling on the pale brown bleaching herbage of the fields at this season– There is no redness in it–

This is november sunlight.

Much cold slate-colored cloud–bare twigs seen gleaming toward the light like gossamer––pure green of pines whose old leaves have fallen–reddish or yellowish brown oak leaves rustling on the hillsides–very pale brown bleaching–almost hoary fine grass or hay in the fields–akin to the frost which has killed it–& flakes of clear yellow sunlight falling on it here & there–such is november

The fine grass killed by this frost– withered & bleached till it is almost silvery has clothed the fields for a long time.

Now as in the Spring we rejoice in sheltered and sunny places. (11/18/1857, Journal Transcript 24:638)

A cold day–. . . seek sunny & sheltered places as in early spring–the S. side the island e.g. Certain localities are thus distinguished. And they retain this peculiarity permanently, (unless it depends on a wood which may be cut)–thousands of years hence this may still be the warmest & sunniest spot in the spring & fall. (11/11/1858, Journal Transcript 28:11–12)

In "A Winter Walk," Thoreau had written of the special gratitude and joy elicited by winter sun and "sheltered places." "When we feel his beams on our backs . . . , we are grateful as for a special kindness, and bless the sun which has followed us into that by-place." The phenomenon exemplified the experience of friendship with the seasons described at greater length in *Walden*:

While I enjoy the friendship of the seasons I trust that nothing can make life a burden to me. The gentle rain which waters my beans and keeps me in the house today is not drear and melancholy, but good for me too. Though it prevents my hoeing them, it is of far more worth than my hoeing. If it should continue so long as to cause the seeds to rot in the ground and destroy the potatoes in the low lands, it would still be good for the grass on the uplands, and, being good for the grass, it would be good for me . . . . In the midst of a gentle rain while these thoughts prevailed, I was suddenly sensible of such sweet and beneficent society in Nature, in the very pattering of the drops, and in every sound and sight around my house, an infinite and unaccountable friendliness all at once like an atmosphere sustaining me, as made the fancied advantages of human neighborhood insignificant, and I have never thought of them since. Every little pine needle expanded and swelled with sympathy and befriended me.

"Friendship" is not being used metaphorically in this passage: central to Thoreau's life was the sense of real and reciprocal sympathy he experienced in the more-than-human world. The "kindness" and "bless[ing]" afforded by the winter sun in "A Winter Walk," like the "infinite and unaccountable friendliness" of nature in the *Walden* passage, reflect feelings of deep and personal interconnection, feelings capable of healing despair and restoring meaning, even to one for whom life threatens to become a burden, as the first sentence of the passage quietly reveals to be the case for Henry Thoreau.

In November of 1861, as he felt his decline sharpen, it is no wonder that Thoreau inscribed this salvific phenomenon—the special balm afforded by "sheltered places" in late fall and winter—in the November chart, even though he could find only two corresponding Journal entries for data points (November 18, 1857, and November 11, 1858). In recording the entry for 1853, Thoreau carefully transcribes "rejoice in" along with the date—as though to preserve in particular this aspect of the phenomenon. As he would have known—etymologist that he was—*rejoice* has a second, archaic meaning: "to own (goods, property), possess, enjoy the possession of, have the fruition of." To "rejoice in sheltered and sunny places" was thus not only to experience joy, but to possess the fullness of the season, to take into oneself and make one's own this special blessing of November. In preserving the memory of this rejoicing in the charts, Thoreau was asserting the continuity of its operation. Homebound, he could still feel the sun on his back.

"Seek sheltered places" exemplifies Thoreau's understanding of natural phenomena as involving both the human subject and the experienced object in a way that reveals these terms to be inadequate. The central tenet of his critique of science, Thoreau's perception of the way observation changed the character of what is observed (and vice versa) anticipates the discoveries of modern physics as well as criticism of scientific language levied by, among others, feminists and philosophers of science. While it may be seen as anthropocentric to understand a place in terms of the value it gives to humans—in this case a warm respite from a cold walk—Thoreau's aim was not to redescribe nature in human terms but rather to redescribe the human as participant in the rhythms and cycles of natural life. Human seeking and rejoicing are as essential to this November phenomenon as the geographical "peculiarity" of the locations in which shelter is to be found. In 1857 he had written,

> I think that the man of science makes this mistake–& the mass of mankind along with him, that you should coolly give your chief attention to the phenomenon which excites you–as something independent on you–and not as it is related to you. . . . With regard to such objects I find that it is not they themselves–(with which the men of science deal) that concern me. The point of interest is somewhere between me & them (i.e. the objects) (11/5/1857, Journal Transcript 24:609–10)

This redescription of knowing as a matter of *relation* ("as it is related to you"), rather than a result of coolly detached observation, unites the ethical and religious aspects of Thoreau's orientation toward nature—visible in the language of the passage above ("bless[ing]," "beneficen[ce]," "sweet[ness]")—with the data-gathering impulses animating so much of the late work. It also helps explain why Thoreau kept up his list making and chart keeping even after he knew that the work they were originally intended to facilitate would now never be accomplished. These activities, now perused only for their own sake, were a continuation of the relational rhythm Thoreau had steadily developed over the years as a way of *seeing* the world in a special, heightened sense. This form of seeing, Walls writes, "required a daily investment of energy and study. It was a sustained interaction among senses, mind, and object, an activity of the mind engaged in a reciprocal process: the mind enters nature, nature is taken into the mind; self and nature react on and finally make, and remake, each other."

The 1857 passage is typical of Thoreau's late descriptive writing in several respects: its attention to the particulars of the landscape—the "reddish or yellowish brown oak leaves rustling on the hillsides–very pale brown bleaching–almost hoary fine grass or hay in the fields," the grass "withered & bleached till it is almost silvery"—is matched by the lyricism and poetry of the description—"bare twigs seen gleaming toward the light like gossamer." That the twigs are "seen gleaming" subtly reminds us that it takes a human perceiver to complete the magic circuit of light, object, and eye. The passage also features Thoreau's drive to know the essence of the month, to *rejoice in* November by mentally taking hold of its key phenomena: "Such is november," and "This is november sunlight."

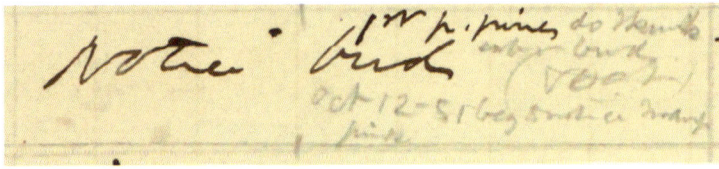

*Notice Buds*

The river is peculiarly sky blue today–not dark as usual. It is all in the air– The cinque-foil on Conantum. Counted 125 crows in one straggling flock moving westward.

The red shruboak leaves abide on the hills.

The witch-hazel . . . have mostly lost their blossoms– perhaps on account of the snow. The ground wears its red carpet under the pines. The pitch pines show new buds at the end of their plumes– How long this? (11/1/1851, *Journal* 4:160)

I see no birds–but hear methinks 1 or 2 tree sparrows. No snow–scarcely any ice to be detected it is only an aggravated November– I thread the tangle of the spruce swamp admiring the leafets of the swamp pyrus which had put forth again now frost-bitten–the great yellow buds of the swamp pink–the round red buds of the high blueberry & the fine sharp red ones of the pannicled Andromeda– Slowly I worm my way amid the snarl, the thicket of black alder–& blueberry &c See the forms ap. of rabbits at the foot of maples–& cat birds' nests now exposed in the leafless thicket. (12/11/1855, Journal Transcript 19:208)

If you are afflicted with melancholy at this season– go to the swamp & see the brave spears of skunk cabbage buds already advanced toward a new year–. Their grave-stones are not bespoken yet– Who shall be sexton to them? Is it the winter of their discontent? Do they seem to have lain down to die–despairing of skunk cabbage-dom. "Up & at 'em" "give it to 'em" "excelsior" "put it thro"– these are their mottoes mortal human creatures must take a little respite in this fall of the year–their spirits do flag a little–there is a little questioning of destiny–& thinking to go like cowards to where the "weary shall be at rest". But not so with the skunk-cabbage. Its withered leaves fall & are transfixed by a rising bud. Winter & death are ignored–the circle of life is complete. Are these false prophets– Is it a lie or a vain boast underneath the skunk cabbage bud pushing it upward–& lifting other dead leaves with it? They rest with spears advanced–they rest to–shoot! (10/31/1857, Journal Transcript 24:592–93)

The November charts articulate an interest that deepens as winter unfolds, becoming a central focus in December: the conspicuousness of bright color and new life in an apparently dying and fading landscape. This seeking out of signs of life—like the seeking out of sheltered places—reflects Thoreau's lifelong tendency to respond to loss and alienation with a determined effort to refocus his attention to the season through which he was living. In an extraordinary Journal passage from April 1852, a few days after a devastating argument with Emerson, Thoreau interrupts his narration of the previous day's observations with a real-time response to Sophia's piano playing.

> I hear the sound of the piano below as I write this and feel as if the winter in me were at length beginning to thaw– for my spring has been even more backward than nature's. For a month past life has been a thing incredible to me. None but the kind gods can make me sane– If only they will let their south winds blow on me. I ask to be melted. You can only ask of the metals that they be tender to the fire that *melts* them. To naught else can they be tender. (4/11/1852, *Journal* 4:434)

The fires that melted Thoreau's inner metal, a cool hardness that he sometimes felt in relation to others or the world—this entry was written just days after Emerson had accused him of being "a cold intellectual skeptic"—were music and nature, and especially signs of warmth and life. His bouts of most profound alienation came when his inner season failed to conform to the outer one, as in this entry, when his "spring has been even more backward than nature's." He knew that the dissolution of such feelings would come with the beneficent influence of the more-than-human world—later in the entry he writes, "If I am too cold for human friendship–I trust I shall not soon be too cold for natural influences" (4/11/1852, *Journal* 4:435)—but also that he had to avail himself of their influence: to actively seek the sanity they could restore. Among other things, the charts of general phenomena represent the persistence and determination of this seeking.

In Thoreau's descriptions of buds in November and December we can feel the inspiration they afforded: his perspective in the November 1, 1851, entry is precise and painterly, panoramic: "Counted 125 crows in one straggling flock moving westward. The red shruboak leaves abide on the hills." The passage ends with a question that, as Peck observes, echoes throughout the Journal in slightly varying forms. "How long?" The question expresses the combination of delight and yearning that Thoreau experienced with every seasonal "first" that he observed. On the one hand, each new appearance was a source of delight. On the other, it prompted the thought of all his limited perspective might have missed. In charting the dates of many firsts across the decade of his Journal keeping, Thoreau sought accurate and identifiable *true beginnings* to each phenomenon, much as he once sought the hard rock bottom of Walden Pond: each plant's flowering, each winter bud appearing. The temporal boundary marking at work in the charts bears an obvious affinity to Thoreau's work as surveyor. Peck writes, "As calendar-maker and surveyor, Thoreau is walking through the world to restore the ancient boundaries of time and space. The larger goal toward which this ambulation works is the restoration of the unity of self and world."

Thoreau's active seeking of inspiration from the natural world in periods of depression and grief is one aspect, perhaps the most personal, of this restorative work. He treats this seeking somewhat comically in the October 31, 1857, entry about skunk cabbage buds, but the point is a deeply serious one, and the "you" to whom this entry is directed is at least in part himself. He was no stranger to feelings of melancholy, even despair. Just two months later he would write, "we do not wonder that so many commit suicide, life is so barren and worthless; we only live on by an effort of the will" (12/27/1857, Journal Transcript 25:25). Part of this "effort of the will" was, for Thoreau, continual reengagement with the annual phenomena of the seasons, in which "winter & death are ignored—the circle of life is complete."

General Phenomena for November

'50   '51   '52   '53   '54   '55   '56   '57   '58   '59   '60   '61

River Lowest

River

Rain in Forth half

Rain in last half

Drizzling & mist rain

N E storm

Thunder & lightning

Rainbow

Still cloudy days

Trial in Am, pleasant in Pm

Fog in morning

1st wreck line

1st really cold & wintry weather

Cold day

Cold day last half

Cold gray days

| 50 | 51 | 52 | 53 | 54 | 55 | 56 | 57 | 58 | 59 | 60 | 61 |
|---|---|---|---|---|---|---|---|---|---|---|---|
| Walks in Snow | | | | | 18ˢᵗ make stubble morning above snow | 30 walks in | | 29ᵗ 8.14 ☾ | | | 22 red cliff N.E. N.E. for sunset |
| 1st tracks | 23ˢ frozen & days before 1ˢᵗ nov | | | | 18 | 30" | | 14 & 29 ☾ | | 24 | 29 |
| Winter coming in | 13 & 1 whit... | winter coming in | Dec 4 | Dec Dec 4ᵗ | after that Dec 5 | Dec Nov 30 | | 14" ☾ ... | Dec cold | 25 snow for winter | |
| Get in boats | Dec 28... | | Dec 2ᵈ | | 30" | | | 26 make up fence | Dec 10 | 29 | 5 clean & pleas... 13 fine day... |
| Fine days... | 1ˢᵗ bright clear, warm day | 1ˢᵗ Pleas & hot blue | | | 9 clear & warm | 16 very warm after rain in night | 26 Pleasant & v. warm 46 at 90 | 8ᵗ a pleasant day | | | |
| Fine days... | 25 again day | 29-30-8 Dec | 20 "A warm day | 28 very clear & | | | 22 quite pleasant | 30 & Dec | | 22 | |
| Bright but cool day... | | | 8ᵗ fine autumn day | 28 31" above | | | 9 warm & cloudy | | | | |
| Nights in last half... | nov 11 but mild | Pleas 20 & 22 Oct 28 | 23 fine week so mild | | | Oct 21 ... clean | 9" | | | | |
| After glow (warm) | 25 Pleas & calm | 24" warm - 7 years | 24 clear & warm | | | | | | | 21 short at sunset | |
| After glow cold (9 years) | 22 frozen | 22 cold & windy | 30 strong cold wind | | 23 strong & warm SW | 14 cold & windy wind NW | 11 windy & cooler | | | 2" Nov cold night cloudy | |
| Windy weather | 30 warm cold & windy | cold & very windy 15 - before snow | | | 25 cold NW wind | 14" probable | | 25 last night & oday very cold & blustering | | | |
| Rain cloudy day | | 9" high in night | | 19 th cold & blustering 20 " sparkling blustering | 24 cold & blustering | & hail & blustering wind our last | | | | | |
| Wind shakes house | | | | | 20 in night | | | 25 last night | | | |
| ... | 8 cold... | | | | | 13" | | | | | |
| Thin Yellow sunlight | | | | | 18 very calm at noon sun | 25 Pale yel. light g... | | | | Oct 19... winter | |
| Cold... | 30" | | | | | Oct 22 - hits ... | 22 | | | | |
| Sparkling windows at sunset | | | | | 4ᵗ for fine fires | 17 13" | | 2 gulls Z Z Z Y | | | |

MA 610

| | 54 | 55 | 56 | 57 | 58 | 59 | 60 | 61 |
|---|---|---|---|---|---|---|---|---|
| Too cold to ... | | 27 | | | 18 rejoice in | 11 seek a warm place | 25 | 19° |
| Make sheltered place | 5° deg. to be | | | | | 12" | | |
| Much interesting warm | | | | | | | | |
| End of sauntering walks | | | | | | 1st... | | |
| Northern lights | | | | | | | 4 with ... | |
| Ice during day | 16 ... | ... | 9 ... | 15 ... | 11 ... | 25 ... | 19 ... | |
| Ice 6 inches thick | 23 ... | 14 ... | 6... | 25 ... | 26 ... | | | |
| Pools in woods bear | | | | | | | | |
| F.H. Pond skimmed over | 21 ... 23 ... | Dec 9 | ... Dec 8 | ... | 18 ... | Dec 9 | 29 ... | 19½ ... |
| River skimmed over | 21 ... | | 30 ... | Dec 6 ... | 30 ... | | | 22 ... |
| Frost about cisterns | 13 Dec ... | 17 abundant 25 | | 5° ... | 11" ... | | | Dec 8 |
| Ground frozen | | 6 ... | | Below 15 | 17 ... | | | 13·14 ... |
| Ground thaws in ... | Nov 7... | | | 15 ... ± 23 | | | | 13 North ... |
| Frozen ground covered & freed | 12" at night | | | | 12" | | | 14 warm ... |
| Feather frost about holes | | 15 a little 25 | | 15 ... | 11" ... | | | |
| Frozen window | | 25 | Dec 14° heavy | 27 ... | | | 25 ... | |
| Skating | | 2 ... | | | | | 26 ... | |
| Long white ... twilight | | 2 | | | | | | |
| | 13 ... | | | | | | | |
| | | 25 ... | | | | | | |
| Snow | 26 ... Nov 1st | Feb 15 ... | 1 ... | 15 1st ... | 2 Nov | 20 a slight flurry | 13 1st ... | 24 1st ... 16 ... 3 ... |
| Winter sun after ... snow | a 10" ... | 23 ... | | 17 ... | 2 Nov | 15 ... | 22 ... | Dec 4 |
| Deeper snow | Dec 26 ... | Dec 30 ... | Dec 30 ... | 29 ... | Dec 22 ... | 28 ... 30 ... | Dec 4 ... | 25 ... |

## General Phenomena for November

| | For order see pencil sheet within | | | lowest say 30 | say 1st lowest | say lowest 1st |
|---|---|---|---|---|---|---|
| | 50 | 51 | 52 | 53 at heights Oct 31 | 54 | 55 |
| 6+ | | Nov 9 fallen more than 1 foot since last observed.<br><br>**River Lowest**<br><br>say 10th | | 5 recent flood gone down in a great measure<br>14 risen surprisingly to spring height owing to rain of 13th - higher than before since spring - 15 still higher so I cross Hubbard with ease - 16 still higher | 2 begins to rise - 10 still at Sum. Level 13 at last decidedly rising on ac. of rain of 11-12-13 - 14 sightly over meads - 16 almost all cabins covered - but R. not nearly as high as last year - | 4 though ap. risen consid. is not more than 9 or 10 in above "Lowest S.L." 7 risen a little more at Assabet esp. & much up other 14 rain has raised R. an additional foot or more - its creeping over the weeds - |
| 5<br>14+ | | Nov 1 raised at least 2 feet (?) by rain in night of Oct 30-the mass of stems of but-bush submerged & - Nov 2 musquash cabins<br><br>**River Highest**<br><br>mostly covered 21 rained hard & so R. raised much higher than it has been this fall | | paddle from Boat to I. straight—19 Ap. at same level<br>20 begins to fall unchecked by rain of 21 - 23 going down but still far over meads<br>25 meads rapidly becoming bare<br><br>highest say 18th | 28 not so high as 16th - 30 slightly over meads<br>highest 16th | 15 rising<br><br>Highest say 15th or later perhaps 2 ft. above S.L. |
| 11<br>9 | | 15 rainy day keeps in house<br><br>**Rain in first half** | ^ | 12 4 pm clears off<br>8-9 rain in night & hard rain in Pm 9th<br>13 rain all day | 11th 12 & 13th hard | 12-13 heavy rain in night |
| 22 | | 21st rained hard<br><br>**Rain in last half** | | 18 a drizzling day | | x |
| 17 | 26-8-9 - 50<br><br>**Drizzling & misty rain** | | 1st warm mizzling rain today & 2 days past | 18 a drizzling day 21 a fine mizzling day all night & to-day 24 drizzling forenoon | | 6 mizzling rain drives me home - a great many mizzling days the last fortnight yet little rain. 7 another mizzling day as fine as mist can fall |
| 18 | | **NE storm** | | | | |
| 22<br>25 | | **Thunder & lightning** | | | | |
| 4+ or 9 | | **Rainbow** | ^ | 12 Pm a very bright rainbow | | |
| 3 & 4 | | 3 - 50 a cloudy still moist Pm<br>**Still cloudy days** | | 3rd rather cloudy Pm | | 4 dark almost rainy day 7 still, dark, mizzling thoughtful Pm |

| very pleasant Nov. was in Perth Amboy 56 | 57 | 58 | 59 lowest 6 (or later) | 60 Lowest say 1st | 61 Lowest say 1st |
|---|---|---|---|---|---|
| | 2nd falling fast - push direct over Lee's mead prob. for the last time - scraping the ground | 22 quite low - almost as low as it has been - for it has not been very low. lowest prob 1st | 6 quite low - 3¼ in below S.L. - lower than before this year — 24 risen consid. at last owing to rain of 22 - had been very low before | 10 & 11 raining raising R consid. onto meadow 14 2 ft 4 in above S.L. accordingly & at height 30 rain raising R. some what | 5 raised 8 ⅛ inch above S.L. by rain of 2-3 nights 14 2½ in above S.L. 17 about 1¼ in below S.L. |
| | prob 1st highest | 5 rises some on ac. of rain of 4th & Oct 30th-so lowest the 30th | Highest say 24 | Highest say 14th | 20 almost 1½ in. below S.L. Highest 5th 28th 2 Pm 2¼ above S.L. |
| | 9 rainy in am 13 some rain in night | 4th a rainy day 6 another " " & nights much fair weather last 3 months | 10 warm rain | 3 more or less rainy 6 a shower in Pm 10 & 11 rainy | 2 fine rain in pm 9th all day consid. 11 rain |
| | 17 last night 23 evening & night, heavy | | 22 after snow | 30 rain | 23 Pm a mizzling rain with a very little fine hail - in night becomes a NE rain storm ([this section unclear] |
| | | 24 dark & drizzling still with a little snow falling | | | 2nd fine rain in Pm |
| | | 23 with sugarings of snow | | | 3rd last night till noon to day - & [unclear] wreck 23 (v above) |
| | 23rd after warm S.W. wind | | | | |
| | | | | | |
| | 1st cloudy pm after clear morning. | 5 a still cloudy day 28 a gray overcast still day. | | | |

| | | | | | |
|---|---|---|---|---|---|
| 23 | rain & clears up cold at night<br>**Foul in <u>Am</u>, pleasant in <u>Pm</u>** | | 24th but very cold | | 11 warm & pleasant <u>Pm</u><br>14 clear bright warm <u>Pm</u> |
| 13<br><s>12</s> | **Fog in morning** | | | | 8 quite warm & foggy morn-<br>ing - 13 misty morn |
| <s>9</s> 6<br>14 | **1st wreck line** | | 5 river wreck<br>7 notice a wreck | 14 1st observable | |
| 14<br>15<br>or 13? | 19 - 50 1st really      perhaps 11th<br>cold day<br>**1st really cold & wintery weather** | 16 colder weather | 11 ice on River bank<br>5 or 6 rods wide[unclear] | 6 dif to drive<br>stake in frozen ground | 20 a cold day |
| 10 | 11 - 51 bright but<br>cold day<br><br>**Cold day 1st half**<br><br>13 cold & dark <u>Pm</u> | | 7 shallow pools in woods<br>skimmed over<br>clear cold frosty morning | 6 sudden cold-<br>pools bear. | |
| <s>26</s><br>28 & 29 | 19th - 50    22nd cool/ <u>Pm</u><br><br>**Cold day last half**<br><br>23-50 finger cold during<br>day 28-50 gloves com-<br>fortable a day or 2 past | ^ | 16 colder weather<br>21 river skimmed over<br>23 F. H. P. "   "<br>24 wintry freezing cold<br>in <u>Pm</u><br>mild swell early 25 cold<br>          27 - 28 | | 20 a cold day<br>24 last 3 or 4 days<br>quite cold sidewalks a<br>    glare of ice<br>30 river skimmed over |
| <s>17</s> 16 | Perhaps 13th <u>Pm</u><br>**Cool gray days** | ^ | 18 cold gray days | 17 raw cloudy<br><u>Pm</u> | 17 chilly <u>Pm</u> with<br>cold gray clouds<br>19 cold gray day |

| | | 50 | 51 | 52 | 53 | 54 | —55 |
|---|---|---|---|---|---|---|---|
| | | | | **General Phenomena for November** | | | |
| 1<br>21<br><s>22</s> | **Walk in Snow** | | | | | | 18th 1st mark stubble &c.<br>rising above snow |
| 2<br>21 | **1st Tracks** | | | 23rd sportsmen & dogs<br>improve 1st snow | | | 18 |
| v. Dec— | finally set in say | 13 C.I think of going<br>into [unclear]<br><br>**Winter setting in**<br><br>Dec. 6 - 50 | winter may be<br>said to have beg.<br>12th of Dec. | Perhaps about Dec 12th<br>(if not. 5th ) | say Dec 4th | ap. about Dec. 13th |
| <s>v Dec</s><br>Dec 3 | **Get in Boat** | | Dec. 28 from<br>Walden | 5th Dec. | Dec. 2nd | 30th<br>8- warm & foggy morn +<br>open window |
| 7 | .    1st bright clear, warm day<br>**Fine days, not Ind. Sum. in 1st half**<br>7 cold morn. bright<br>& pleasant day<br>(go to Chituate) | | | 1st pleasant but breezy<br>1st & 2nd fine days<br>3rd warm westerly wind<br>15 some hazy Ind. Sum like<br>but rather windy | | 9 clear & beautiful<br>day after a hard frost<br>11 warm & pleasant pm<br>while sun shines<br>13 first clear pm after<br>mist & rain Nov. pleasant<br>        thus far |

| | | | | | |
|---|---|---|---|---|---|
| | | | | 2 as several days past cloudy & misty in morning & fairer warmer, if not Pm Ind. sum. in Pm | 22nd cloudy Am Pm all in after-glow |
| | | | 17 & 18 till almost noon | | 6 touch of Ind. sum in Pm |
| | | | | | |
| | 14 very much colder than before - hands stiff - then 27° at 6 Pm | 12th much the coldest day yet | | 20th & 21st cold | 16 colder |
| | 15 pools in woods skimmed over | 3rd colder<br>11 a cold day<br>12 much the coldest day yet | | | |
| | 24- & 25 cold Thanks-giving weather | 14 very cold<br><br>16 cold & blustering Pm<br>18 F. H. P. completely frozen<br>during last 4 days<br>29 river froze | | cold 20th & 21st<br>25 very cold | |
| | | 2 a cool gray day | | | 16<br>21 |

| 56 | 57 | 58 | 59<br>a very pleasant Nov. | 60 | (22 - wind chiefly N & NE for several weeks)<br>61 |
|---|---|---|---|---|---|
| 30 walk in | | 29th & 14 (?) | | | 25 |
| 30th | | 14 & 29<br>2<br>v.8th | | 24 | 25 |
| say Nov. 30th | | ^14th(?) genial Nature sealed up leaves you outside<br>29th a winter landscape & phenomenon - a clear pleasant winter day-v 30 | say Dec. 4 | 25 now for winter | |
| Dec. 2 | | 26 on ac. of fence | Dec.10 | 29th | |
| | 6 very warm after rain in night - wind SW Therm. 70 afternoon Ind. summer & 7th<br>8th warm cloudy morning | 10 Pleasant, esp. am 46+ at Pm | 8th a pleasant day | | 5 clear & pleasant with W. wind<br>13 fine day but cool |

| | | | | | |
|---|---|---|---|---|---|
| 26<br>25 | 25 - a fine day<br><br>**Fine days, not Ind. Sum. in last half** | 29 - 30- & Dec 1st mildest & pleasantest days since Nov. came in. 27 almost Ind. summer | 20th a warm day | 28 very clear & bright as well as comfortable weather | 14 clear bright warm Pm 16 Minott calls last fortnight good weather to complete harvest |
| 26<br>26 or 27<br>25' | **Bright but cool day to walk** | | 11th fine calm frosty morning-cold    ? | 28 (?) v above | |
| 26 | **Nights, in last half, without freezing** | | 23 for week or more past no freezing days or nights, Ends 24th | | |
| 2'<br>25' | Nov. 11 Nut mead.<br><br>**After-Glow (warm)** | Perhaps Oct 22 Oct 28 | | | |
| | **Pleasant calm Spring-like morning** | | 23rd by 8 am—pleasant calm spring-like morn. | | |
| 25<br>27 | 22nd of year<br><br>**After glow cold (of year)** | 29th warm - of year | 24 clear yellow sunsets & after glow this month as to-night 29 a Nov. Russet one clear yel. light after clouds | | |
| 15 | 22 cold & windy Pm<br><br>**Windy weather.**<br>30 rather cold & windy Pm & some snow still | | at sunset<br>6 windy Pm<br>14 clear—with strong NW wind drying the earth.<br>25 clear cold windy | 30 strong cold wind | |
| 19<br>17 | 4th truly so<br><br>**Raw & Gusty day** | cold & very windy 16 - but no snow | | | 19th cold & blustering 20th exceedingly blustering |
| 19'<br>18 | **Wind shakes house** | | 9th high in night ( with rain) still stronger & gustier but warmer S.W. by day | | |
| 4<br>10 | 8 stillness of woods & fields remarkable<br>**Stillness which precedes winter** | | | | |
| 21<br>20 | **Thin yellow sunlight** | | | | |
| 20 | 7th on Dudley Pond<br>**Sparkle on Ponds [unclear] (to Oct)** | | | | |
| 8 | 11th of 51<br>**Cool silvery light in white pines** | | | | |
| 14th<br>16 | **Sparkling windows at sunset** | 30th | | | |
| | & 15 - 58<br>**Reflection of boat on bank**<br>v Oct    (v. Oct ) | | | 2 | |

| | | | | | |
|---|---|---|---|---|---|
| | 9 warm but raining<br>28 - & 29th remarkably warm days<br>30 warm but cloudy | 22 quite pleasant day but hardly Ind. sum | 30 & Dec 1st & 2nd remarkably warm & spring like days - a moist warmth | | |
| | | | | 22 beautiful day - cool but crystalline air | |
| | | | | | |
| | Oct 21<br>Oct 28 bright gleam before sunset after long storm | 9th | | | |
| | | | | | 21 start at sunset |
| | 23 strong & warm SW | 14 cold & windy - wind NW | 11th windy & cooler | | 2nd Pm cold windy & cloudy |
| | 25 cold NW wind Pm<br>24 cold & blustering | 14th probably<br>16 cold & blustering - mostly overcast Pm | | 25 last night & today very cold & blustering | |
| | 20 in night | | | 25 last night | |
| | | 13th | | | |
| | 18 & no red in it—<br>Novemberish | 25 pale yel. light of Sun | | | |
| | ~~Oct 14 Walden~~ | ~~Oct 20 White Pond~~ | | | ~~Oct 17 Walden~~ |
| | | Oct 25 - 58 | | 22 | |
| | 4th from Pine Hill | 17<br>13th | | | |
| | | | | | |

| | 51 / 50 | 52 | 53 | 54 | 55 |
|---|---|---|---|---|---|
| say 28 / v. ~~Dec~~ | 28 gloves com[50]fortable. 51 / a day or 2 past / **Wear gloves** / 23 finger cold during day | not yet, though it has been finger cold 23rd | 11th wear mittens / 7 clear cold frosty morn. hands in pockets | | Dec 8 no gloves yet. — / 1st time 11 but have not walked early / 20 as usual no gloves |
| ~~27~~ 28 | Beg. to think of outside coat & boots / 28th **Too cold to Paddle** | | 27 | | |
| | ~~or in Oct~~ commonly / **Seek sheltered places** ^ | | | | |
| 10 | **Sunset interestingly warm** | 3rd beg. to be | | | |
| 14th | **End of sauntering walks** | | | | |
| | ~~Wooding up v. Oct~~ | | | | ~~1st 6th – & 9th~~ |
| 10 (?) | **Northern Lights** | | | | |
| 14? | Throw stones on ice at Hey-? / Wood's mead / [unclear] 7th / **Ice during day** | 16 by edges of river which does not melt | 8th 7th shallow pools in woods skimmed over this am / 7 a very little ice by river still at eve -11 in river bays 5 or 6 rods wide at 9am | | 9th a little on my boat seat, / 26 ice next to shore bore me & my boat / 27 a little along shore most of day |
| put with next ~~19~~ | 23 by brooks 1 inch thick in pm / 8th 1 in. thick at 4 Pm under N side of woods / **Ice 1 inch thick** | | | | v above 26 |
| ~~19th~~ | 23 walk across pond of an acre in woods / 14th Haywood's little pond thinly / **Pools in woods bear** | | | 6th | |
| v Dec. 28 | 25th skimmed over (1st) / **F. H. Pond ^ skimmed over** / open Dec. 2nd | 21 1/3 skimmed over 23rd entirely | Dec 4th | Before Dec. 8(?) | Dec 21 prob some days |
| v Dec. 23 24? | 13 Dec 1st / **River ^ skimmed over** / 16 prob open again | 21 in some places this Pm | Dec. 2 still no ice except in morn. by sides - Dec. 5 thinly in most places frozen over | Dec 5 prob. in some places / Dec. 8 in many places / Dec.14 Assabet mostly open | 30 for all day behind Dodds' / Dec 20 greater part open |
| say 7th | **Frost about cistus** | 13 Dec. 52 | 7 abundant 25 | 19 closed almost every-where | 5th has been prob. |
| 10th | **Ground frozen** | | | 6 frozen ground dif. to force a stake down | |
| 11th | Nov 7th first observe it / **Ground thaws in sun** | | | | |
| 11th | 12th at night / **Frozen ground resounds to tread** / morn & eve | | | | |
| 11th | **Feather frost about holes** | | 11th a little 25 | | |
| ~~26~~ 28 | **Frost on window** | | 25 | | Dec 14 heavy |

| 56 | 57 | 58 | 59 | 60 | 61 |
|---|---|---|---|---|---|
| Buy boots Dec. 3rd on ac. of                snow | | Oct 26. shops hang out gloves | put on boots Dec 5 | 20 & 21 decidedly finger cold tonight<br>25 need mittens<br>& great coat | 40<br>1<br>≤ |
| | | | 25 | | |
| | 18 rejoice in | 11 seek a warm place | | | 19th |
| | | | | | |
| | | 12th | | | |
| | | 1st Goodwin still | | | |
| | | | | 4 with some redness above - weather being cooler | |
| | 15 in woods N side hills - skimmed ¼ inch thick | 11 a pool in woods skimmed over in Pm<br>12 river side skimmed in Pm | 25 thin ice along shore in Pm | 22. consid. lasts all day on river meadows & cold pools | 19th a rod wide by river in a sheltered place perhaps on 16 61 |
| | | | | | |
| | 25 shows nearly 1½ inch thick | 26 Pout's Nest just bears | | | |
| some formed on Dec 6 must have been frozen 4th at least | | 18 completely during last 4 days - 24 still | Dec. 9th | 29 all but the channel | 19 ½ skimmed over - Dec 3rd skimmed over |
| Dec. 4 open with long white strips of ice each side<br>Dec. 5 well skimmed over in most<br>6 generally frozen | places | 30 froze generally last night<br>say 18 | Dec. 9th generally last night | prob. 29th or 25 | 22nd at eastward shore —<br><br><br>as for river on Hub. |
| 13 gen. open again | | 11th not melted in Pm | | | bridge Dec. 3rd |
| | Before 15th | 17 has remained frozen since morn. of 12th | | | 13-14 &c |
| | 15 in Pm & 23rd | | | | 13 N side walls |
| | | 12th | | | 14 morn & eve for a few days past |
| | 15 asbestos like in earth | 11th many ice crystals heaved up<br>13th | | | 3rd |
| | 27 beautiful | | | 25 handsome as ever | Dec 14 handsome |

| | | | | | | |
|---|---|---|---|---|---|---|
| v Dec. say 8 or 9 | of Dec. **Skating** | 14 - 51 boys been skating a week | Dec 18 - . Loring's Pond | 28 in Cambridge Dec. 22 10 days old | Dec 6 on way to Providence- frozen prob. 5th | Dec 15 boys 2 or 3 days past - not borne a man yet Dec. 20 pretty good skating |
| v Oct. | **Long White Aut. Twilight** | | | 2 | | |
| 14th | still more **Mts ^distinct (v. Oct)** | 13 very dark blue | | 25 very distinct | | |
| 6 | 19 heard of in neighbor **Snow on mts. (v. Oct)** hood | Nov. 13 - 51 | | | Oct 19 sugared with 1st above Littleton | at eve |
| 12 | Nov 26 inch this morn the 1st **1st snow** | Oct 27 - 51 1st snowing this morn at end of rain | Oct 15 1st snow - a whitening about half an hour then rain | 10 Am 8th Nov. very fine white mist toward wood - by 2 has not whitened ground- only sugared plowed ground at eve turns to rain | 15 1st sugaring | 17 ^ about an inch [unclear] clears up at noon 18- not gone 24 |
| say perhaps 19-24 21 | ,10th whitened once more **Whitening after 1st snow** but will soon be gone 13 see it on Peterboro hills | | 23 whitens ground for a day or 2 | Dec. 5 1st whitening | | Dec 9 & turns to rain |
| v. Dec say Dec 11th or 12th | 25 deeper than before lies still on 30th **Deeper snow** Dec 15 half a foot | | | Dec. 26 - 3 inches 1st of any consequence | Dec 3rd 5 or 6 inch | Dec 30 1 foot much deepest yet |

| 15² 17 | 50 **Willow osier bright** Dec 29- 51 | 52 | 53 | 54 | 55 |
|---|---|---|---|---|---|
| | | | | 14 as in spring | Dec 3rd Shattuck's |
| 8th | 9 a. scoparius **November Lights** (v oct) | | | | |
| | **Twigs like cobwebs** (v oct) | | | | |
| 10² | ^ **Mazes - birch &c &c** | | | | |
| | **Gossamer** (v 15-58 (v oct) | | 19 but not as perfect as 31st Oct. Ind Sum. Rm ? | | 7 much & some 13 after rain |
| v. Dec. | **Notice colored twigs** or above snow? | | | | Dec. 14 |
| 8³ | **Water blue as indigo** | | 14th | | |
| 15² | **Colors of Andromeda in dif lights** | | | | |
| 5 [unclear] | 1st p. pines do skunk cab. bud (v oct) **Notice buds** Oct. 12-51 beg. to notice swamp pink | Dec. 1 alder, birch catkins &c. Oct. 19- Skunk cab. Nov 2. high blueberry | Oct. 23 high blueberry Oct. 26 leaves chiefly off notice buds | Bass buds &cc 15 | Dec. 11 in Holden swamp |

| | | | | | |
|---|---|---|---|---|---|
| Dec. 6 fairly begun | Dec. 13 Goose Pond | | | 26 some boys skated on Goose P. | |
| | 4 & decided purple at eve on Pine Hill | | | | |
| | | 8 2 or 3 inch in Bangor yesterday morn. 7 [unclear] white | Oct 20 snow fell in N.H. | | 9th in Maine |
| in Nov. (Nov. 5 in Amboy- flakes in air) | 20 a slight flurry | 13 1st sugaring 9 Pm not gone 14th | 12 a short time - whitening ground in spots | 24 1st spitting - a flurry - perhaps $1/8$ in. or less in diameter | 16 2 or 3 [unclear] no whitening. wind NW |
| Nov. 29 | Dec. 16 | 15 a very fine snow 16 ground still greyed with it 23 occasional sugarings in a NE storm - 24 little falling | 22 white a few hours | Dec 4 | Nov 25 |
| 29 all day with a little hail - several inches deep - or Dec 24 - 9 or 10 inch deep | Dec. 26 1st of consequence 3 or 4 inch deep | 28 [unclear] a reg. snow storm 3 inch in eve 30 saw it snow for 20 mil. off | Dec 4 2 or 3 inch Dec 20 3 or 4 inch | Dec 4 - 4 or 5 inch | 25 from NE -night say 5 inches- after rain & fully all day of 25 until sunset. |

| 56 | 57 | 58 | 59 | 60 | 61 |
|---|---|---|---|---|---|
| | | 18th | (Oct. 16th | | 19 ? red        scop |
| | Dec. 6 - sweet fern | 10 on hazel 14 sweet fern 15 & 17th & say 1st half Nov. | ^8a. scoparius^ fair as ever- also 15th ? Oct. 16 some bare twigs and some weeds beg. to glitter with hoary light | A. Scop. silvery Sep 30 | Oct. 30 A. [unclear] bright |
| was 28 - (^at Amboy before) 3rd birch twig | | Oct. 25. birch twigs at sunset began with an alder 8 many mazes 15th & esp 17th | Oct. | | |
| | | | | 1st a good deal | 22 some |
| in blueberry Dec. 13 - growth of young birches | | 12 in marsh | | | |
| | | | | 4 river | |
| | | 14 | 17 | | |
| 8 swamp pink & clethra Dec. 6 & 21st | Oct. 31 skunk cab. | say 1st half Nov. after Oct. 22nd of S. discolor | Oct 18 of S. discolor Dec 31 sweet gale | Oct 24 S. discolor | |

| | | | | | |
|---|---|---|---|---|---|
| 12[1] | **Willow & alder buds at last** | 30 Early tremblers & early willows | | | |
| | Oct 16-51 shadbush nearly leafing **Shadbush &c &c leaf** | | 1st & 6th shadbush | 4th shadbush (Sep. 19th hardhack puts forth new leaves) | 5th checked by frost Oct. 22 - shadbush leafing again. |
| 8th | **Observe Rad. leaves** | | 3rd of many plants - primrose - thistle & frag. everlasting 14th winter rye the most conspic. | | Dec. 23rd at Lee's Cliff 9th |
| 2 [unclear] | 19th-50 evergreens   22-cress **Notice evergreen ferns &c &c** perhaps v back – to winter rye green in Oct. | | 3rd ev. trees more distinct. 15 ev. ferns - Dec 7 latter part Nov. & now before snow attracted by small evergreens | | Oct. 22 rad. shoots of lechea more conspic. Oct 28 polypody more conspic. |
| 10[3] | **Sap flows in Scar. Oak** | | | | |
| v Dec. | Dec 31-51 **A Lichen day** | | | | |
| 3rd | **Woodchoppers' axe** | | 3rd | | |
| 1st | 13th think of going into **Short Pm** Contemplate going into winter quarters. | | | | |

| | | | | |
|---|---|---|---|---|
| 4 <u>not</u> swollen yet | ^ | 18 willow peeps ¹/₄ inch | Oct 18 - peeps from the S. discolor bud | |
| 8<sup>th</sup> swamp-pyrus also clethra decidedly ex-panded showing leaflets | ^ | 25 some high blueberry buds fairly started - into red leaves (V Oct. 13-59) | Oct 13 - shadbush swamp one | |
| | | 8<br>Oct 28 - beg. notice ev. ferns<br>Sep 18 young w. pines green | | |
| | Oct 13 green begs to be a rare & interesting color | 5 Glyceria fluitans more noticeable.<br>8 broom distinct<br>(v. 17 & 18-58)<br>in list<br>oct 6 evergreens greener | Ev. ferns grow more distinct after Sep 16<br>Oct 12 very few ferns but ev. ones left | |
| | | oct 18 wintergreen [unclear]<br>10 | | |
| | | 24 | Dec 6 somewhat<br>Dec 18<sup>th</sup> | |
| | | | | |
| | | 1<sup>st</sup> at almshouse<br>v8<sup>th</sup> | | |
| | | | | |

All Phenomena for December. Henry David Thoreau Collection.
Yale Collection of American Literature, Beinecke Rare Book & Manuscript Library.

DECEMBER:

# *Green in Winter*

---

"ALL THE NEW THINKING IS ABOUT LOSS," ROBERT HASS WRITES
in his poem "Meditation at Lagunitas." "In this it resembles all the old thinking." In December we rise in darkness and return in darkness, feeling our
way from grief to grief. Mid-month I haul out the box of lights, a heavy-duty
extension cord, and two tires from the garage. The yard is pitched too steep
for a ladder, so I stack the tires against the ancient and moss-covered birch
in front of the house and balance with a foot on each side to wrap the lights
around the tree. It's an amateur job—the extension cord visible along the
ground, a few dull bulbs skewing the pattern, the lines uneven—but this is a
tolerant neighborhood. The stove groans and clanks and keeps its little fire lit.

It is the month of my best friend's suicide, and though I can't imagine
ever not knowing the date, I have started having to count the years. Loss is
like that. We pull our chairs closer to the fire.

There is no snow this December, only days of ceaseless rain, which floods
the riverbanks and closes the roads and takes out the power all over town. The
kids miss a week of school. Line workers come from Canada and New Jersey
and Vermont and sleep in rows of cots in the college gym. People stand in
their ruined yards and talk, loan out generators and invite each other over for
hot showers and charging in the old rural ritual of human solidarity against
the elements. When the power comes back, neighborhood by neighborhood,
the lights lining trees and doorways and eaves of houses turn on again, like
little green shoots, I think, coming up out of the dirt.

✳

In December of 1861, Thoreau suffered an attack of pleurisy, which further
limited his mobility. Another loss came with the death of George Minott,

about whom he'd written, "Minott is perhaps the most poetical farmer–who most realizes to me the poetry of the farmer's life–that I know. He does nothing (with haste and drudgery–) but as if he loved it" (10/4/1851, *Journal* 4:116). It is unclear why, in this season of losses, Thoreau altered his habit of drawing up charts of general phenomena for each month, instead choosing to title the December charts "*All* Phenomena for December," but one senses in this gesture a final pull toward the whole living earth, an impulse toward that repleteness that for him signaled life. This sense of the intricate abundance of the natural world was for Thoreau the opposite pole of the feeling of barrenness, a common December phenomenon. In 1858 he'd recorded in his Journal "The ground is still for the most part bare. Such a December is at least as hard a month to get thro' as November– You come near eating your heart now–" (12/25/1858, Journal Transcript 28:94). In the long winter of 1861, he makes "Walker eats his heart" a regular category for the December chart. In 1857, he'd written,

> In sickness & barrenness–it is encouraging to believe that our life is dammed & is coming to a head so that there seems to be no loss–for what is lost in time is gained in power– All at once unaccountably, as we are walking in the woods–or sitting in our chamber–after a worthless fortnight–we cease to feel mean & barren. (12/13/1857, Journal Transcript 25:19)

In the sickness and barrenness of December of 1861, Thoreau could not wait for his life to come to a head, but sought his own fullness and power in a final, newly expansive set of charts. The December charts detail not only weather patterns and atmospheric phenomena but also woodpeckers, snow buntings, grosbeaks, geese, tree sparrows, owls, golden-crested wrens, bullfrogs and trout.

If, as I have suggested, the charts Thoreau drew up in 1861 functioned as a way for him to experience the season, the December he sought to experience was one full of living creatures. The pendulum swing between barrenness and abundance is apparent throughout Thoreau's December Journal entries, and attention to these entries can attune us to the role played by desire in Thoreau's habits of observation. Typically in these entries, an absence calls forth a presence: the very bareness of the landscape provokes a desire in the walker, who then trains his observant eye, or the eye of memory, on the subtle signs of life beneath or behind the apparent stillness and emptiness of the natural world. On December 8, 1855, he writes, "This P. M. I go to the woods down the RR–seeking the Society of Some flock of little birds, or some squirrel–but in vain. . . . Let a snow come & clothe the ground & trees & I shall see the tracks of many inhabitants now unsuspected & the very snow covering up the withered leaves will supply the place of the green ones which are gone" (12/8/1855, Journal Transcript 19:205). An entry written a few days later follows the same pattern:

> I see no birds–but hear methinks 1 or 2 tree sparrows. . . . .
>
> Standing there though in this *bare* . . . landscape–I am reminded of the incredible phenomenon–of small birds in winter. That ere long amid the cold powdery snow–as it were a fruit of the season will come twittering a flock of delicate crimson-tinged birds (lesser red-polls) to sport & feed on the seeds & buds now just ripe for them on the sunny side of a wood–shaking down the powdery snow there in their cheerful social feeding–as if it were high mid summer–to them. (12/11/1855, Journal Transcript 19:208–9)

In both cases, the absence of the birds calls forth their presence in his mind, reminds him of what he knows from past Decembers: that the woods, though seemingly desolate, are still full of life. Knowing that "a man receives only what he is ready to receive," that "we hear & apprehend only what we already half know," Thoreau, walking in the bare winter landscape actively anticipated what he hoped and believed he would receive: evidence of life's continuity through the dark months of the year (1/5/1860, Journal Transcript 30:230).

The December charts reflect this process on a larger scale: coming to terms with the mysterious ravishing of his body by disease, with physical weakness, limited mobility, and increasing dependence on others, Thoreau sought, as he always did in periods of barrenness, evidence of life going on. Fortunately, his Journal provided plenty: its pages were nearly as replete with creaturely life as the woods in which its contents had been painstakingly gathered.

As accounts of his friends and family attest, Thoreau knew he was dying, and seemed to give himself over to the experience of it, to live his dying as fully as he'd lived every other chapter of his life. Several of these accounts emphasize his patience and peace. In a letter to Daniel Ricketson shortly after Thoreau's death, Sophia wrote,

You asked for some particulars relating to Henry's illness. I feel like saying that Henry was never affected, never reached by it. I never before saw such a manifestation of the power of spirit over matter. Very often I heard him tell his visitors that he enjoyed existence as well as ever. He remarked to me that there was as much comfort in perfect disease as in perfect health, the mind always conforming to the condition of the body. The thought of death, he said, could not begin to trouble him. His thoughts had entertained him all his life, and did still.

An account by Ellery Channing, while corroborating Sophia's sense of Henry's acceptance of illness and death, also gives us a sense of its deep and alienating pain:

The wasting away of his body, the going forth & exit of his lungs, which, like a steady lamp, gave heat to the frame, was to Henry an inexplicably foreign event, the labors of another party in which he had no hand; though he still credited the fact to a lofty inspiration. He would often say that we could look on ourselves as a third person, and that he could perceive times that he was out of his mind. Words could no longer express these inexplicable conditions of his existence, this sickness which reminded him of nothing that went before: such as the dream he had of being a railroad cut, where they were digging through and laying down the rail,—the place being in his lungs.

If we believe both of these accounts, written by the two people closest to him in his final months, Thoreau stayed awake to the experience of living, *enjoyed* the experience of living, even as it became inexpressibly painful. "His thoughts had entertained him all his life," Sophia explains, "and did still." It seems likely that by the spring of 1862, Thoreau's embodied consciousness had come to hold the intricate sense of the seasons he'd spent so long recording. In the dream reported to Channing, Thoreau's body had become the land itself, cut open for the laying of railroad track. No doubt the first flowers of spring opened inside him too. The final charts of his monumental Kalendar speak to his faith that they would.

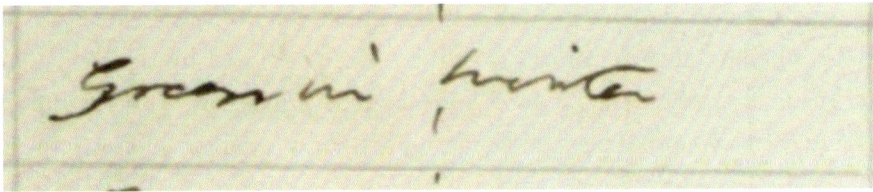

*Green in Winter*

In November & now before the snow I am attracted by the numerous small evergreens on the forest floor–now most conspicuous. –Especially the very beautiful Lycopodium dendroideum (somewhat cylindrical–& also *in this Grove* the var obscurum) of various forms surmounted by the effoete spikes–some with a spiral or screw-like arrangement of the fan like leaves–some spreading & drooping–  It is like looking down on evergreen trees– –  And the L. lucidulum of the swamps forming broad thick patches of a clear liquid-green–with its curving fingers–Also the pretty little fingers of the zigzagging cylindrical L. clavatum a clubmoss zigzagging amid the dry leaves not to mention the spreading openwork umbrellas of the L. complanatum or Flat club moss. all with spikes still  Also the liquid wet glossy leaves of the Chimaphila–(winter or snow-loving–)umbellata–with its dry fruit. Not to mention the still green-mitchella repens–& checquer berry in shelter both with fruit–goldthread–goldthread–P. secunda with drooping curled back leaves . . . (12/7/1853, *Journal* 7:193)

We pause & gaze into the Mill brook on the Turnpike bridge. C. says that in Persia they call the ripple marks on sandy bottoms chains or chain work–

I see a good deal of cress there– on the bottom for a rod or 2–the only green thing to be seen. No more slimy than it usually is beneath the water in summer– Is not this the plant which most, or most conspicuously preserves its greenness in the winter? Is it not now most completely in its summer state of any plant? So far as the water & the mud & the cress go– It is a summer scene. It is green as ever & waving in the stream as in summer. (12/22/1859, Journal Transcript 30:186–87)

In the December charts, Thoreau is especially concerned with color: In this month in 1855, he had written, "Particularly are we attracted in the winter by greenness and signs of growth– as the green & white shoots of grass & weeds pulled–or floating on the water–& also by color–as cockspur lichens & crimson birds–&c" (12/26/1855, Journal Transcript 19:233). These vibrant flashes, winged or rooted, stood out against the seeming blankness of the winter landscape to the expectant eye, training the observer's focus on signs of life. Thoreau was particularly fascinated by what he called "radical leaves," the new growth visible close to the stem or root of perennial plants in winter.

> At Lee's Cliff I notice these radical (?) leaves quite fresh–Saxifrage sorrel–polypody–mullein–columbine–veronica–Thyme-leaved sandwort–spleenwort–strawberry–buttercup–radical johnswort–mouse-ear–rad–pinweeds–cinquefoils–checkerberry–winter green–thistles–catnep–Turritis stricta especially fresh & bright–& what is that fine very minute plant thickly covering the ground–like a young arenaria? (12/23/1855, Journal Transcript 19:230)

One pictures him close to the ground, kneeling or even lying down to witness the new growth beneath dead outer leaves. In 1853, he comes close to the ecstatic mood of the famous thawing sandbank passage in *Walden* in describing the "curving fingers" and "spreading openwork umbrellas" of the evergreen undergrowth. In the "Spring" chapter of *Walden*, he'd described the way "innumerable little streams overlap and interlace one with another," on the thawing bank,

> exhibiting a sort of hybrid product, which obeys half way the law of currents, and half way that of vegetation. As it flows it takes the forms of sappy leaves or vines, making heaps of pulpy sprays a foot or more in depth, and resembling, as you look down on them, the laciniated, lobed, and imbricated thalluses of some lichens; or you are reminded of coral, of leopards' paws or birds' feet, of brains or lungs or bowels, and excrements of all kinds.

One can feel in this passage Thoreau's ecstatic participation in the abundant energy of spring, the way the continually metamorphosing pulse of life makes its way from the watery foliage of the sandbank through his body to the words on the page, whose materiality Thoreau points to later in the passage, remarking that "The radicals of lobe are *lb*, the soft mass of the *b* (single lobed, or B, double lobed,) with the liquid *l* behind it pressing it forward. In globe, *glb*, the guttural *g* adds to the meaning the capacity of the throat. The feathers and wings of birds are still drier and thinner leaves." Adding the very sounds our inner voice utters as we read to the dizzying number of connections he suggests in this passage, Thoreau pulls our present day reading into direct relation with the thawing bank, his writing hand, and the unfolding power of life that unites them. Strikingly, one feels a similar energy in the December passage, with its exuberant Latin and its "spreading," "drooping," and "zigzagging" forms, its stream of "alsos," "ands," and "not to mentions." This is Thoreau in ecstatic contact with the unfolding season. In December of 1861, he had reason to remind himself that he'd found such contact possible not only in the brilliant days of spring thaw, but also in the seeming barrenness of winter.

"Green in winter" also speaks to Thoreau's love of paradox. This affinity was not, as Emerson believed, a superficial verbal trick, but rather a fascination with the interpenetration and interdependence of opposites: in nature, as well as in language. The habit of reversing conventional perspective that allows Thoreau to imagine "fish[ing] in the sky, whose bottom is pebbly with stars," and to point out at the end of *Walden* that "the sun is but a morning star," also allows him to perceive the summer within winter, and more broadly, to experience time in its full complexity, the past still alive in the unfolding of the present moment. In Thoreau's always evolving but never abandoned transcendentalism, time, like space, is discovered to contain both the near and the seemingly distant. At Walden Pond,

> both place and time were changed, and I dwelt nearer to those parts of the universe and to those eras in history which had most attracted me. Where I lived was as far off as many a region viewed nightly by astronomers. We are wont to imagine rare and delectable places in some remote and more celestial corner of the system, behind the constellation of Cassiopeia's Chair, far from noise and disturbance. I discovered that my house actually had its site in such a withdrawn, but forever new and unprofaned, part of the universe.

Just as the Walden experiment teaches Thoreau to be "expert in home-cosmography"—to perceive the cosmos in his neighborhood—the Kalendar enables him to perceive all seasons within his present moment. Connected to the perception of the losslessness of seasonal time developed in the wake of his brother John's death, Thoreau's understanding of the deep imbrication of past and present becomes a lasting consolation, affording him a vision in which "the age of miracles is each moment thus returned– Now it is wild apples–now river-reflections–now a flock of lesser red-polls. In winter too resides immortal youth–& perennial summer" (12/11/1855, Journal Transcript 19:211–12).

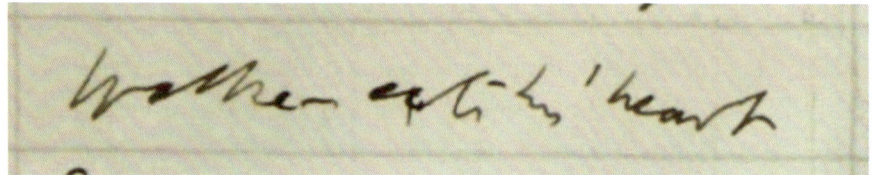

*Walker Eats His Heart*

It is pretty poor picking out of doors to day–there is but little comfort to be found– . . .

　When I returned from the south the other day–I was greeted by withered shrub oak leaves which I had not seen there– It was the most homely & agreeable object that met me. I found that I had no such friend as the shrub-oak hereabouts. A farmer once asked me what shrub oaks were made for–not knowing any use they served. But I can tell him that they do me good. They are my parish ministers regularly settled. (12/17/1856, Journal Transcript 22:145–46)

Pm up river on ice to FH. & across to Walden–

　The ground is still for the most part bare. Such a December is at least as hard a month to get thro' as November– You come near eating your heart now–. (12/25/1858, Journal Transcript 28:94)

Thoreau's Journal is sprinkled with references to eating his own heart. Mostly these occur in the month of November—he associates this expression with a bare landscape before it is covered in snow. In November of 1853, for example, he wrote, "Now a man will eat his heart if ever—now while the earth is bare barren & cheerless— and we have the coldness of winter without the variety of ices & snow" (11/27/1853, *Journal* 7:176).

　The phrase is conspicuous in its vivid, if metaphorical, evocation of self-harm, and it is an unusually strong emotional note for the Journal. Thoreau would have been familiar with the phrase—related to but distinct from the idiom "eat your heart out," used as a command, which suggests the raving jealousy of the addressee—as an expression of deep grief used frequently by Homer. "How long will you eat your heart out here in tears and torment?" the goddess Thetis asks her son Achilles in the *Iliad*, after the death of Patroclus. The expression signals a kind of unhealthy inwardness—a grief that turns away from the outside world, doubling in on and devouring the griever. It seems likely that these precise lines of the *Iliad* were the source of Thoreau's fondness for the expression: the lonely Achilles, withdrawn from his comrades and turned inward in grief, would have been a resonant figure for Thoreau in his most heartsick moods. This is the mood he associates with the November landscape:

> A cold & dark afternoon the sun being behind clouds in the west  The landscape is barren of objects– – the trees being leafless– & so little light in the sky for variety. Such a day as will almost oblige a man to eat his own heart. A day in which you must hold on to life by your teeth–  You can hardly ruck up any skin on nature's bones– The sap is down– she won't peel. Now is the time to cut timber for yokes & ox bows–leaving the tough bark on–yokes for your own neck. Finding yourself yoked to matter & to Time.
>
> Truly a hard day–hard Times these.  not a mosquito left  Not an insect to hum. Crickets gone into winter quarters– Friends long since gone there– & you left to walk on frozen ground–with your hands in your pockets. Ah but is not this a time for your deep inward fires? (11/13/1851, *Journal* 4:180–81)

The image of the yoke, which links Thoreau (who is both the speaking subject and the *you* of this passage) "to matter & to Time," signals the brutal triumph of linear time—with its law of continual loss and its ever-nearer end point—over the cyclical, self-renewing time evidenced by "Green in winter." "Such a day as will almost oblige a man to eat his own heart," Thoreau writes, and one can feel here his temptation to despair, Achilles-like, over the loneliness of the season. But that *almost* is significant, and the passage ends with a tentative renewal of faith in the "inward fires" that connect him to the still-living, if seemingly barren, natural world.

The appearance of this category in the December charts, rather than in the charts for November, the month with which he most often associated it, adds another dimension to the phenomenon. In December, the persistence of a pre-snow barrenness in the month in which snow is expected signaled an especially long period of near despair: "Such a December is at least as hard to get thro' as November." As a December phenomenon, "Walker eats his heart" thus represents both an objective, external and an internal, emotional experience: a single pattern of both inward and outward weather. Recording this category in the December chart, Thoreau was able to bring despair helpfully down to size: those days when "Walker eats his heart" were after all merely another recurrent annual phenomenon, like the first snowfall or the boys skating. They, too, were part of the pattern, and the pattern was ongoing.

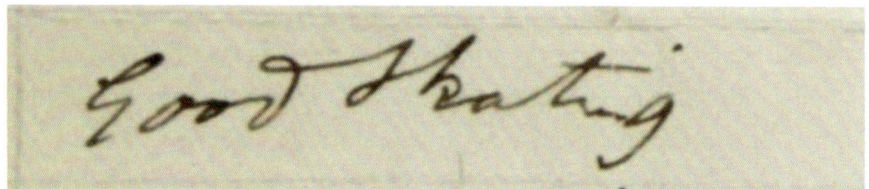

*Good Skating*

Pm Skated ½ mile up Assabet & then to foot of Fair Haven Hill. This is the first tolerable skating. Last night was so cold that the river closed up almost everywhere–and made good skating where there had been no ice to catch the snow of the night before. First there is the snow ice on the sides – somewhat rough & brown or yellowish-spotted where the water overflowed the ice on each side yesterday–& next over the middle the new dark smooth ice–And where the river is wider than usual a thick fine grey ice–marbled–where there was prob. a thin ice yesterday–probably the top froze as the snow fell. I am surprised to find how rapidly & easily I get along–how soon I am at this brook or that bend in the river which it takes me so long to reach on the bank or by water. I can go more than double the usual distance before dark– It takes a little while to learn to trust the new black ice– I look for cracks to see how thick it is– (12/19/1854, Journal Transcript 18:95–96)

Take my first skate to Fair Haven P. It takes my feet a few moments to get used to the skates. I see the track of one skater who has preceded me– this morning– This is the first skating–
  I keep mostly to the smooth ice about a rod wide next the shore

commonly–where there was an over-flow a day or 2 ago– There is not the slightest over flow today & yet it is warm (thermometer at 25+ at 4 ½ Pm). It must be that the river is falling. Now I go shaking over hobbly places–now shoot over a bridge of ice only a foot wide between the water & the shore at a bend. . . . – Now I suddenly see the trembling surface of water where I thought were black spots of ice only–around me– The river is rather low–so that I cannot keep the river above the Clam Shell bend–I am confined to a very narrow edging of ice on the meadow–gliding with unexpected ease through withered sedge–but slipping some times on a twig– Again taking to the snow to reach the next ice–but this rests my feet–Straddling the bare Black willows–winding between the button bushes–& following narrow threadings of ice amid the sedge–which bring me out to clear fields unexpectedly– Occasionally I am obliged to take a few strokes over black & thin looking ice where the neighboring bank is springy–& am slow to acquire confidence in it–but returning how bold I am! Where the meadow seemed only sedge & snow I find a complete ice connexion – . . .

That grand old poem called Winter is round again without any con-nivance of mine– . . . An epic, in blanc verse–enriched with a million tinkling rhymes. (12/7/1856, Journal Transcript 22:120–24)

I think more of skates than of the horse or locomotive as annihilators of distance . . . The skater can afford to follow all the windings of a stream & yet soon leaves far behind & out of sight, the walker who cuts across–Distance is hardly an obstacle to him. I observe that my ordinary track like this

the strokes being 7 to 10 feet long The new stroke is 18 or 20 inches one side of the old– The briskest walkers appear to be stationary to the skater–The skater has wings–balance to his feet– (12/29/1858, Journal Transcript 28:102–3)

Skating was among the chief joys of winter for Thoreau, who found in this activ-ity not only amplified power of bodily extension and "annihilation of distance," but increased access to aspects of the natural world that were normally remote. In "A Winter Walk," he had written, "No domain of nature is quite closed to man at all times, and now we draw near to the empire of the fishes." The closeness opened by the frozen pond offers a winter counterpoint to the modes of proximity afforded by summer: "Our feet glide swiftly over unfathomed depths, where in summer our line tempted the pout and perch, and where the stately pickerel lurked in the long corridors formed by the bulrushes."

As Ian Marshall observes in his essay "Winter Tracings and Transcendental Leaps: Henry Thoreau's Skating," "Thoreau celebrates skating as a liberating endeavor, opening up much of the natural world not only for our perusal, but for our participation in its life." His Journal entry from 1856 reflects this sense of both speed and ecstatic participation, moving quickly from phenomenon to phenomenon, the sense of immediacy and motion underscored by the entry's repeated "now."

Along with the feeling of power derived from speed and access to "the empire of the fishes," skating provided Thoreau with seasonally specific powers of perception. In *Walden* he had written,

> If we knew all the laws of Nature, we should need only one fact, or the description of only one actual phenomenon to infer all the particular results at that point. Now we know only a few laws, and our result is vitiated, not, of course, by any confusion or irregularity in Nature, but by our ignorance of essential elements in the calculation. Our notions of law and harmony are commonly confined to those instances which we detect; but the harmony which results from a far greater number of seemingly conflicting, but really concurring laws, which we have not detected, is still more wonderful. The particular laws are as our points of view, as, to the traveller, a mountain's outline varies with every step, and it has an infinite number of profiles, though absolutely but one form. Even when cleft or bored through it is not comprehended in its entireness.

Skating on the river, Thoreau rapidly collected such "points of view," gathering more of the river's "infinite number of profiles," and bringing these impressions together in a synthesized whole. "I still recur in my mind to that skate of the 31st" he wrote in February of 1855,

> I was thus enabled to get a bird's eye view of the river to survey its length
> & breadth within a few– hours–connect one part on the shore with

another in my mind & realize what was going on upon it– from end to end to know the whole as I ordinarily knew a few miles of it only– (2/3/1855, Journal Transcript 18:199)

This desire to realize the whole of a phenomenon—in this case, the river—by multiplying his perspective is the impulse that drives the Kalendar project. In both cases, the single or static view is amplified—in the one case via the phenomenon of motion through space, and in the other through the multiplication of discrete moments in time.

The phenomenon of ice itself, as well as the reversals of ordinary perception it effected, added to Thoreau's delight in skating. Walking on water, seeing the sky reflected on this new ground, Thoreau experienced the world with new eyes, awakening to its wonder. Like "green in winter," the radical reorganization of the landscape afforded by frozen ponds and rivers was the sort of natural paradox that provided intensified perception, an experience he continually sought—and sought to communicate in his own, paradox-infused representations of these encounters:

> Not only the earth but the heavens are made our footstool. That is what the phenomenon of ice means– The earth is unusually inverted & we walk upon the sky–the ice reflects the blue of the sky–The waters become solid & make a sky below–the clouds grow heavy & fall to earth & we walk on them. We live & walk on solidified fluids. (2/12/1860, Journal Transcript 30:312)

In January of his final winter, Thoreau was visited by his friends Theo Brown and Harrison Blake. In a letter to Daniel Ricketson, Brown describes skating to Concord from Framingham to spend "some hours with [Thoreau] in his mother's parlor, which overlooks the river that runs all through his life." Outside was a beautiful snowstorm, and "his talk was up to the best I ever heard from him—the same depth of earnestness and the same infinite depth of fun going on at the same time." One can imagine this complex, paradoxical tone—serious, earnest, attentive, but somehow full of fun, full of the deep joy that was for him the condition of life—in Thoreau's remark to his friends that afternoon: "You have been skating on this river. Perhaps I am going to skate on some other."

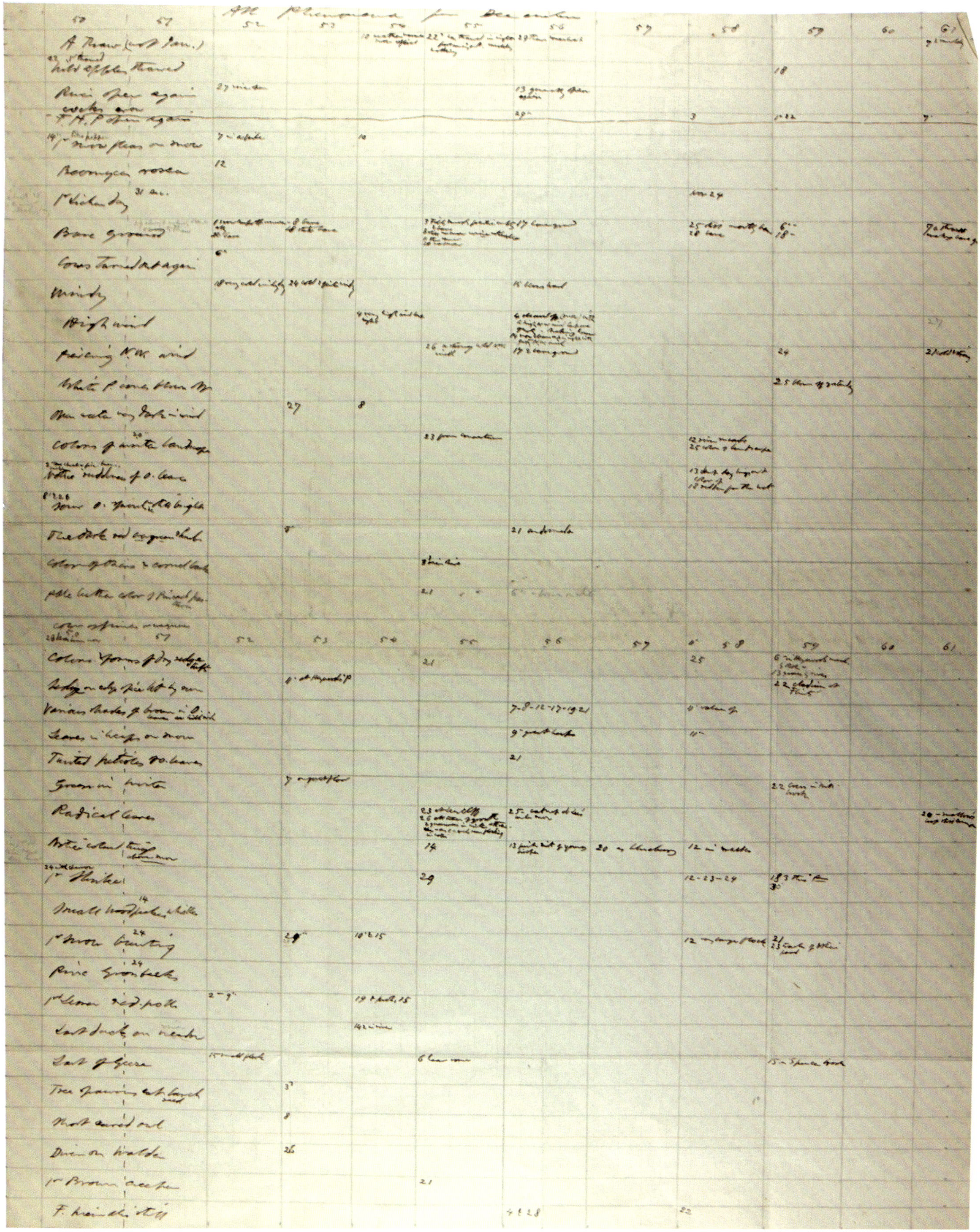

All Phenomena for December

| | 50 | 57 | 52 | 53 | 54 | 55 | 56 | 57 | 58 | 59 | 60 | 61 |
|---|---|---|---|---|---|---|---|---|---|---|---|---|

_(Handwritten phenological table; most cell entries are illegible.)_

| | 52 | 53 | 54 | 55 | 56 | 57 | 58 | 59 | 60 | 61 |
|---|---|---|---|---|---|---|---|---|---|---|
| Hooting owl | | | | | 9 & 19 | | | | | |
| Woodcock's ? | | | | | 17 | | | | | |
| Partridge ? more | | | | | | 15 | | | | |
| Musk rats in Walden | 27 ? | | | | | | 3 ducks ? | 10 sheldrake / 17 ducks ? | | |
| Geese ... ? | | | | | | | | 25 | | |
| Pond not in Walden? | 56 | | | | | | | | | |
| 1st frost through ice | | 15 ... | | 21 ... | 7 ... / 29 ... | | | 22 ... | | |
| Trout | | | | | | | | | | |
| Frog up ? | | 3 ... | | | | | | | | |
| Bullfrog out | | | | | | 31 | | | | |
| 1st snow & ice | | | 15 | | | 3 | 29 | 25 | | |
| Ants in winter quarters | | | | | | | | | | |
| Dogwood fruit | | | | | | | | | | |
| ...berries | | | | | | | | | | |
| Woodchuck ... | 19 ... | 23 ... | | 14 ... | | | | | | |
| Write ... from T.H. ... | 14 | 27 | | 26 | | | 3 ... | 13 ... | | |
| ... first ... | | | 8 ... | | | | | | | 11 ... / 7 ... |
| ... color of wood & earth | 22 | | | | | | | | | |
| Reflection ... | | | | 80 | | | | | | |
| Rain green | | | | 30 | | | | | | |
| Mother o' pearl sky | 52 | 51 | 20 ... | 30 | | | | | | |
| Walks in woods | | | | 29 ... | 6 ... | | | | | |
| Weather ...'s heart | | | | 8 ... | 17 ... | | 25 ... | | | |
| Skull ... | | | | | 12, 17 ... / 6 ... | | | | | |
| ... | | | | | 10 | | | 5 ... / 12 ... | | |
| Winter ... of Walden | | | | | 9 ... | | 25 | | | |

Phenomena for December

| | 50 | 51 | 52 | 53 | 54 | 55 | 56 | 57 | 58 | 59 | 60 | 61 |
|---|---|---|---|---|---|---|---|---|---|---|---|---|
| Birds feeding on ... | | | | | | | 1 & 4 | | | 19 (19-22-3-5 + 2, 24-31) 31 ... | | |
| Blue shadows | | | | 20 | | | | | | | | |
| ... boats | | 28 from Walden | 5 | 2 | Nov. 30 | 2 | | | Nov. 26 or x.t | 10 | Nov 29 | |
| Meat pie ... | | | 8" | | | | | | | | | Nov 19 ... |
| 1st cold morning ... | | 12 cold at last | | 5 very cold but | | | | | | 3" ... | 9" ... | |
| Clear off cold after rain | | | 18" | | | | | | | | | |
| Very cold, zero or below | | 18 ... | | 20 ... coldest | | 19 ... cold – 90 | | | 23° colder | 24 cold min. | 25 ... | |
| | | | | | | | | | | 28 cold. 29 at 3 a. 19° | | |
| F.H.P. frozen again | | | | | | | | | | | | |
| River frozen again | | | | | | | | | | | 21 ... again | |
| First ... frozen | | 22 yesterday | | 11" ... | | 3 at least 4... | | | | | | |
| ... began to freeze | | 27 ... today | | 23 ... | | 21 about an acre ... | 29 8 or 10 ... | 27 ... | Nov 11 1/3 ... | 24 1/3 ... | | 25 ... |
| Walden frozen | | 9 in 5 (2-3) | | night of 30-31 | | | Dec 28 | | 25 4 ... | 24-5 | | |
| Goose Pond skimmed over | | 13" | | ... | | | | | | | | |
| Shady ice crystals | | | 16" | | | | | | | | | |
| ... apple frozen | | | | | | | | | | | | |
| 1st walk on ice | | | | | | | | | 12 min ... | 13" ... | | |
| Skating | | 18 ... P. | | 6 or ... | | 15 boys 2 or 3 day | 6 boys ... | 13 ... | | Nov. 26 ... | 23 ... | |
| Good skating | | ... | | 24 ... | 19 ... skating | 20 ... | 7 ... F.H.P. | | 29 ... River | 26 ... | | |
| ... on ice | | | | | | | | | | | | |
| Rosettes on ice | | | | 20 on river | | | | | | 29° | | |
| | | | | 21 on Walden | | | | | | | | |

| | 50 | 51 | 52 | 53 | 54 | 55 | 56 | 57 | 58 | 59 | 60 | 61 |
|---|---|---|---|---|---|---|---|---|---|---|---|---|
| River a... frozen everywhere | | | | | 19 ... | | | | | Nov 30 & Dec 1 (2) | | |
| Turtle under ice | | | 3 (3 in. ...) 9" | | | | | 2 & 13 | | | | |
| Lizard under ice | | | 4" | | | | | | 3 & 25 | | | |
| Ice sloops | | | | 20 on river | | | | | 28 ... | 23 ... 24-5 | | |
| Boys skate on crust | | | | | | 27 & 28 ... | | | | | | |
| Level bars of frozen mist | | | | | | | 10 | | | | | |
| Rake toothed icicles | | | | | | | 15 ... | | | | | |
| Kill fish under ice | | | | | | | | | 18 ... | | | |
| Ground cracks | | | | | | | 18 ... (23) | | | | | |
| Walk on Walden ... | | | | | | | | | 28° | | | |
| Vapor from river ... | | | | | | | | | | 29 (& 31) | | |
| Teaming ice | | | | | | | | | | 29 | | |
| Plants, buds, fruits in ... | | | | 14 along river | | | | | | 25 ... 31 | | |
| ... remarkable day | | | | | | | | | 3 ... | Nov 30. Dec 1 ... | | 7 ... |
| Gnats in air | | 6 | | | | | | | | | | 7 in ... |
| Gossamer | | 6 ... | | | | | | | | | | |
| Morning ... | | | | | | 14 ... 10 ... 31" | | | | | | |
| | | | | 31 ... | | | | | | 22 | | |
| Fair days ... | | 9 & 3 ... 10 ... | | 20 ... | 3 & 9. 29 ... | | 6 min ... 27 | | 21 ... 22 & 23 ... | | 2 ... | |
| A leaf ... | | 9" – 16 | | | 31 ... 10 ... | | | | 31 ... | | 12 – 8 ... | |

| | '50 | 57 | 52 | 53 | 54 | 55 | 5-6 | 57 | 58 | 59 | 60 | 61 |
|---|---|---|---|---|---|---|---|---|---|---|---|---|
| Rive when lowest | | | | | | | | | 26 nine being low | | | |
| Rive when highest | | | | | | 20 meads much over flowed | | | | | | |
| Rain | | | | | | 22 warm rain | 31 some yesterday | | | 28 | | |
| Drizzling rain & driving mist | | | | | | 16 | | | | | | |
| Warm foggy day | | | | | | | | | | | | |
| Mist reaching near object | | | | | | 16 | | | | 6 | | |
| P prieit[?] grain like lichen | | | | | | | | | | 18 | | |
| Rain here snow on Mts | | | | | | | | | | | | |
| Rain ends in snow | | | 23 | | 22 | | | | | | | |
| A glittering of snow | | | | | | | | | | | | |
| Snow turns to rain | | | | | 24 | | | | | | | |
| Deeper snow | | | | | | | | | | | | |
| Thick book[?] with snow | | | | | | | | | | | | |
| Bring home box traps | | | | | | | | | | | | |
| A great snow storm | | | | | | | | | | | | |
| Snow blows over | | | | 27 | | | | | | | | |
| Snow on trees | | | | | | | 24 | 27 | | 10-20 | | |
| Damp snow plasters tree | | | | 27 | 4 | | | | | | | |
| Slosh | | | | | | | | | | | | |
| Snow on ground | | | 52 | 53 | 54 | | | 57 | 58 | 59 | 60 | 61 |
| Hard snow frozen solid | | | | | | | | | | | | |
| Dry snow squeaks | | | | | 20 | | | | | | | |
| Sleighing | | | | | | | | | | | | |
| Bare snow | | | | | | 14 | | | | | | |
| Coarse snow | | | | | | 30 | 4 | | | | | |
| Snow rolled up by wind | | | | | | | | | | | | |
| Drifts | | | | | | | | | | | | |
| Thaw drifts | | | | 27 | | | 25 | | | 15 | | |
| Days lengthened | | | | | | | | | | | | |
| Snow reflected from snow crust | | | | | | | | | | | | |
| Cows kept at home | | | | | | | | | | | | |
| Tracks | | | 22 | 27 | 18-21 | | | 27 | 22 | | | |
| Snails revealed | | | | | | | | | | 5 | | |
| Hunters out with dogs | | | | 26 | | | | | | | | |
| Bare ground above snow | | | | | 15 | | | | | | | |
| Weeds above snow | | | | | | 29 | | | | | | |
| Many pine seeds on snow | | | | | | | | | 12 | | | |
| Bird seeds on snow | | | 18 | | 4 | | | | | 6 | | |
| See what squirrels have eaten | | | | | | | | | | | | |

## All Phenomena for December

| | 50 | 51 | 52 | 53 | 54 | 55 |
|---|---|---|---|---|---|---|
| **A Thaw ( not Jan. )** | | | | | 10 weather warmer snow softened | 22nd has thawed in night frost coming out muddy walking |
| | 22 1st thawed **Wild apples Thawed** | | | | | |
| **River open again** | | | 27 river open | | | |
| **cocks crow** | | | | | | |
| **F. H. P open again** | | | | | | |
| **1st snow fleas on snow** | 14th like pepper | | 7 in a pile | | 10 | |
| **Baeomyces rosea** | | | 12 | | | |
| **1st Lichen day** | about 10th a [unclear] or lichen day | 31 Dec. | | | | |
| **Bare ground** | | 29 almost entirely bare or [unclear] to thaw | 1 snow keeps off unusually 28 bare | 8 bare 18 still bare | | 3 fields & woods partic. empty & bare 8 still no snow nor ice noticeable 11 still no snow 20th no snow |
| **Cows turned out again** | | | 6th | | | |
| **Windy** | | | 18 very cold windy day | 24 cold & quite windy | | |
| **High wind** | | | | | 4 very high wind last night | |
| **Piercing N.W. wind** | | | | | | 26 a strong cold N.W. wind |
| **White p. cones blown off** | | | | | | |
| **Open water very dark in wind** | | | | 27 | 8 | |
| **Colors of winter landscape** | | 20th | | | | 23 from Conatum |
| **Notice redness of O. leaves** | 2 the shrub o. fire burns briskly | | | | | |
| **Some O. [unclear]- still bright** ↓c | 8 & 26 | | | | | |
| **The dark red evergreen shrubs** | | | | 5th | | |
| **Color of osiers & cornel bark** | | | | | | 3rd [unclear] |
| **Pale leather color of Pinweed pasture** | | | | | | 21 |
| **Color of pines or evergreens** | 50 26 dark brown now | 51 | 52 | 53 | 54 | 55 |

| 56 | 57 | 58 | 59 | 60 | 61 |
|---|---|---|---|---|---|
| 29 thaws somewhat | | | | | 7th muddy |
| | | | 18 | | |
| 13 generally open again | | | | | |
| 29th | | 3 | 1st & 2 | | 7th |
| | | | | | |
| | | | | | |
| | | Nov. 24 | | | |
| 17 bare ground | | 25 still mostly bare<br>28 bare | 6' —<br>18 — | | 7 a thaw<br>  making bare gr |
| | | | | | |
| 15 blows hard | | | | | |
| 4 cleared off (snow) with a high N.W. wind last eve. greatly - shaking house<br>14 snow clears up in night with<br>  gusty N.W. wind | | | | | 27 |
| 17 & bare ground | | | 24 | | 21 cold & strong |
| | | | 25 blown off yesterday | | |
| | | 12 River meads<br>25 color of landscape | | | |
| | | 13 damp day brings out color of<br>18 redder for the wet | | | |
| | | | | | |
| 21 andromeda | | | | | |
| 6  brown on white | | | | | |
| | | | | | |
| 56 | 57 | 11th    58 | 59 | 60 | 61 |

| | | | | | |
|---|---|---|---|---|---|
| | Colors & forms of dry sedge hills | | | | 21 |
| | Sedge on edge of ice lit by sun | | 11 at Haywood's P. | | |
| | Various shades of brown in O. leaves on hillside | | | | |
| | Leaves in heaps on snow | | | | |
| | Twisted petioles of O. leaves | | | | |
| | Green in winter | | 7 on forest floor | | |
| | Radical leaves | | | | 23 at Lee's Cliff<br>26 all types of growth & greenness in winter attract-ive – as e.g. weeds seen floating in water |
| Say 1st or later before deep snow | Notice colored things <u>above snow</u> | | | | 14 |
| | 24 with sparrow<br>1st Shrike | | | | 29 |
| | 14<br>Small woodpecker whistles | | | | |
| | 24<br>1st snow bunting | | 29th<br>29 | 10 & 15 | |
| | 24<br>Pine grosbeaks | | | | |
| | 1st Lesser redpolls | 2 —9th | | 19 & prob. 15 | |
| | river<br>Last ducks on meadow | | | 14 2 in river | |
| | Last of geese | 15th small flock | | | 6 hear some |
| | Tree sparrows eat larch seed | | 3rd | | |
| | Short barred owl | | 8 | | |
| | Diver on Walden | | 26 | | |
| | 1st Brown creeper | | | | 21 |
| | F. hyemalis still | | | | |

*December 1850–1861 pg. 2*

| All Phenomena for December | | | | | |
|---|---|---|---|---|---|
| 50 | 51 | 52 | 53 | 54 | 55 |
| Hooting Owl | | | | | |
| Woodcock still | | | | | |
| Partridge in snare | | | | | |
| Sheldrake in Walden | | 27 a black & white duck on it | | | |

| | | | | | |
|---|---|---|---|---|---|
| | | 25 | 6th in Haywoods meads. by RR — 13 grows by river | | |
| | | | 22 cladium at Flint's | | |
| 7 - 8 - 12 - 17 - 19 - 21 | | 11th value of | | | |
| 9th great heaps | | 11th | | | |
| 21 | | | | | |
| | | | 22 cress in Mill-brook | | |
| 25- catnip at Lee's under snow | | | | | 20 mallows' leaf still common |
| 13 pink tint of young birches | 20 a blueberry | 12 in masses | | | |
| | | 12 - 23 - 24 | 18 3 this $\underline{Pm}$ 30 | | |
| | | 12 very large flock | 21 23 tracks of & [unclear] [unclear] | | |
| | | | | | |
| | | | | | |
| | | | 15 in Spencer brook | | |
| | | 1st | | | |
| | | | | | |
| | | | | | |
| 4 & 28 | | 22 | | | |

| 56 | 57 | 58 | 59 | 60 | 61 |
|---|---|---|---|---|---|
| 9th & 19th | | | | | |
| 17 | | | | | |
| | 15 | | | | |
| | | 3 ducks in | 10 sheldrake 17 duck in | | |

| Phenomenon | 50 | 51 | 52 | 53 | 54 | 55 |
|---|---|---|---|---|---|---|
| Golden-crested wren | | | | | | |
| Perch rise on Walden ? | | | 5(?) | | | |
| 1st fish through ice | | | | 15 yesterday on Flint's & F.H. first | | 21 yesterday fish on F.H.P. |
| Trout | | | | | | |
| Dig up frog | | | | 3rd at a spring | | |
| Bullfrog out | | | | | | |
| 1st larvae &c on ice | | | | | 15 | |
| Ants in winter quarters | 22 | 21 | | | | |
| Dogwood fruit | | 21 | | | | |
| Prino berries | | | | | | |
| Woodchopping fairly begun | | 19 sound of in all woods | | 23 Therien in rain | | 14 hear sound of |
| Winter sunsets from F.H.H.& elsewhere | | 23- 4 & 27th | 14 | 27 | | 26 |
| Splendid sunsets | | | | | 8 a fine one  11th Early still clear winter sunsets now | |
| Notice color of woods I cut | | | 22 | | | |
| Reflections in open parts of river | | | | | | 20 |
| River green | | | | | | 30 |

| | 50 | 51 | 52 | 53 | 54 | 55 |
|---|---|---|---|---|---|---|
| Mother o' pearls sky | | | | | 20th at sunrise | 30 |
| Walk in swamps | | | | | | 29 good walk |
| Walker eats his heart | | | | | | 8 solitude & [unclear] [unclear] walk now |
| Shrub O. leaves [unclear] | | | | | | |
| Short Pms | | | | | | |
| Winter eve at Walden | | | | | | |

## All Phenomena for December

| Phenomenon | 50 | 51 | 52 | 53 | 54 | 55 |
|---|---|---|---|---|---|---|
| Birds feeding on seeds above snow | | | | | ~~20~~ | |
| Blue shadows | | | | | 20 | |
| Get in boat | 3 | | 28 from Walden | 5 | 2 | Nov. 30 |
| Sheets of ice float down river in [unclear] (in eve) | | | | 8th | | |

| 56 | 57 | 58 | 59 | 60 | 61 |
|---|---|---|---|---|---|
| | | | 25 | | |
| 7 some fishers on F.H.P. yesterday<br>28 on Walden ice about 4 inches thick<br>29 - in Miles' brook | | | 22- on Flints P. | | |
| | 31 | | | | |
| | | 29 - | 25 | | |
| | 3 | | | | |
| | | | | | |
| | | | | | |
| | | 3rd warm sunset | 13 from R.R. | | |
| | | | | | 11th splendid glittering scarlet sunset |
| | | | | | |
| | | | | | |
| 56 | 57 | 58 | 59 | 60 | 61 |
| 6 observe dry swamp fruit | | | | | |
| 17th poor picking for | | 25 hard Dec to get thro' | | | |
| 1st & 17-19th<br>6th far greater part fallen | | | | | |
| 10th | | | 5th early candle light<br>12th short Pm | | |
| 9 (v [unclear] 15th) | | 25— | | | |

| 56 | 57 | 58 | 59 | 60 | 61 |
|---|---|---|---|---|---|
| 1st & 4th | | | 17 - (19 - 22 - 3 - 5 - 9 & esp 31st)<br>31 - hemlock seeds | | |
| | | | | | |
| 2 | | Nov. 26 on ac. of fence | 10 | Nov. 29 | not taken out in 61 |
| | | | | | Nov. 19 at eve |
| 5th clear cold winter weather | | | | | |

| | | | | | |
|---|---|---|---|---|---|
| | 1st cold morning, say 14° + | 12th cold at last | 4th coldest day yet + clear with consid. wind - after 1st cloudless morn. for a week or 2 24 is cold | 5 very cold last night | |
| | 17th piercing cold Pm Clears off cold after rain | | 18th | | |
| | Very cold, zero or below | 18 very cold windy day | 28 perhaps coldest night - pump slightly frozen | 20 said to be coldest morning yet 31 a very cold day | 31 |
| | F.H.P. frozen again | | | | |
| | River frozen again | | | | |
| | Dec 16th Flint P. frozen | 22 yesterday | 4 only skimmed a little at the shore Dec. 5 | 11th how long | |
| | 26 not more than 1/2 frozen 17 it was only slightly skimmed Walden begun to freeze a rod from shore on the 23rd 1/3 frozen | 27 no ice in to-day | 22 a few acres of it freeze 24 almost entirely open again - 30 not quite | | 21 all but an acre in my cove |
| Av. of 13 years Dec. 25 | 27(?) Walden frozen | Jan. 5 (52-3) | night of 30-31st | ap. 2 inch thick prob night of 18th | |
| | Goose Pond skimmed over | 13th | 8* 1st [unclear] frozen (was skimmed over night of 3-4) | | |
| | Study ice crystals | | 10th | | |
| | 19 Wild apples frozen | | | | |
| | 1st walk up river | | | | |
| V. Nov Say 8 or 9 | 14 boys been skating a week Skating | 18th Lorings P. | Nov. 28 in Cambridge Dec. 22 10 days old | 6 on way to Providence from prob. the 5 | 15 boys 2 or 3 days but not firm for men yet 20 pretty good |
| | Good skating | 18th Lorings Pond good there | 24 skate across Flints P. 25 skate to F. Haven & [unclear] | 19th tolerable skating - 20 skate to F. Haven | 20 pretty good on meadows & side of river |
| | 17th Attend to bees | | | | |
| | Rosettes on ice | | | 20 on river 21 on Walden | |
| | 50   51 Spring like   days | 52 | 53 | 54 | 17 remarkably fine spring like morn- ing 55 23 & some previous days- pleas- ant & spring like weather |
| | River ap. frozen everywhere | | | 19 last night so cold R. closed almost every where - 20 ap. every- where | |

| | | | | | |
|---|---|---|---|---|---|
| 8th at 8am 8°+ prob coldest day yet 10th at 7 ½ 3°+ | | | 3rd suddenly quite cold freezes in the house ^ | 9th sudden cold last night 9 | 3rd colder yet 14°+ [unclear] 4° at 7 am |
| 17 cold with wind | | | | | |
| 18 very cold - go to Amherst | | 23rd colder | 24 cold wind ^ 28 cold. 29 - at 8 am 15°— | 25 the last the coldest night yet. | 26 - 5°— coldest morning yet |
| | | | | | 21 skimming over again |
| 9 at least 4 inch thick yesterday. | | | | | |
| 29 8 or 10 acres open 9 scarcely a particle of ice | 27 almost skimmed over will be to-night | 11 1/3 skimmed over 13 not so much as 11th 18 merely a little edges 20 frozen except 2 spots in mid. | 24 ½ for more than a week - an acre or 2 open yet | | 21 none is there |
| Prob night of 30 19 last night - 21 open again owing to rain of 20th— 27 still open in one place - 28 froze again | Dec. 28 | same 23 25th at length was skimmed over last night | 24-5 | C says 1st frozen the 16th | 29th |
| last night | 13 just frozen to bear | | | | |
| | | | | | |
| | | 12 on ice to F. H. Hill also 25 to Pond | 13th to F.H.P. | | |
| 6 fairly begun | 13 Goose pond | | | Nov. 26 some boys skated on G. pond | 23 only on G. Pond commonly for a week or 2 past |
| 7 to F.H.P. | | 29 to I. Rice's | 26 to Lee's bridge 29 to Ball's Hill | | |
| | | | | | |
| | | | 29th | | |
| | | | Nov. 30 & 1st & 2nd | | |
| 56 | 57 | 58 | 59 | 60 | 61 |
| | | | | | |

| | 50 | 51 | 52 | 53 | 54 | 55 |
|---|---|---|---|---|---|---|
| **Turtle under ice** | | | | 3rd (7th in a brook?) 9th | | |
| **Lizards under ice** | | | | 4th | | |
| **Ice whoops** | | | | | 20th at eve | |
| **Boys skate on crust** | | | | | | 27 & 28 in streets |
| **Level bars of frozen mist** | | | | | | |
| **Raked-toothed icicles** | | | | | | |
| **Kill fishes under ice** | | | | | | |
| **Ground cracks** | | | | | | |
| **Walk on Walden & study shores** | | | | | | |
| **Vapor from open parts of river in morning** | | | | | | |
| **Teaming ice** | | | | | | |
| **Plants, buds, fruits &c above ice** | 14 sweet gale etc &c at Loring P | | | | 14 along river | |
| **Ind. summer-like days** | 4 beautiful - almost In Sum pure glassy air | 6 warmest & pleasantest yet | Nov 29-30 & Dec 1 pleasant-^est days since Nov. came in 7th True Ind. summer day 8th another | 11 almost Ind. sum. clear & warm - without greatcoat | | |
| **Gnats in air** | | | 6th | | | |
| **Gossamer** | | | 6 across Corner causeway | | | |
| **Mornings of creation** | | | | | | 14 a fine winter morning 31st |
| **Can walk in road, enough to see sky & breathe air** | | | | | 31 beautiful clear very cold day | |
| **Fine days though cold** | 2nd pleasantest day of all | v. Ind. Sum. days | | 9 3rd glorious days - clear & not too cold 10 another, among finest in year | 20th sharp clear air & still- white snow & polished ice - 21 among finest in year | 3rd & 4th 23 a remarkably bright & pleasant day with a very soft wind a little N of W |
| **A leaf frost on trees & [unclear]** | | | | 9th — 16 | | 31 after mist in night a fog still |

*December 1850–1861 pg.4*

## All Phenomena for December

| | 50 | 51 | 52 | 53 | 54 | 55 |
|---|---|---|---|---|---|---|
| | | 14 gone down about 2 feet leaving ice for most part without water on mead. | | | | |
| **River when lowest** | Say 4?? | Say 15 | | | | |
| **River when highest** | Say 20 | Say 1st | 2 risen a few feet since last rain & partially floods mead. | | | 20 mead. somewhat overflowed say 24 (?) |

| | | | | | |
|---|---|---|---|---|---|
| | 2 & 13 | | | | |
| | | 3rd & 5th | | | |
| | | 28 now the ice cracks | 23 at eve 24-5 | | |
| 10 | | | | | |
| 15 Walden on ac. of wind of morning | | | | | |
| | | 18 at Walden | | | |
| 18th at Amherst (v.23rd) | | | | | |
| | | 28th | | | |
| | | | 29 (v.31) | | |
| | | | 29 | | |
| | | | 25 sweet gale<br>31 "    " | | |
| | | 3 delicious mild Pm through gr. covered with snow | Nov 30 - Dec 1 & 2 very warm & spring-like | | 7th & esp. 8th when 60°+ at 1 ½ pm |
| | | | | | 7 in a thaw |
| 10 (?) | | | | | |
| | | | 22 | | |
| | 6 amid sweet fern<br>27 | | 21 rather mild<br>22 & 23 all fine<br>clear bright & rather mild | | 12th but colder (20°+ at 8 am) |
| 10 small one | | | 31 some | | 12— & several bet this & 18th |

| 56 | 57 | 58 | 59 | 60 | 61 |
|---|---|---|---|---|---|
| 7 rather low - am con fined skating to a very narrow strip of ice on mead. side of button bush.<br>was raised by rain of 14th & ran partly over meads | | 26 "river being low" | | | Prob. 1st<br>8th 2 Pm 4 ¼ inch above S.L. |
| the 17<br><br>say 22 | | | 23 Great mead. more than half covered with ice | Rain of yesterday (Nov. 30) raising R. somewhat | prob. end of month |

| | | | | | |
|---|---|---|---|---|---|
| | **Rains**    . 1st half / - - - - / last half | | | | 22 warm rain in Pm |
| | 28 **Drizzling rain & driving mists** | | | | 16 Pm steady gentle warm rain & mist & mizzling |
| | 29 - 30 - 31st **Warm foggy days** This with some thaw | | | | |
| | **Mist revealing near objects** | | | | 16 |
| | **P. pine lit by rain like lichen** | | | | |
| | **Rain here snow on Mts** | 12 last night's rain, snow there | | | |
| | **Rain ends in snow** | | 23 | 23 | |
| | 1st snow night of 6 ^ & still covered 2 inch the 8th     23rd snows in forenoon **Whitening snow** | 13th the 3rd snow | 5 a little this morn. 22 slight last eve - 2nd of the winter 23 | 18 a little finely last night & this am 21½ inch this am 24 some 3 inch last night | 13th snowing & ground whitened     3rd Begs. to snow again in eve. 15 this morn ap. in earnest |
| 4th or 5th | Fairly set in say 6th     (?) 13 think of going into ⊔ winter quarters **Winter setting in** | Winter may be said to have begun the 12th | Perhaps about 12th, if not 5th | say 4 | ap. about 13 |
| | **Snow turns to rain** | | | 24 fine rain | 9th 15 turns to gentle warm rain in Pm 25 pm NE turn partly to rain & hail at midday |
| Say 11 or 12 | Nov 25 deeper than before & still lies the 30th **Deeper snow - 3 inch or more** Dec. 15 half a foot | | 26 in am 3 inch deep 1st snow of any consequence & more added night before 27th | 3rd 5 or 6 inch | 30 began last night & is now a foot deep - ceases at 9 am much the most yet |
| | **Thick boots, with 1st deeper snow** | | | | |
| | **Bring home box traps** | | 5 too late to use them | | |
| | **A great snow Snow storm** old fashioned snow storm 23rd said to be 3 feet above us | | 29 driving & blocking up - no travel 20 inch 31 4 inch more last night in all 2 feet | | |
| | 24 **Snow blows over crust on ice like steam** | | 27 | | |
| | 24th     17- & 23 **Snow lodged on trees &—** | | | | |
| | **Damp snow plasters trees** | | 27 | 4 NE sides | |
| | **Slosh** | | | | |

| | | | | | |
|---|---|---|---|---|---|
| 12 began yesterday <u>Pm</u> snow turns to rain all day 14/20<sup>th</sup> more or less all day | 31 some yesterday | | 18 | | 2 warm rain last nights 23 - 24 - 27 |
| 3<sup>rd</sup> mizzles & rains all day | | 5 fine mizzling 13 fine mizzling rain | 18 misty rain in <u>Pm</u> | | |
| | | | 6 Walden in mist | | |
| | | | 18 | | |
| 3<sup>rd</sup> about as much as 29<sup>th</sup> fell last night 23 all day one inch or 2 | 5 a few flakes at noon 16 a whitening | 5 yesterday <u>Pm</u> 3 or 4 inch | 10 2 <u>Pm</u> till night - still storm & large flakes 14 2 <u>Pm</u> again fine & dry - horizontally - 3 inch | -9 | 1<sup>st</sup> a little falls 23<sup>rd</sup> 2 inch [unclear] 6 at night 24 as much more |
| Say Nov. 30 | v. 8<sup>th</sup> | v. 8 - (14 (?) genial Nature sealed up leaves you outside 29 winter landscape & phenom- -ena - a clear pleasant winter day v 30 | 26 little say 4 | Nov. 25 now for winter | |
| 14<sup>th</sup> turns to rain all day | 30<sup>th</sup>-1 | | 8 in night 20 fast & large flakes & very lodging snow -rain in <u>Pm</u> when 3 or 4 inch | | |
| 24 snow in the night making 9 or 10 inches Pm still snowing | 26 all day - 1<sup>st</sup> of consequence 3 or 4 inch in all | 4 awake to winter & snow 2 or 3 inch deep- 1<sup>st</sup> of any con- sequence Nov.28 at length a reg. snow storm 3 inches in eve - Nov. 30 see it | ^ 20 3 or 4 inches 14 <u>Pm</u> & night 3 inch. 30 fast - 7 or inches fallen deepest yet | 1<sup>st</sup> snow 4 or 5 inch this eve – 4<sup>th</sup> 22 2<sup>nd</sup> important snow 23 7 or 8 in at least now | Nov 25 from NE last night say 2 inch new snow [unclear] all 25<sup>th</sup> |
| Nov. 29 all day, with a little hail several inches | | | | | |
| 3<sup>rd</sup> —56 on ac. of slosh. | | snow 20 miles off | 5 (v end of 6<sup>th</sup>) | | |
| | | | | | |
| | | | | | |
| 24<sup>th</sup> light snow | 27 | | 10 - 20 | | |
| | | | | | |
| 3<sup>rd</sup> | | | | | |

| | 50 | 51 | 52 | 53 | 54 | 55 |
|---|---|---|---|---|---|---|
| **Snow on ^ground** | 2nd no snow — before it was mostly bare frozen ground. (20 since 15th ground covered ½ foot or more ^ | | | | 3rd no | 3rd no snow yet since the 1st whitening which lasted so long. |
| **Sloshing snow frozen solid** | | | | | 5th snow with water beneath 5-6 inch deep frozen solid bears well | 26 inch or 2 of crusted snow on ground / 29 3rd day of hard crust— can skate anywhere |
| **Dry snow squeaks** | 23 snow of last 7 or 10 days remarkably light & dry ^ | | | | 20 | |
| **Sleighing** | | | | | 14 good still with but little snow / 26 excellent since the 5th | |
| **Star-snow** | | | | | | 14 |
| **Coarsened & furrowed snow surface** | | | | | | 30th |
| **Snow rolled up by wind** | | | | | | |
| **Drifts** | | | | | | 14th / 30th |
| **Wall drifts** | 25 [unclear] ^ | | | 27 | | |
| **Day lengthened by reflected lights** | 8 (described 17th) | | | | | |
| **Moon reflected from snow crust** | 8 | | | | | |
| **Cows kept at home** | 8th | | | | | |
| **Tracks** | 19th | 22 | | 27  26 & ^ | 18-31st | 14th in ½ inch snow / 30 |
| **Quails revealed** | | | | | | |
| **Hunters out with dogs** | | | | 26 | | |
| **Observe plants in & above snow** | 22   14 blue curls | | | | 15 sweet fern | |
| **Weeds above snow** (also blue-curls ly-copodium &c - ) | blue-curls full since 8th | 14 rhexia | | | | 29th |
| **Many pine needles on snow** | 24 | | | | | |
| **Birch scales on snow** | | 18th | | | 4 | |
| **See what red-squirrels [uncl.] have eaten** | 22 | 18  sweet-briar hips | | | | |

| 56 | 57 | 58 | 59 | 60 | 61 |
|---|---|---|---|---|---|
| 18 snows enough to whiten ground beyond Littleton<br>56<br>12 in one [unclear] 1/2 the snow gone<br>13 snow mostly gone | 57<br>11th snow on ground | Dec. 3 covered with snow<br>58<br>11th snow on ground | 59<br>20 since Dec. 4th | 60 | 61 |
| | 31 ground still white<br>more snow last night | | | | |
| | | | | | |
| 1st still pretty good sledding with the little snow the 29th left | | | | 22 since the 4th | 24th 1st sleighs |
| | | | | | |
| 4th | | | 21 (v. end of 22) for figure | | |
| | | | 13th yesterday night | | |
| 25 so drifted there were as many carts as sleighs | | | | | |
| 25 with a strong N.W. wind | | | 15th | | |
| 28 since snow of 23rd days seem consid. lengthened owing to increased lights at twilight | | | | | |
| | | | | | |
| 6 rabbits in slosh | 27 mice &c | 22nd -& 25th | 12-13-17<br>24 partridge | | |
| | | | 5th | | |
| | | | 13 yesterday | | |
| | | | 31st sweet gale &c | | |
| 1st 2nd 3rd 4th - 5- 6 | | | 9th & 14th | | |
| | | 12 | [9th | | |
| | | | 6 | | |
| | | | 22 chestnut burs | | |

# *Afterword*

AFTER THOREAU'S DEATH IN MAY OF 1862, HIS MANUSCRIPTS passed into the possession of his sister Sophia. "Housed in three trunks, two wooded, one leather—of his own making, these papers covered Thoreau's entire literary career, from student compositions written at Harvard to essays dictated at his deathbed." The collection included "about sixty bound volumes, mostly Journal and extract books . . . supplemented by several thousand leaves of notes and rough drafts." Henry and Sophia had always been close, sharing a deep affinity for nature and natural history as well as a fierce commitment to abolition, and the death of the other Thoreau siblings, their brother John in 1842 and sister Helen in 1849 (both from tuberculosis), united them further. That Henry was able to continue work in his final year—and Sophia herself reported that "he did not cease to call for his manuscripts till the last day of his life"—was due almost entirely to the extraordinary degree of intimacy that they achieved during Henry's final illness. As Kathy Fedorko writes,

> When advanced tuberculosis rendered Henry bedridden in late 1861, Sophia took on a professional role as his amanuensis and assistant editor, in addition to being his caretaker and companion. . . . Sophia competently and gladly helped her brother revise his manuscripts and conduct business with Ticknor and Fields. During his illness Sophia assisted Henry in revising and editing *A Week on the Concord and Merrimack Rivers* and began the process of negotiating for new editions of *A Week* and *Walden*. She also ensured that "Autumnal Tints," "The Higher Law," "Wild Apples," and "Walking," which they had worked on together, were published in the *Atlantic Monthly* after Henry's death in May.

Much as Channing and Horace Mann acted as extensions of Henry's own body in his final months, bringing him samples and reports of the seasons, Sophia now became his eyes and hands: copying, editing, organizing, and negotiating with publishers. In the four years after Henry's death, "Sophia's major task was to supervise final publication of various essays and books that Henry had partially edited: *Excursions* (1863), *The Maine Woods* (1864), *Cape Cod* (1865), and *A Yankee in Canada, with Anti-Slavery and Reform Papers* (1866)."

The story of what befell Thoreau's manuscripts after Sophia's own death in 1876 is a long and dismaying one, including a good deal of carelessness and greed (William L. Howarth describes negotiations "amusingly similar to shrewd Yankee horse-trading") on the part of subsequent inheritors. Houghton Mifflin cannibalized one stash of now-disorganized manuscripts, cutting individual leaves from their texts and tipping them into printed volumes for a special Manuscript Edition in 1906. The result was a wide scattering of Thoreau's manuscripts, which delayed progress on scholarship on the previously unpublished work for decades. My work on the manuscripts transcribed in this volume was made possible by pioneering detective work by Howarth and by more recent contributions by Elizabeth Witherell and *The Writings of Henry D. Thoreau.*

Neither clearly literary nor, by contemporary standards, clearly scientific, Thoreau's Kalendar has long been of interest to Thoreau scholars but has remained largely unknown to the public. In his eulogy for his friend, Emerson famously referred to Thoreau's late-life projects—which were, to his mind, woefully incomplete.

> The scale on which his studies proceeded was so large as to require longevity, and we were the less prepared for his sudden disappearance. The country knows not yet, or in the least part, how great a son it has lost. It seems an injury that he should leave in the midst his broken task, which none else can finish,—a kind of indignity to so noble a soul, that it should depart out of Nature before yet he has been really shown to his peers for what he is.

But if the Kalendar is indeed a "broken task"—or part of one—it is broken in the same way we are: finite, human, ever reaching beyond what is possible to hold. I hope this book extends that reach a bit further.

# *Notes*

---

Introduction

ix     ***This is June***  Henry David Thoreau, Online Journal Transcripts, Volume 23, p. 118, The Writings of Henry D. Thoreau, manuscript vols. 18–33, http://thoreau.library.ucsb.edu/writings_journals.html.

        Journal entries from October 22, 1837, through September 3, 1854, are reproduced from the Princeton University Press edition of Thoreau's writings: Henry David Thoreau, *The Journal of Henry D. Thoreau*, 8 vols. to date, Princeton, 1981–. (Hereafter cited parenthetically by volume and page number as *Journal*.) Entries after September 3, 1854, are reproduced from the online transcripts of Thoreau's Journal published by The Writings of Henry D. Thoreau: Henry David Thoreau, Online Journal Transcripts, The Writings of Henry D. Thoreau, manuscript vols. 18–33, http://thoreau.library.ucsb.edu/writings_journals.html. (Hereafter cited parenthetically by transcript volume and page number as *Journal Transcript*.) Brackets, cross-outs, and other editorial markings present in the Journal transcripts have been omitted for ease of reading.

xi     ***A more immediate predecessor***  Robert D. Richardson, *Henry Thoreau: A Life of the Mind* (University of California Press, 1986), 305–9.

xi     ***dedicated student of native cultures***  John J. Kucich, "Thoreau's Indian Problem: Savagism, Indigeneity, and the Politics of Place," in *Thoreau in an Age of Crisis: Uses and Abuses of an American Icon*, ed. Kristen Case, Rochelle L. Johnson, and Henrik Otterberg (Brill, 2021),127–44, 128.

xii     ***plan for a larger work***  Laura Dassow Walls, *Henry David Thoreau: A Life* (University of Chicago Press, 2017), 648.

xiii     ***what such a book***  Henry David Thoreau, *Wild Fruits: Thoreau's Rediscovered Last Manuscript*, ed. Bradley P. Dean (Norton, 2001).

xiii     ***unfolded in the present tense***  In "The Story of March," Thoreau shifts between present and future tense, and first and second person, clearly working through the question of how to represent seasonal time grammatically.

xiii     ***By the thirteenth of May***  Thoreau, *Wild Fruits*, 11.

xiii     ***part of Thoreau's critique***  For an evocative description of Thoreau's temporal thinking in *Walden*, see Alexandra Manglis, "Thoreau's Myth as Temporal Alternative," *The Concord Saunterer* 23 (2015), 1–18.

xiii     ***rise of industrialization and capitalism***  E. P. Thompson, "Time, Work-

Discipline, and Industrial Capitalism," *Past & Present*, no. 38 (December 1967): 56–97. See also Barbara Adam's important corrective to the idea of "traditional" time as uniformly cyclical and "modern" time as uniformly linear. Adam argues that human beings have always experienced time as both linear and circular. In my view it is possible to hold this position while recognizing a general ascendancy of "clock time" corresponding to industrialization, per Thompson's argument.

xiii   ***it is not therefore desirable***   Henry David Thoreau, *Walden*, ed. J. Lyndon Shanley (Princeton University Press, 1971), 44.

xiv   ***active suppression of the worker's knowledge***   Jenny Odell, *Saving Time: Discovering a Life Beyond the Clock* (Random House, 2023), 8, 31–33.

xiv   ***Thoreau designed a life***   Thoreau, *Walden*, 87.

xiv   ***that same spring the Smithsonian Institute***   Bradley P. Dean, introduction, Henry David Thoreau, *Wild Fruits: Thoreau's Rediscovered Last Manuscript*, ed. Bradley P. Dean (Norton, 2001), x–xi.

xiv   ***the project may have inspired***   With thanks to Beth Witherell for pointing me to the circulars, and to this Journal entry: "It is remarkable how the American mind runs to statistics. Consider the number of meteorological observers & other annual phenomena. The Smithsonian Institute is a truly national Institution. Every Shop keeper makes a record of the arrival of the first martin or blue-bird to his box. Dod the broker told me last spring that he knew when the first blue-bird came to his boxes–he made a memorandum of it. John Brown Merchant tells me this morning that the martins first came to his box on the 13th ult he & made a minute of it. Beside so many entries in their day books & ledgers— They record these things" (*Journal* 8:68).

xvi   ***allowed Thoreau to envision his world***   Charles Darwin, *On the Origin of Species by Means of Natural Selection* (London, 1859), 73.

xvi   ***This system allowed Thoreau to navigate***   William Rossi, "Making *Walden* and Its Sandbank," Digital Thoreau, https://digitalthoreau.org/making-walden-and-its-sandbank/#fn26. I am grateful to Beth Witherell for her careful explanation of the hash mark system via email.

xvi   ***while lists exist for all months***   A composite chart of February, March, and April phenomena, not included in this book, seems to have been an early experiment that gave way to the monthly charts. See Beth Witherell, "An Introduction to Henry David Thoreau's Phenological Data, Collected in Concord, Massachusetts, Between 1851 and 1861," The Writings of Henry D. Thoreau, 16, https://thoreau.library.ucsb.edu/project_resources_essays/NCEAS_talk_final_March_27,_2008,_with_images_sm_rev.pdf.

xvi   ***Thoreau winnowed once again***   Witherell, "An Introduction," 29.

xviii   ***a material memory, a book***   H. Daniel Peck, *Thoreau's Morning Work: Memory and Perception in "A Week on the Concord and Merrimack Rivers," the Journal, and "Walden"* (Yale University Press, 1990), 45.

xx   ***a system of mutually glossing works***   Michael Benjamin Berger, *Thoreau's Late*

*Career and the Dispersion of Seeds: The Saunterer's Synoptic Vision* (Camden House, 2000), 339.

xxi **Thoreau's decades-long grappling**  For a rich and detailed discussion of Thoreau's relationship to the science of his day, and of the tensions between idealism, materialism, and holism in nineteenth-century intellectual life more generally, see Laura Dassow Walls's *Seeing New Worlds: Henry David Thoreau and Nineteenth-Century Natural Science* (University of Wisconsin Press, 1990)

xxii **what I am calling a second or virtual nature**  My use of this phrase differs from William Cronin's in *Nature's Metropolis: Chicago and the Great West* (New York: Norton, 1991), where he uses it to describe a landscape altered by human presence and economic activity. My own useage emphasizes the mediation of Thoreau's access to the natural world, and is in line with Lawrence Buell's in *Literary Transcendentalism: Style and Vision in the American Renaissance* (Cornell University Press, 1973), 149.

xxii **in this it will be retained**  Thoreau, *Walden*, 1.

xxiii **linked to larger, more collective losses**  Richard Primack, *Walden Warming: Climate Change Comes to Thoreau's Woods* (University of Chicago Press, 2014).

xxiv **His world is replete with ghosts**  Rochelle L. Johnson, "Broken Birds, Broken Body, Broken World." Unpublished talk.

xxv **Chronoception—our sense of**  I am grateful to James Finley for introducing me to chronoception and for suggesting the ways in which Thoreau extended his own time-sense outward beyond human time scales.

xxv **There can be no un-ageing**  Barbara Adam, *Timewatch: The Social Analysis of Time* (Polity Press, 1995), 22.

xxv **on the experience of awe**  Melanie Rudd, Kathleen D. Vohs, and Jennifer Aaker, "Awe Expands People's Perception of Time, Alters Decision Making, and Enhances Well-Being," *Psychological Science* 23, no. 10 (August 10, 2012).

## PART I: SYNOPTIC VISION

April: Sea Turn

4 **The United States have a coffle**  Henry David Thoreau, "A Plea for Captain John Brown," in *Reform Papers*, ed. Wendell Glick (Princeton University Press, 1973), 130.

4 **The slave-ship is on her way**  Thoreau, "A Plea," 124.

5 **All afternoon the four friends read**  Walls, *A Life*, 458.

5 **Darwin's revolutionary book**  Walls, *A Life*, 459.

6 **this text was read by**  Walls, *A Life*, 472.

6 **a pioneering document**  Berger, *Thoreau's Late Career*, 4.

6 **a small text book**  Walls, *A Life*, 462.

6 **If we knew all the laws**  Thoreau, *Walden*, 290–91.

6 **The unstated assumption of the Journal**  Peck, *Thoreau's Morning Work*, 75.

8 **telescopes, instruments of vision**  Walls, *A Life*, 268.

10    *sweet and beneficent society in Nature* Thoreau, *Walden*, 131–32.

11    **In his description of the German** Hans Ulrich Gumbrecht, *Atmosphere, Mood, Stimmung: On a Hidden Potential of Literature*, trans. Erik Butler (Stanford University Press, 2012), 3.

11    *references to music and weather* Gumbrecht, *Stimmung*, 4.

12    *the landscape radiated from me accordingly* Thoreau, *Walden*, 81.

14    *designates certain privileged experiences* Alan D. Hodder, *Thoreau's Ecstatic Witness* (Yale University Press, 2001), 5.

14    *every natural fact is an emanation* Ralph Waldo Emerson, "The Method of Nature," *Emerson: Essays and Lectures*, ed. Joel Porte (Library of America, 1983), x.

14    **Time is but the stream** Thoreau, *Walden*, 98.

May: Washing Day

29    **The Boston papers reported** Walter Harding, *The Days of Henry Thoreau: A Biography* (Dover Publications, Inc., 1982), 424.

29    *unless he is continuously inspired* Thoreau, "A Plea," 133.

29    *when good seed is planted* Thoreau, "A Plea," 119.

31    *infinite and unaccountable friendliness* Thoreau, *Walden*, 132.

32    *the symbolic potential of* **spiritus** Thomas Pribeck, "A Note on the Winds of Walden," *CLA Journal* 34, no. 3 (1991): 359.

36    **As Dean notes, the dramatic contrast** Bradley P. Dean, "Science, Poetry, and 'Order among the Clouds': Thoreau and Luke Howard," *The Thoreau Society Bulletin*, no. 253 (Fall 2005), 1–5.

37    **The world globes itself** Ralph Waldo Emerson, "Compensation," in *Emerson: Essays and Lectures*, ed. Joel Porte (Library of America, 1983), 289.

38    **The phenomena of the year** Thoreau, *Walden*, 301.

38    **As fruits and leaves** Henry D. Thoreau, "Autumnal Tints," in *The Essays of Henry D. Thoreau*, ed. Lewis Hyde (North Point Press, 2002), 218.

38    *wheels within wheels* Walls, *A Life*, 468.

38    **The basis of Transcendentalist thinking** Buell, *Literary Transcendentalism*, 149.

38    **Only in the incremental development** Peck, *Thoreau's Morning Work*, 54.

June: Shadows of Clouds

50    **This orientation toward the pictorial** Richardson, *A Life of the Mind*, 261, 359.

51    **Nature is the symbol of spirit** Emerson, "The Method of Nature," 20.

51    **The perception of solid Form** John Ruskin, *The Elements of Drawing* (Dover, 1971 [1857]), 27. Quoted in Richardson, *A Life of the Mind*, 359.

52    *the term Thoreau most often uses* Peck, *Thoreau's Morning Work*, 68.

54    *several intense relationships with women* Walls, *A Life*, 239–41.

55    **Thoreau conceives of chastity** Cristin Ellis, "Chastity and Vegetality: On Thoreau's Eco-erotics," in *Dispersion: Thoreau and Vegetal Thought*, ed. Branka Arsić (Bloomsbury, 2021), 165–88, 166.

55    **The generative energy** Thoreau, *Walden*, 219.

56    *landscapes radically integrated with* James Finley, "'Justice in the Land': Eco-

logical Protest in Henry David Thoreau's Antislavery Essays," *The Concord Saunterer* 21 (2013): 15.

56    ***Ultimately, as Finley writes***  Finley, "Justice in the Land," 17.

58    ***the Romantic view of clouds***  Dean, "Science, Poetry," 1–5.

58    ***castles in the air***  Thoreau, *Walden*, 324.

58    ***The radicals of lobe***  Thoreau, *Walden*, 306–7.

58    ***to trace relations horizontally***  Peck, *Thoreau's Morning Work*, 54.

60    ***a foundation for harmony***  Quoted in Richardson, *A Life of the Mind*, 264.

60    ***When the past is viewed***  Peck, *Thoreau's Morning Work*, 45.

61    ***To affect the quality of the day***  Thoreau, *Walden*, 90.

## PART II: SECOND NATURE

### October: Gossamer Days

79    ***the way of life is wonderful***  Emerson, "Circles," in *Essays and Lectures*, ed. Joel Porte (Library of America, 1983), 414.

80    ***set off still hopeful***  Walls, *A Life*, 494.

80    ***added amanuensis to her other roles***  Walls, *A Life*, 494. Among the manuscripts he prepared for publication that final winter was an essay derived from "Autumnal Tints," a lecture he'd delivered first in Worcester on February 22, 1859, and then in Waterbury, Connecticut on December 11, 1860. This second occasion was his final lecture. "October, or Autumnal Tints" was sent to Ticknor and Fields on February 20, 1862, and appeared in *The Atlantic Monthly* in November of that year, six months after Thoreau's death.

80    ***views from this frame***  Robert Thorson, *The Boatman: Henry David Thoreau's River Years* (Harvard University Press, 2019), 9.

81    ***This is the only way***  Thoreau, *Walden*, 11.

81    ***to describe all these bright tints***  Thoreau, "Autumnal," 218–19.

83    ***a double shadow of myself***  Thoreau, *Walden*, 293.

83    ***partly the voice of the wood***  Thoreau, *Walden*, 123.

85    ***the value of a fact***  Henry David Thoreau, "A Natural History of Massachusetts." *Excursions*, ed. Joseph A. Moldehhauer (Princeton University Press, 2008), 27.

85    ***he never stopped seeking***  For a fuller discussion of the complex relation between "facts" and "truths" in Thoreau's evolving epistemology, see Walls, *Seeing New Worlds*, especially chapter one, "Facts and Truth: Transcendental Science from Cambridge to Concord," 15–52. See also David M. Robinson, *Natural Life: Thoreau's Worldly Transcendentalism*, especially chapter eight, "Leaf, Fruit, Seed: Nature's Great Circle" (Cornell University Press, 2004), 176–201. For a discussion of Thoreau's "horizontal" analogical tendencies, see Peck, *Morning Work*, 53–55.

85    ***its tendency toward reproductive superabundance***  "In short, the spirit and peculiarity of that impression nature makes on us, is this, that it does not exist to any one or to any number of particular ends, but to numberless and endless benefit; that there is in it no private will, no rebel leaf or limb, but the whole is oppressed

by one superincumbent tendency, obeys that redundancy or excess of life which in conscious beings we call *ecstasy.*" Emerson, "The Method of Nature," 121.

86    ***I wash off all my chagrins***  I am indebted to H. Daniel Peck's brilliant analysis of this Journal passage in *Thoreau's Morning Work*, 109–10.

89    ***measure and catalog the width***  Daegan Miller, *This Radical Land: A Natural History of American Dissent* (The University of Chicago Press, 2018), 23.

89    **Statistics of the Bridges**  Miller, 250, n.32.

90    ***what plants grow where***  Miller, 16.

90    ***Below the notch in my willow***  Henry David Thoreau, *Plan of Concord River* . . . Concord Free Public Library, https://concordlibrary.org/special-collections/thoreau-surveys/107a.

90    ***located on Channing's property***  Thorson, *The Boatman*, xii.

91    ***Indian Summer***  Thoreau's use of the widely used term "Indian Summer" to describe a warm stretch of weather in fall follows the settler-colonial pattern of appropriation and erasure. The term likely derives from colonists' encounter with Algonquin peoples, who believed that such periods of unseasonable warmth in fall were a gift from the Creator, Cautantowwit. Thoreau used the expression frequently, typically only with regard to weather, but on at least a couple of occasions, also making reference to Indigenous peoples. For example:

> Everywhere in our corn and grain fields the earth is strewn with the relics of a race, which has vanished as completely as if trodden in with the earth– When I meditate on the destiny of this prosperous branch of the Saxon family, and the unexhausted energies of this new country–I forget that what is now Concord was once Musketaquid, And that the American race has had its history– The future reader of history will associate this generation with the red man in his thoughts, and give it credit for some sympathy with that race– Our history will have some copper tints at least and be read as through an Indian summer haze– (1842–1844 [undated entry], *Journal* 2:38–50)

This passage, which rehearses the "vanishing Indian" myth while also holding up sympathy with Native people as a cultural virtue, is typical of Thoreau's complex relation to Native peoples, a relation characterized by both lifelong interest and engagement and savagism and appropriation. See Jamie K. Oxendine, "Indian Summer: Untold Story, Etymology, and History," https://www.powwows.com/indian-summer/, and Kucich, "Thoreau's Indian Problem," ed. Case, 127–44.

92    ***These dates are taken from***  Henry Youle Hind, "North-West Territory: Reports of progress, together with a preliminary and general report on the Assiniboine and Saskatchewan exploring expedition, made under instructions from the Provincial Secretary, Canada" (Toronto, 1859).

92    ***Thoreau copied the dates***  Henry W. and Albert A. Berg Collection of English and American Literature, The New York Public Library, "[Notes on general phenomena]. Holograph notes," New York Public Library Digital Collections, accessed August 30, 2023, https://digitalcollections.nypl.org/items/d69df600

-7347-0132-95d6-58d385a7bbd0. With gratitude to Beth Witherell for solving the mystery represented by these entries.

92    ***Nature is not ruffled***  Henry David Thoreau, *The Correspondence of Henry David Thoreau: Volume 1: 1834–1848*, ed. Robert N. Hudspeth (Princeton University Press, 2013), 104–5.

November: Seek Sheltered Places

106    ***great monument to self-registering***  Walls, *A Life*, 493.

107    ***treading some snowy dell***  Henry David Thoreau, "A Winter Walk," in *Excursions*, ed. Joseph A. Moldehhauer (Princeton University Press, 2008), 30–31.

108    ***Interestingly, this entry occurs***  (Journal Transcript 20:139–40). I follow Walls in reading the second friend mentioned in this entry as Channing.

108    ***Channing's irresponsibility and dark moods***  Walls, *A Life*, 323, 138, 324.

108    ***often assisted by Channing***  Walls, *A Life*, 442.

110    ***This composite picture***  Berger, *Thoreau's Late Career*, 39.

110    ***categories were sliding out of focus***  Peck, *Thoreau's Morning Work*, 105.

111    ***river at 11 am***  The Morgan Library and Museum, *Nature Notes*, MA 610.

112    ***grateful as for a special kindness***  Thoreau, "Walk," 31.

112    ***the friendship of the seasons***  Thoreau, *Walden*, 131–32.

113    ***have the fruition of***  "Rejoice," Online Etymology Dictionary.

114    ***It was a sustained interaction***  Walls, *A Life*, 147.

117    ***hard rock bottom of Walden Pond***  "Let us settle ourselves, and work and wedge our feet downward through the mud and slush of opinion, and prejudice, and tradition, and delusion, and appearance, that alluvion which covers the globe, through Paris and London, through New York and Boston and Concord, through church and state, through poetry and philosophy and religion, till we come to a hard bottom and rocks in place, which we can call reality, and say, This is, and no mistake." Thoreau, *Walden*, 97–98.

117    ***As calendar-maker and surveyor***  Peck, *Thoreau's Morning Work*, 100.

December: Green in Winter

138    ***comfort in perfect disease***  Alan D. Hodder, *Thoreau's Ecstatic Witness* (Yale University Press, 2001), 304.

138    ***The wasting away of his body***  William Ellery Channing, *Thoreau The Poet Naturalist* (Boston, 1873), 339. Quoted in Hodder, *Thoreau's Ecstatic Witness*, 305.

140    ***laciniated, lobed, and imbricated thalluses***  Thoreau, *Walden*, 305.

141    ***The feathers and wings of birds***  Thoreau, *Walden*, 306.

141    ***whose bottom is pebbly with stars***  Thoreau, *Walden*, 98.

141    ***We are wont to imagine***  Thoreau, *Walden*, 87–88.

143    ***How long will you eat***  Homer, the *Iliad*, trans. Robert Fagles (Penguin, 1990).

146    ***long corridors formed by the bulrushes***  Thoreau, "A Winter Walk," in *Essays*, ed. Hyde, 37.

146    ***Thoreau celebrates skating***  Ian Marshall, "Winter Tracings and Transcendental Leaps: Henry Thoreau's Skating," *Papers on Language & Literature* 29, no. 4 (1993): 463.

146     *If we knew all the laws*   Thoreau, *Walden*, 290–91.

147     *to skate on some other*   Quoted in Hodder, *Thoreau's Ecstatic Witness*, 302–3.

Afterword

167     *several thousand leaves*   William L. Howarth, *The Literary Manuscripts of Henry David Thoreau* (Ohio State University Press, 1974), xix.

167     *sharing a deep affinity*   Kathy Fedorko, "'Henry's Brilliant Sister': The Pivotal Role of Sophia Thoreau in Her Brother's Posthumous Publications," *The New England Quarterly* 89, no. 2 (2016): 222–56, http://www.jstor.org/stable /24718239.

167     *he did not cease to call*   Sophia Thoreau to Daniel Ricketson, 20 May 1862, Anna and Walton Ricketson, *Daniel Ricketson and His Friends: Letters, Poems, Sketches, Etc.* (Houghton Mifflin, 1902), 142.

167     *Sophia took on a professional role*   Fedorko, "Henry's Brilliant Sister," 226.

168     *to supervise final publication*   Howarth, *The Literary Manuscripts*, xix.

168     *shrewd Yankee horse-trading*   Howarth, *The Literary Manuscripts*, xxiii–xxv.

168     *how great a son it has lost*   Ralph Waldo Emerson, "Thoreau," *The Atlantic Monthly*, August 1862, https://www.theatlantic.com/magazine/archive/1862 /08/thoreau/306418/.

# Bibliography

Adam, Barbara. *Timewatch: The Social Analysis of Time.* Polity Press, 1995.

Berger, Michael Benjamin. *Thoreau's Late Career and the Dispersion of Seeds: The Saunterer's Synoptic Vision.* Camden House, 2000.

Borst, Raymond R. *The Thoreau Log: A Documentary Life of Henry David Thoreau.* G. K. Hall, 1992.

Buell, Lawrence. *Literary Transcendentalism: Style and Vision in the American Renaissance.* Cornell University Press, 1973.

Cronin, William. *Nature's Metropolis: Chicago and the Great West.* Norton, 1991.

Darwin, Charles. *On the Origin of Species by Means of Natural Selection.* London, 1859.

Dean, Bradley P. "Science, Poetry, and 'Order among the Clouds': Thoreau and Luke Howard." *The Thoreau Society Bulletin*, no. 253 (Fall 2005): 1–5.

Dean, Bradley, ed. *Wild Fruits: Thoreau's Rediscovered Last Manuscript.* By Henry David Thoreau. Norton, 2001.

Ellis, Cristin. "Chastity and Vegetality: On Thoreau's Eco-erotics." In *Dispersion: Thoreau and Vegetal Thought.* Edited by Branka Arsić. Bloomsbury, 2021.

Emerson, Ralph Waldo. "Circles." In *Essays and Lectures.* Edited by Joel Porte. Library of America, 1983. 401–414.

Emerson, Ralph Waldo. "Compensation." In *Essays and Lectures.* Edited by Joel Porte. Library of America, 1983. 283–302.

Emerson, Ralph Waldo. "The Method of Nature." In *Essays and Lectures.* Edited by Joel Porte. Library of America, 1983, 115–132.

Emerson, Ralph Waldo. "Nature." In *Essays and Lectures.* Edited by Joel Porte. Library of America, 1983. 283–302.

Emerson, Ralph Waldo. "Thoreau." *The Atlantic Monthly*, August 1862. https://www.theatlantic.com/magazine/archive/1862/08/thoreau/306418/.

Fedorko, Kathy. "'Henry's Brilliant Sister': The Pivotal Role of Sophia Thoreau in Her Brother's Posthumous Publications." *The New England Quarterly* 89, no. 2 (2016): 222–56. http://www.jstor.org/stable/24718239.

Finley, James. "'Justice in the Land': Ecological Protest in Henry David Thoreau's Anti-slavery Essays." *The Concord Saunterer* 21 (2013): 1–35.

Gumbrecht, Hans Ulrich. *Atmosphere, Mood, Stimmung: On a Hidden Potential of Literature.* Translated by Erik Butler. Stanford University Press, 2012.

Harding, Walter. *The Days of Henry Thoreau: A Biography.* Dover Publications, Inc., 1982.

Hodder, Alan D. *Thoreau's Ecstatic Witness*. Yale University Press, 2001.

Homer. The *Iliad*. Translated by Robert Fagles. Penguin, 1990.

Howarth, William L. *The Literary Manuscripts of Henry David Thoreau*. Ohio State University Press, 1974.

Johnson, Rochelle L. "Broken Birds, Broken Body, Broken World." Unpublished talk.

Kucich, John J. "Thoreau's Indian Problem: Savagism, Indigeneity, and the Politics of Place." In *Thoreau in an Age of Crisis: Uses and Abuses of an American Icon*. Edited by Kristen Case, Rochelle L. Johnson, and Henrik Otterberg. Brill, 2021.

Manglis, Alexandra. "Thoreau's Myth as Temporal Alternative." *The Concord Saunterer* 23 (2015): 1–18.

Marshall, Ian. "Winter Tracings and Transcendental Leaps: Henry Thoreau's Skating." *Papers on Language & Literature* 29, no. 4 (1993): 459–74.

Miller, Daegan. *This Radical Land: A Natural History of American Dissent*. The University of Chicago Press, 2018.

Odell, Jenny. *Saving Time: Discovering a Life Beyond the Clock*. Random House, 2023.

Peck, H. Daniel. *Thoreau's Morning Work: Memory and Perception in "A Week on the Concord and Merrimack Rivers," the Journal, and "Walden."* Yale University Press, 1990.

Pribeck, Thomas. "A Note on the Winds of Walden." *CLA Journal* 34, no. 3 (1991): 354–63.

Primack, Richard. *Walden Warming: Climate Change Comes to Thoreau's Woods*. University of Chicago Press, 2014.

Richardson, Robert D. *Henry Thoreau: A Life of the Mind*. University of California Press, 1986.

Robinson, David M. *Natural Life: Thoreau's Worldly Transcendentalism*. Cornell University Press, 2004.

Rossi, William. "Making *Walden* and Its Sandbank." Digital Thoreau. https://digitalthoreau.org/making-walden-and-its-sandbank.

Rudd, Melanie, Kathleen D. Vohs, and Jennifer Aaker. "Awe Expands People's Perception of Time, Alters Decision Making, and Enhances Well-Being." *Psychological Science* 23, no. 10 (August 10, 2012): 1130–36.

Thompson, E. P. "Time, Work-Discipline, and Industrial Capitalism." *Past & Present*, no. 38 (December 1967): 56–97.

Thoreau, Henry David. "Autumnal Tints." In *The Essays of Henry D. Thoreau*. Edited by Lewis Hyde. North Point Press, 2002.

Thoreau, Henry David. Charts of General Phenomena for April, May, June, October. The Morgan Library & Museum. MA 610.

Thoreau, Henry David. *The Correspondence of Henry David Thoreau: Volume 1: 1834–1848*. Edited by Robert N. Hudspeth. Princeton University Press, 2013.

Thoreau, Henry David. "General Phenomena for October" and "An[nual] Phenomena for December." Henry David Thoreau Collection. Yale Collection of American Literature, Beinecke Rare Book and Manuscript Library.

Thoreau, Henry David. *The Journal of Henry D. Thoreau*. 8 vols. to date. Princeton University Press. 1981.

Thoreau, Henry David. Online Journal Transcripts. The Writings of Henry D. Thoreau, manuscript vols. 18–33. http://thoreau.library.ucsb.edu/writings_journals.html.

Thoreau, Henry David. "A Natural History of Massachusetts." In *Excursions*. Edited by Joseph A. Moldenhauer. Princeton University Press, 2008.

Thoreau, Henry David. "A Plea for Captain John Brown." In *Reform Papers*. Edited by Wendell Glick. Princeton University Press, 1973.

Thoreau, Henry David. *Walden*. Edited by J. Lyndon Shanley. Princeton University Press, 1971.

Thoreau, Henry David. "A Winter Walk." In *Excursions*. Edited by Joseph A. Moldenhauer. Princeton University Press, 2008.

Thorson, Robert. *The Boatman: Henry David Thoreau's River Years*. Harvard University Press, 2019.

Walls, Laura Dassow. *Henry David Thoreau: A Life*. The University of Chicago Press, 2017.

Walls, Laura Dassow. *Seeing New Worlds: Henry David Thoreau and Nineteenth-Century Natural Science*. The University of Wisconsin Press, 1990.

Witherell, Elizabeth. "An Introduction to Henry David Thoreau's Phenological Data, Collected in Concord, Massachusetts, Between 1851 and 1861." The Writings of Henry D. Thoreau. 16. https://thoreau.library.ucsb.edu/project_resources _essays/NCEAS_talk_final_March_27,_2008,_with_images_sm_rev.pdf.

# *Acknowledgments*

As I wrote the essays and transcribed the charts collected in this book, I worked with stacks of books around me. Many of these were the volumes that shaped my understanding of Thoreau when I first read them as a graduate student. Since then, I have had the good fortune to meet many of their authors—Thoreau studies is a surprisingly small world, comprised of extraordinarily generous people, and my felt sense of the presence of these friends and colleagues in their words has been one of the joys of working on this book.

First among these ministering angels are Daniel Peck and Laura Dassow Walls. Dan answered an email from a stranger about the Kalendar in 2006 or so and bequeathed to me a roll of microfilm once belonging to Sherman Paul. I was a graduate student just beginning a dissertation chapter, and it felt like a benediction. Laura's book, *Seeing New Worlds: Henry David Thoreau and Nineteenth-Century Natural Science*, exploded most of what I thought I knew about nineteenth-century American literature and left a complex ecology of thinking and writing in its wake. Work on Thoreau's manuscripts and late career by William Howarth, Michael Berger, Bob Richardson, Bradley Dean, and Beth Witherell has likewise been essential to my understanding of the Kalendar. This book would not exist without those books.

Many place-names listed in the charts were identified with the help of Ray Angelo's extraordinary project "Thoreau Place Names: A Guide to Place Names in Concord and Lincoln, MA in the Journal of Henry David Thoreau," now housed on the Internet Archive at https://archive.org/details/thoreau-place-names.

The charts transcribed for this book first appeared on the Thoreau's Kalendar site, transcribed and encoded with the help of a host of brilliant UMF students, including Diana Allen, Carinne Haigis, Richard Johnson, Joey LeBlanc, Holland Corson, Anastasia Mertz, and Liz Niznik. The work of transcribing demands patience, curiosity, and care, and these students have inspired me with their capacities for all three. A special thank you to Liz and

Anastasia, who stayed on past graduation to help with the final transcription push this past year, and without whose help this book would still be a Word document. The Thoreau's Kalendar site was designed and is maintained by the almost unfathomably generous Jonathan Martin, whose beneficent presence first welcomed me into the world of digital humanities and whose ongoing willingness to support this project is a gift I can never repay.

A team of Thoreau scholars strained their eyes and devoted their time to reviewing transcriptions, catching many significant oversights and errors on my part. Beth Witherell, Laura Walls, Brent Ranalli, Henrik Otterberg, Michael Berger, and Sandy Petrulionis, thank you for your invaluable contributions to this collective endeavor. John Kucich and Beth Witherell answered nagging last-minute questions, and Anastasia Mertz was my long-distance comrade in arms in assembling and formatting the manuscript. Dear friends and trusted readers James Finley, Rochelle Johnson, and Dan Gunn provided invaluable feedback on the essays. This book has benefitted from their intelligence and care, as have I.

Making this book a material reality has presented a number of challenges that few, if any, other publishers would have been willing to face. I am grateful beyond reckoning to Daniel Slager, Lauren Langston Klein, Mary Austin Speaker, Alex Guerra, and the rest of the team at Milkweed Editions for their Thoreauvian commitment to imagining possibility.

I am grateful to the Thoreau Society for over a decade of conversation, support, and friendship. I chose Thoreau for many reasons, but the Thoreau *people* are very close to the top of the list. Thank you for teaching me the difference that community, generosity, and shared enthusiasm can make in an academic life.

Finally, thank you Avery and Wyatt for your patience with my absorption in this project and for the sustaining joy of being your mom. And to Aaron Wyanski, partner in the truest sense, who reminds me there is more day to dawn.

KRISTEN CASE is a poet and scholar. She is the author of *American Pragmatism and Poetic Practice: Crosscurrents from Emerson to Susan Howe* and three books of poetry, most recently, *Daphne*. She is co-editor of the *Oxford Handbook of Henry David Thoreau*; *William James and Literary Studies*; *Thoreau in an Age of Crisis: Uses and Abuses of An American Icon*; *21|19: Contemporary Poets in the 19th Century Archive*; and *Thoreau at 200: Essays and Reassessments*. She is Executive Director of the Monson Seminar and Director of *Thoreau's Kalendar: A Digital Archive of the Phenological Manuscripts of Henry David Thoreau* and lives in Maine.

milkweed
EDITIONS

Founded as a nonprofit organization in 1980, Milkweed Editions
is an independent publisher. Our mission is to identify, nurture,
and publish transformative literature, and build an
engaged community around it.

We are based in Bde Óta Othúŋwe (Minneapolis) in
Mní Sota Makhóčhe (Minnesota), the traditional homeland of the
Dakhóta and Anishinaabe (Ojibwe) people and current home to
many thousands of Dakhóta, Ojibwe, and other Indigenous
people, including four federally recognized Dakhóta nations
and seven federally recognized Ojibwe nations.

We believe all flourishing is mutual, and we envision a future in
which all can thrive. Realizing such a vision requires reflection on
historical legacies and engagement with current realities.
We humbly encourage readers to do the same.

milkweed.org

Milkweed Editions, an independent nonprofit literary publisher, gratefully acknowledges sustaining support from our board of directors, the McKnight Foundation, the National Endowment for the Arts, and many generous contributions from foundations, corporations, and thousands of individuals—our readers. This activity is made possible by the voters of Minnesota through a Minnesota State Arts Board Operating Support grant, thanks to a legislative appropriation from the Arts and Cultural Heritage Fund.

MᶜKNIGHT FOUNDATION

MINNESOTA STATE ARTS BOARD

NATIONAL ENDOWMENT for the ARTS
arts.gov

CLEAN WATER LAND & LEGACY AMENDMENT

Interior design by Alex Guerra
Typeset in Adobe Caslon Pro

Adobe Caslon Pro was created by Carol Twombly
for Adobe Systems in 1990. Her design was inspired by
the family of typefaces cut by the celebrated engraver
William Caslon I, whose family foundry served
England with clean, elegant type from the early
Enlightenment through the turn of the
twentieth century.